Each Winding Path

Each Winding Path

Stories of Faith from Florida College Female Faculty

Jena Aitchison • Becky Barlar • Elizabeth Behle • Bonny Cable
Hope Chandler • Julie Gant • Annetta Hastings, PhD
Minerva Holk, EdD • Jennifer Kearney • Jessica Miles, PhD
Abigail Orf • Melissa Paquette • Molly Taylor
Kathleen Trigg • Brooke Ward

FLORIDA COLLEGE
PRESS

Each Winding Path: Stories of Faith from Florida College Female Faculty

Florida College Press
119 N. Glen Arven Ave.
Temple Terrace, Florida 33617

ISBN: 978-0-9674231-8-0

Printed in the United States of America.
Due to the nature of this writing, different translations of the Holy Bible are used by the various writers. These translations include:

CONTENTS

ABBREVIATIONS

Bible Translations

CSB	Christian Standard Bible
ESV	English Standard Version
NASB	New American Standard Bible
NASB95	New American Standard Bible 1995 Update
NIV	New International Version
NKJV	New King James Version
NRSV	New Revised Standard Version

Bible Books

Gen	Genesis	2 Chr	2 Chronicles	Dan	Daniel
Exo	Exodus	Ezr	Ezra	Hos	Hosea
Lev	Leviticus	Neh	Nehemiah	Joe	Joel
Num	Numbers	Est	Esther	Amo	Amos
Deu	Deuteronomy	Job	Job	Oba	Obadiah
Jos	Joshua	Psa	Psalms	Jon	Jonah
Jdg	Judges	Pro	Proverbs	Mic	Micah
Rut	Ruth	Ecc	Ecclesiastes	Nah	Nahum
1 Sam	1 Samuel	Son	Song of Solomon	Hab	Habakkuk
2 Sam	2 Samuel	Isa	Isaiah	Zep	Zepheniah
1 Kin	1 Kings	Jer	Jeremiah	Hag	Haggai
2 Kin	2 Kings	Lam	Lamentations	Zec	Zechariah
1 Chr	1 Chronicles	Eze	Ezekiel	Mal	Malachi

Mat	Matthew	Eph	Ephesians	Heb	Hebrews
Mar	Mark	Phi	Philippians	Jam	James
Luk	Luke	Col	Colossians	1 Pet	1 Peter
Joh	John	1 The	1 Thessalonians	2 Pet	2 Peter
Act	Acts	2 The	2 Thessalonians	1 Joh	1 John
Rom	Romans	1 Tim	1 Timothy	2 Joh	2 John
1 Cor	1 Corinthians	2 Tim	2 Timothy	3 Joh	3 John
2 Cor	2 Corinthians	Tit	Titus	Jde	Jude
Gal	Galatians	Phl	Philemon	Rev	Revelation

FOREWORD

Ralph Waldo Emerson observed that "there is no history, only biography" and thereby describes the deep influence of individuals on our collective life and the way their personal stories represent us. The fifteen autobiographies in this volume portray women faculty who have shaped young lives for the highest good at Florida College and who reflect generations of Christian educators past, present, and future. Each chapter is a reason that Florida College is following Christ today: these women have led the way in their service to God and others. But these stories also represent us: they are windows into the character of other men and women, past and present at Florida College, whose own stories are continued in the narratives that you will read here. Perhaps most importantly, these fifteen reflections are mirrors in which future faculty and students might see what kind of people they can become, by God's grace.

It is an honor for me to have served at Florida College with all the faculty who have authored this volume. In their service to Jesus through countless students, they have "done a beautiful thing," and I'm grateful for the publication of each of these faithful reflections so that "what she has done will also be told in memory of her" (Mat 26:10,13).

Dr. John B. Weaver
President, Florida College
August 10, 2024

PREFACE

The inspiration for this book emerged from a conversation in Dr. John Weaver's office in November 2022. At the time, I was serving as his Chief of Staff, and we would meet every Monday morning to go over our weekly agenda. Our discussions covered a range of topics, but that particular morning, our focus was on donor gifts.

Dr. Weaver often gives a book authored by one of our Bible professors as a token of appreciation to constituents or friends of the College following a personal visit. I suggested that it would be meaningful to have a book specifically authored by the female faculty of FC. My proposal was to use this opportunity not only to showcase the work of our women faculty but also to honor all the women who have contributed to the College over the years.

This book, published nearly two years later, is the result of that initial idea. In December 2022, I met with the female professors to formulate our plan. We agreed to meet monthly to brainstorm and develop our approach. We decided to model our book after a lecture series format, with each faculty member contributing a chapter.

We decided to share our personal stories about what led us to work at the College to provide a meaningful context. Each chapter would reflect the individual experiences of the contributors, and we chose themes based on these stories. To make the book a practical resource, we included discussion questions at the end of each chapter, making it suitable for use in women's study groups.

I am deeply grateful to Brooke Ward for meticulously examining the archives to identify all the former female faculty members of Florida College since its founding in 1946. We aimed to acknowledge these pioneering women who forged paths during a time when working outside the home was far less common. In the early years, women were notably underrepresented both as students and faculty members in higher education.

This project is a tribute to these remarkable women who served as role models and mentors to countless young Christians throughout their college years. Their contributions have had a lasting impact, and this book seeks to honor their legacy and the trail they blazed.

In the Book of Acts, we meet several women who were actively engaged in their work, contributing significantly to their communities and to the early church. Lydia, a seller of purple goods, is mentioned in Acts 16:11-15. She was a successful businesswoman whose home became a center for early Christian fellowship. Tabitha, also known as Dorcas, was a seamstress who dedicated her skills to making garments for the poor, as detailed in Acts 9:36-43. Priscilla, a tentmaker alongside her husband Aquila, is noted in Acts 18:1-4 for her role in supporting Paul and the early church through her work and teaching.

Additionally, in Romans 16:1-2, we read about Phoebe, a deaconess in the church at Cenchreae, who played a crucial role in the early Christian community. These examples illustrate that women have historically been active both in the church and in the marketplace, working diligently for God's purposes. Their contributions, whether through business, craft, or ministry, were integral to the growth and support of the early Christian movement.

Solomon wisely observed in Proverbs, "The heart of man plans his way, but the Lord establishes his steps" (Pro 16:3). He further advised, "Trust in the Lord with all your heart and lean not on your own understanding; in all your ways submit to him, and he will make your paths straight" (Pro 3:5-6). Reflecting on the narratives of the female faculty, it is clear how providence plays a crucial role in guiding our lives. Life often unfolds like a winding road, filled with unexpected turns and challenges.

This metaphor of the "long and winding road" aptly represents the journey of life, highlighting both the unpredictability and the divine guidance that shapes our paths. The stories of these women illustrate how faith and providence have influenced their personal and professional journeys. This demonstrates that despite the twists and turns, their commitment to their work and their trust in God have led them to impactful and meaningful outcomes.

I want to extend my heartfelt gratitude to Dr. John Weaver for his support and for allowing me to lead this project. I also deeply commend the women who dedicated their time and energy to writing their chapters for this book. Their diligence and commitment are evident throughout the pages.

Additionally, I am grateful for the invaluable assistance of our former and current English faculty members who took on the time-consuming task of editing the manuscripts. Their meticulous work ensured the high quality of the final product.

A special thanks goes to Adam Shanks, our new publisher at the Florida College Bookstore, whose patience and guidance were instrumental in bringing this project to completion. David Barlar, the owner of Lam.Agency, Inc. in Franklin, TN, who received his AA from FC in 2002, provided his expertise in graphic design for the book cover. Carrie Black, the bookstore manager, also played a crucial role in overseeing the publication process. Each person involved has contributed significantly to making this book a reality, and I am deeply appreciative of their efforts.

It is my sincere prayer that this book will guide and inspire women of all ages to discover their place in God's kingdom. May the narratives shared within these pages encourage you to lead your best life moving forward. Whether you are young, old, or somewhere in between, I hope that the stories resonate with you and spark a desire to connect with the authors on our campus.

I am confident that these women exemplify true heroism in service and faith within the kingdom. Working closely with them on this project has been a profound honor, and I trust that their experiences and dedication will touch your heart as much as they have touched mine.

Dr. Annetta Hastings
Major Gift Officer
Florida College

FEMALE FACULTY 1946-2024

* Sorted chronologically by the approximate date of hire

1946-1947	
Higgins, Myrtle	English
McCann, Jean	Librarian/English
Tinius, Mildred	Home Economics
1948-1949	
Alexander, Emalene	Science
Lanier, Joy	English
May, Catherine	Piano
Qualls, Norma Jean	Home Economics
Waters, Marjorie	Home Economics
1949-1950	
Catauro, Lucille	Art
Hanks, Kitty	English
Lindsey, Floye	Business
Miller, Bobbie	Business/Home Economics
Neville, Mary	Biology
Reagan, Jo	Home Economics
1950-1951	
Downey, Magdalene (Ragsdale)	Home Economics
Galloway, Mary Elizabeth (Morris)	Librarian
Garrett, Margie	Piano
Kopel, Rachel (Dare)	Chemistry/Mathematics
1951-1952	
Brown, Dorothy	Journalism
1953-1954	
Meek, Betty	Home Economics
1954-1955	
Lewis, Olive	Home Economics
Tacker, Margaret	Piano
1960-1961	
Meier, Geneva	Art
1962-1963	
Wiley, Annette	Business
1963-1964	
Cook, Reba	Fine Arts
Focht, Joan (Norvell)	Fine Arts
Swahn, Mildred	Home Economics/Library
1965-1966	
Burgess, Evelyn	Science & Mathematics
Evans, Hazel Fern	Languages
Morris, Mary Elizabeth	English
Tyler, Frances Kay	Home Economics
Weaver, Eleanor	Fine Arts
Wynn, Lucille	Home Economics
1966-1967	
Lehman, Jane	PE
1969-1970	
Banta, Lena	Business
Mann, Joyce S. "Judy"	Home Economics
1971-1972	
Koonce, Gladys	English, Spanish
1972-1973	
Himmel, Doris	Music
Jenkins, Elizabeth	Secretarial/Business
Pickup, Joella	Music
1974-1975	
MacDonald, Norene	English
Watson, Peggy	Home Economics, PE
1975-1976	
Bingham, Nancy	English
Wilson Sharman G.	French
1976-1977	
Barlar, Rebecca "Becky"	Music
1980-1981	
Cooke, Janetlyn	German, English, Drama
Hunter, Crystal	Education

1981-1982	
Hudson, Karen	PE
1984-1985	
Gibson, Julia J. (Bryant)	Art
Walker, Darlene (Anderson)	Humanities
1985-1986	
Witherington, Karen (Taylor)	English, Humanities
1986-1987	
Atherton, Loretta	Education, English, Journalism
1987-1988	
Sheahan, Judy	Home Economics
1988-1989	
Chandler, Hope	Modern Language
1989-1990	
Moss, Christie	Forensics
1992-1993	
Pope, Mary Ann	Librarian
1993-1994	
Hastings, Annetta (Mauck)	Mathematics
Wagner, Shannon	Aerobics
1994-1995	
Johnson, Laura	English
McCray, Sherri	Aerobics
1995-1996	
Rymal, Becky	Mathematics
1996-1997	
Lacquement, Tandie	Mathematics
Dickey, Wanda	Librarian
1997-1998	
Bourquardez, Nancy	English
Bowman, Denise	English/Librarian
Madrigal, Sandy	Mathematics
Rice, Barbara	Business
Wyatt, Shawn	Music (Piano)

1998-1999	
Maravilla, Monica	English
Parimore, Donna	PE
1999-2000	
Barlar, Nancy	Music/Education
Moody, Marianne	PE
2000-2001	
Jamison, Karen	Education
2002-2003	
Kearney, Jennifer	Librarian
2004-2005	
Hastings, Andrea	Mathematics
Walker, Darlene	Music
2005-2006	
Barlar, Ashley (Reynolds)	Librarian
2007-2008	
Ward, Brooke	Librarian
2008-2009	
Roberts, Suzanne	Education
2009-2010	
Yoho, Tammy	Communications
2010-2011	
Bassett, Jenny	Music
2011-2012	
Cable, Bonny	Education
2012-2013	
Dickey, Lydia	Mathematics
2013-2014	
Crump, Katie	English
Dvorak, Lauren	Science/Nutrition
Price, Anna	Education
Trigg, Kathleen	Communication
2014-2015	
Jones, Cornelia	Mathematics
Peters, Grace	Communication

2015-2016	
Harrell, Sonali	English
Gant, Julie	English
2018-2019	
Baughman, Melody	Mathematics
Brown, Carry	Athletics/Business
Parimore, Jessica	PE
2019-2020	
Ross, Bailey	Science/Mathematics
2020-2021	
Bard, Kim	Art History
Holk, Minerva	Nursing
Moore, Jessica	Music
Oleinik, Tara	PE
Wilson, Roxanne	Marketing

2021-2022	
Aitchison, Jena	Nursing
Amos, Debbie	Science/Mathematics
Behle, Beth	English
Garcia, Angela	Behavioral Science
Miles, Jessica	Kinesiology
Orf, Abigail (Mountford)	Nursing
Rainwater, Lanna	Business
Taylor, Molly	Music
2022-2023	
Paquette, Melissa	Nursing
Scarlett, Alison	English
Thurmon, Joy	Music/Piano
2024-2025	
Chilcote, Kristin	Behavioral Science

PERSEVERANCE

Jena Aitchison

"I have learned, in whatsoever state I am,
therewith to be content."
Philippians 4:11

Many children have dreams they believe they will follow when they grow up. In a young child's mind, anything is possible. Some children may want to be professional athletes or police officers, while others may aspire to be doctors or follow in their parents' footsteps. Some may even imagine where they want to live from a young age, what their profession will be, and how many children they want to have. However, any child's most significant decision is to follow God's plan. Our Father desires that we follow His Word, be baptized for the remission of our sins, and then walk with Him. Impressing upon the next generation the importance of having faith and anchoring themselves in their beliefs is essential to living a godly life.

Sometimes, in our busy, happy lives, we do not realize the extent of our blessings until we face adversity. All families will experience adversities at some point, and when they do, Christians must choose how they will react. Ideally, they will look at God's blessings and be genuinely thankful for them, even in adversity, so that obedience and love for one another will reign when a difficulty arises. Sometimes, however, stresses such as financial crisis, job loss, relocation, and especially health concerns can wear down the family's fabric and foundation. Looking to God and His Word is essential in persevering through such trials.

A good example of faith and perseverance in adversity is when my father, healthy and in his late 30s, suddenly collapsed. In the ER, the doctor treated him for a heart attack; however, a second doctor coming on the shift looked straight into my father's eyes and realized his condition was affecting his brain. After a CT scan and much prayer, we realized he had experienced an arteriovenous malformation rupture in the brain, causing his brain to bleed out. He spent weeks in the ICU and then months in physical therapy, learning to write, walk, drive, and do all the tasks he had done before with little or no thought. Activities that used to seem like second nature took his entire concentration. During these months, I watched my mother, grandparents, aunts, uncles, and other extended family, as well as our church family, rely on God. The day after my dad's collapse was Sunday, and my entire family attended worship together. Their example taught me the importance of worshiping God and putting trust in Him, especially in extremely difficult moments. During this troubling season of our lives, my brother and I were surrounded by those who loved us but who demonstrated to us that they loved the Lord even more. I saw what holding fast to God's unchanging hand looks like. For the next two years, I studied the Bible with family members and eventually was baptized at the age of ten. I understood that what matters is obedience and my walk with God each day. Through the study of the Scriptures, I began to grow in understanding His will for me as well as how much God loves us all.

During my father's many therapy sessions to relearn the functions he had lost, the toll on our family was tremendous. We came to appreciate that family cannot and should not go through significant life-altering events alone. I had many conversations with my mom, grandparents, aunts and uncles, and a counselor. Even though my faith was strong at my tender age, a professional helped me overcome the fears associated with my dad's condition. My relationship with my father had always been special, so seeing him hooked up to a myriad of machines with a tube in his throat and unable to communicate profoundly affected me. I did not know it then, but seeing the healthcare professionals care for my dad is the reason I decided to become a nurse.

As I neared the completion of high school, deciding which college to attend was a new experience for my family. My older brother had attended college, but my parents had not, so it was a learning adventure for us. During my senior year, I visited Florida College, which in the late 1990s was looking to build the girls' volleyball team. I considered FC so that I could play volleyball at the collegiate level and attend a school that fostered my values and my faith, along with fellow brothers and sisters in Christ. Although, in the end, I chose to stay close to home, I believe there is something to be said for taking a step out into the unknown with an opportunity like Florida College and being surrounded by those of faith during those crucial years of development into adulthood. I ultimately attended one college and two universities in Indiana, finally earning a health and physical education degree in the spring of 2005. Still, I had already decided from the time I began student teaching that the school setting was not for me.

I met my husband at a church in Lafayette, Indiana, and we officially started dating after graduation. Our wedding was in March 2006, less than a year later. To some, our dating and engagement time may have seemed too short, but he and I had been extremely close friends for two years before we decided to date officially. He had been commissioned into the Army and was preparing to attend officer training in Arizona just weeks after we married. I still had a job with a traveling health company, and it exposed me to a side of healthcare that piqued my interest: public health, working to help people establish healthier lifestyles. I eventually moved down to Arizona and earned my certificate as a nurse's aide while my husband finished his training. Then, we moved back to Indiana. Having that job also helped me choose a new career- nursing. My husband was often away, training for his first deployment, so I took a leap of faith and applied. Purdue University accepted me into the second-degree BSN program. Changing what I wanted to do so many years after I began working took determination and dedication. Some may feel I should have continued in the same field rather than take a different path, but I was determined to try something new that would ultimately help those who needed that kind of care. With the support and encouragement of my husband and family, I pursued a new career. God gave me the strength to pursue this goal. Working while taking classes was a challenge for me while my husband was away, but focusing on my goals provided strength and a determination to find balance in my life during that busy time.

Constant communication with my spouse, family, and friends, as well as honesty about personal limitations and what I could accomplish, assisted me in making decisions, along with a dedicated prayer life. With my husband's deployment imminent and our desire to start a family, the decision to return to school and become a nurse was right. Time continued to move forward, and I knew that attending my classes with my young children waiting for me at home would make life infinitely more complicated. I enrolled at Purdue; their second-degree nursing program was an intensive, one-year program that offered all the required classes, clinics, and labs in four terms: summer, fall, spring, and summer. I was fortunate to find other students with whom to carpool, as my husband and I had only one car. During the spring semester, I found out I was pregnant with our first child, and he was due just a few days after graduation. Happily, I could walk across the stage at thirty-eight weeks pregnant to get my diploma and receive my nursing pin at a reception following the ceremony.

About eight weeks after Titus, our first child, was born in Indianapolis, my husband was called up by the National Guard and deployed to the Middle East. Though I did not know or understand it at the time, the Department of Defense was conducting a "surge" of military forces into Iraq in an effort to handle and reduce the spreading insurgency in 2008. My husband's twin brother was on his second deployment, so my in-laws had two of their children serving overseas simultaneously. Sacrifice to serve a cause or others takes all types of people and all manner of service. Being a new mother and managing with a husband deployed for the first time was challenging. There were times that I found it difficult to persevere; however, my family, friends, and church members encouraged me through these new experiences.

I knew that after graduating, my first goals would be to pass the National Council Licensure Examination-Registered Nurse (NCLEX-RN) and find a job supporting being a new mother. I took a position on the orthopedic floor of a local hospital in Indianapolis that allowed me to work less than full-time but also gave me the experience I needed as a new nurse. Once I started my new nurse orientation, I realized that without the assistance of nurse educators, my transition was going to be more difficult than I expected. Once orientation was completed, the hospital gave me four or five patients on an orthopedic medical/surgical floor. These patients often needed pain management and physical therapy, which is important in the initial post-operative time frame. As a new nurse, I learned to prioritize patient needs while providing safe nursing care for everyone. During this time, I was also juggling being a mother of a young boy, who stayed with different family members depending on their schedules. I trusted my parents, grandparents, and many other family members to watch my son while I worked, and the saying, "It takes a village to raise a child," took on real meaning for me. In these months, I had infrequent contact with my husband, as these were the days before reliable internet on deployments. He emailed daily, but we were able to speak only when the Morale Welfare and Recreation lines were open and able to connect with Indiana. While it was a hard year starting a new career, taking care of my first child, and coping with our first deployment as a family, I learned that I was loved by so many. As I felt that love from people on this earth, I recognized how much more my Heavenly Father loves me.

When my husband returned from deployment, he received orders to move to Fort Hood (now Fort Cavazos), Texas. We spent Christmas together, packed the entire house, and moved to Texas. This was going to be my first experience gaining a new nursing license in another state. Applying for a license in a new state was a frustrating experience that would replay repeatedly each time we relocated. When nurses apply for licensure in a new state, they must follow its regulations to obtain a new license. Still, many states are part of a compact licensure agreement that accepts licenses from other states in that compact. Getting nursing jobs at that time was never difficult, but finding the right balance between working, rearing a child in the Lord, supporting and leading our family, and increasing my nursing skills was challenging. Each goal has its challenges, and one must consider the positives and negatives. While serving others and helping patients improve are ideal goals, being a mother, raising children, and supporting and leading our families should be the utmost focus.

I took a nursing job in an orthopedic unit shortly after arriving in Central Texas, and I learned I was pregnant with our second child a few weeks after starting my new job. After six months, I gave my notice to stay at home with my son and new baby girl, Ainsley. Six months after her birth, my husband's orders ended, and there was a gap before he went on active duty status. At that time, I was blessed to work as a home health nurse in the same healthcare system as the hospital I worked for in Central Texas. A home healthcare nurse's skills were similar and different from what I had experienced on the orthopedic floor. In home health, one must be self-motivated and able to work independently. My job was to go to the patients' homes and assess both the patients and their surroundings. I gathered as much information as possible to assist patients and get services started for them. A home healthcare nurse needs many nursing skills, creativity, and flexibility to succeed.

Once my husband was issued active-duty orders, we moved to Fort Bliss in west Texas. Shortly after that move, my husband learned he would be deployed to the Middle East in sixty days. Moving to a new location with few friends or acquaintances and having a baby and a toddler was extremely overwhelming. After much prayer and discussion, my husband and I decided to ask my parents if they would move to Texas to help with the care of our children during my husband's second deployment. I accepted a job as a school nurse a few weeks after my husband deployed.

Midway through the deployment, we had a family emergency. My eighteen-month-old daughter was hit by his car as my father backed into the driveway. I received a phone call that I was ill-prepared to hear. Ainsley was taken to the pediatric hospital in town. Once I arrived, I had to wait to see her while she was having a CT scan. When I finally walked into her room, she was intubated and wrapped up. Her prognosis was really good, but she required surgery to clean out and suture up her scalp. She stayed in the hospital for two days before being discharged. My husband received emergency leave and was able to come home with Ainsley from the hospital. God truly blessed us through the traumatic experience and preserved us through this trial.

My husband served as a unit commander for two years while stationed at Fort Bliss, Texas; in that time, he was constantly on call and working through issues at work. In 2013, we had our daughter Sydney, who would be the final addition to our family. As our children became school-age, we had a choice: to send them to public school or to homeschool them. When we first married, we never thought about homeschooling, but as the time drew near for our oldest to go to school, we chose that direction. This meant educating our kids in all subjects, many of which I had not studied or used since grade school. My husband and I both taught, each teaching the subjects we thought we could teach the best. I focused on science and math; my husband took English and social studies. We quickly learned that we were nowhere near organized enough to provide a rigorous, daily, academic schedule. Fortunately, during this time, our moves around the country stationed us where homeschool co-op groups met regularly, providing valuable assistance, resources, and opportunities for our children to interact with other homeschooled children. All parents must decide what is in the best interest of their children.

While educating the children, I took a job teaching clinicals to nursing students in El Paso, Texas. The students were vocational nursing students looking to become LVNs. It was my first real experience teaching and instructing in nursing. The job also taught me the importance of understanding and working on the basics of nursing skills and the value of critical thinking. Both are areas that every nurse should understand and be comfortable using. I also stressed that they should ask questions when unsure of the task. LVNs play a critical role in the nursing community and work directly under Registered Nurses (RNs).

There is a critical shortage in nursing education. Nursing has long had this shortage, and the ability to produce new nurses in a field where burnout is quite high is severely limited. Combining nursing with education brought my educational journey full circle. I was returning to where I had begun, not with physical and health education but with nursing education. I quickly realized to move further into the educator role, I needed more schooling.

Since our family life was busy and my husband had so many responsibilities, I needed to find a program that would allow me to continue to homeschool our kids and take classes at the same time. We were also moving again, reassigned to the Pentagon in northern Virginia. I began my nursing graduate program two months before moving to Virginia. The program confirmed that nursing education was the career field I wanted to pursue, and working through teaching clinicals, I began to explore other areas of nursing in which I had little experience, such as mental health.

Continually being stationed at different locations within the United States allowed us to attend many different congregations. Some congregations were large, some were small, some had leadership in the form of elders, and others were led through men's business meetings. Deciding where we might want to move next with the Army depended on where we could find strong congregations to worship and work. In our minds, there was little profit in going to a location that might help my husband's military career but would be hours away from a group of the Lord's people. You have the right priority if you have that at the forefront of all your decisions, including college, careers, and where to settle down. How can you serve God and be close with fellow brethren if you are not in a location where Christians meet?

My husband's job at the Pentagon required him to work the night shift, four days on and four days off, for months at a time. We were still homeschooling our children, sometimes while he was attempting to sleep during the day and while I was finishing graduate school. Finding a better job for him was of paramount importance. He was able to interview successfully for a job as an aide-de-camp for a general, but it required us to move again, just over a year after we moved to Virginia. This time, we moved to Maryland. I was able to complete my graduate degree and began looking at job opportunities as we moved. We knew that we would be in Maryland for a single year only, so I was able to be picky in my job selection. I secured a position as a nurse educator in a long-term care facility. With my parents' help, we could continue to homeschool the kids, and I gained valuable experience in one kind of nursing education.

After a year in Maryland, we moved to Kansas, where my husband attended Command and General Staff College. Sometimes, God has different plans despite what you think will happen. We planned to be in Kansas for only one year, but it turned into three. While there, I had the opportunity to work for the VA as a nursing clinical instructor for a small college that offered a BSN program. As my husband prepared to deploy on his third mission to the Middle East, we made the decision to send our kids to a public school on post. This happened as our oldest child was ready to begin middle school, and our youngest was in first grade. This time frame was an adjustment for my children because they were starting a new school experience, and their dad deployed for the first time they could remember. Then, COVID broke out at the end of their school year. There were many times when my faith trembled. However, with study under the strong leaders of our local congregation, the support of my family, and, most importantly, our ever-present God, we persevered through this adversity.

Through my quest to become a nursing educator, I always knew Florida College would be the ideal educational environment. Many family members and friends attended Florida College, and I had a working knowledge of the environment and the expectations FC provided its students. In March of 2021, I received an email from Florida College encouraging me to apply to their new nursing program starting in the fall of 2021. My husband was on active duty in the Army at the time, and we were living in Colorado. I hesitated to apply because if I took the position, my children and I would move, and my husband would stay in Colorado. Paul encouraged me to apply and reminded me that God would always be there for us. With much prayer and discussion, I applied to Florida College on the last day the position was to be posted. Shortly after applying, I received an email setting up a virtual interview. Near the end of April, I flew to Florida and spent a day on the campus of Florida College interviewing and taking in the sites and culture that FC had to offer. Once back in Colorado, I received a call from the Academic Dean offering me a position at FC. I had mixed emotions because I knew this opportunity was what I had dreamed about for my future career. However, taking the position at FC meant I would be away from my husband. Through much prayer and deliberation as a family, we decided I would take the position. Our goal was for our three children and me to move to Florida while my husband finished his time in Colorado. While there have been difficult moments starting a new job and career, I thoroughly enjoy the wonderful environment at FC. My children have been able to settle in, make connections, and, very importantly, not concern themselves with moving again and again.

Teaching at FC has been an amazing experience. I have the best colleagues and students. Coming to work is a joy each day, but I also know my professional family supports my prioritizing my own family. I thank God for allowing me to have so many life experiences that guided me to where I am today.

Perseverance is a crucial quality in life as it enables us to face challenges and obstacles. It forces us to keep going even when the going gets tough. Our aim is to explore the topic, examine what the Bible, both Old and New Testament, has to say concerning perseverance, and apply that to daily life.

There are several reasons why each of us should continue to persevere, even when faced with difficulties. First, perseverance builds character and strength. We develop resilience, determination, and perseverance when we face and overcome our challenges. These qualities help us to grow and mature as individuals, enabling us to face future obstacles with confidence and faith.

Let us consider some biblical examples of perseverance. One of the most well-known examples is that of Job. Job was a man who had everything: a loving family, wealth, and good health. However, God allowed Satan to test Job's faith by taking away everything that Job had. He lost his children, his wealth, and his health. Despite all this, Job remained faithful to God and persevered through his trials. Ultimately, God restored everything to Job and blessed him even more. This story is a powerful example of the importance of perseverance in the face of adversity.

Secondly, perseverance leads to growth and progress. When we persevere through life's challenges, we learn valuable lessons, gain new skills, and develop a deeper understanding of ourselves and our faith. Perseverance enables us to overcome obstacles and achieve our goals, leading to personal growth and success. Another biblical example of perseverance is that of Paul. Paul was a man who faced many trials and tribulations in his life. He was imprisoned, beaten, and stoned for his faith. In 2 Corinthians 4:8-9, Paul writes, "We are hard pressed on every side, but not crushed; perplexed, but not in despair; persecuted, but not abandoned; struck down, but not destroyed." Paul's perseverance in the face of trials and tribulations is a testament to the power of faith and the importance of perseverance in our lives. Now, let us conduct a word study of perseverance. The original Greek word for perseverance is *hupomone*, which means to "remain under, to bear up courageously, and to endure." This word appears several times in the New Testament, including in James 1:12, where it says, "Blessed is the one who perseveres under trial because, having stood the test, that person will receive the crown of life that the Lord has promised to those who love him." This definition highlights that perseverance requires courage and endurance in adversity. Perseverance is crucial because it helps us to achieve our goals and dreams.

From the female perspective, the Old Testament is alive with examples of strong, faithful, and devoted women to both God and their respective families. In the Old Testament book of Ruth, the principal character, Ruth, a Moabite wife in the Hebrew family of Emilech and Naomi, turned her back on the faith of her ancestors and followed Naomi and God to an unfamiliar land of Israel. Naomi's relationship with the God of Israel had impacted Ruth. This is striking because Naomi had been widowed and had lost both her sons—her life was not easy. But despite her pain, Naomi had a strong witness in the face of adversity. She did not desert or abandon God. She still honored and loved Him. Ruth saw something in Naomi that made her want to follow after Naomi's God. Characteristics that make up Ruth's character include selflessness, devotion, loyalty, and a willingness to sacrifice and take a risk by leaving everything familiar. She was willing to go to an unknown place, people, and God, facing potential ridicule from both her Moabite people for leaving as well as from the Jews for being both an outsider and a Gentile.

Thirdly, perseverance is a testament to our faith and trust in God. When we persevere through difficulties, we demonstrate our belief that God is with us, guiding and supporting us through every trial and tribulation. Perseverance is an act of faith, showing that we trust in God's plan and believe He will help us overcome any obstacle we face. Perseverance is a key principle emphasized throughout the Bible. It is persistance in the face of challenges, obstacles, and setbacks. The Bible teaches us that perseverance is essential for achieving our goals, overcoming adversity, and growing in our faith. One of the most well-known verses on perseverance in the Bible is Galatians 6:9, which states, "Let us not become weary in doing good, for at the proper time we will reap a harvest if we do not give up." This verse reminds us that perseverance is necessary for reaping the rewards of our efforts. It encourages us to continue doing good and not to lose heart, even when we face difficulties or challenges.

When we face obstacles and challenges, it is easy to become discouraged and give up. However, if we endure bravely through these challenges, we can achieve great things. Perseverance also helps us to grow as individuals. When we face difficulties, we learn important lessons about ourselves and our world. We become stronger, more resilient, and more compassionate. Perseverance is a vital component of faith and spiritual growth. When we face trials and tribulations, we demonstrate our trust in God and commitment to his will. In addition to the biblical examples of perseverance, many Bible verses support the importance of this quality. James 1:2-4 says, "Consider it pure joy, my brothers and sisters, whenever you face trials of many kinds, because you know that the testing of your faith produces perseverance. Let perseverance finish its work so you may be mature and complete, not lacking anything." This verse reminds us that trials and difficulties are a natural part of life and that pressing on through these trials can help us to grow and mature as individuals. Another Bible verse that supports the importance of perseverance is Romans 5:3-4, in which Paul writes, "Not only so, but we also glory in our sufferings, because we know that suffering produces perseverance; perseverance, character; and character, hope." This verse reminds us that perseverance is important for achieving our goals and developing our character and cultivating hope in our lives.

Additionally, Paul persevered in the face of physical harm and limitations. Despite the beatings and unjust imprisonments, Paul wrote in Philippians 4:11, "I have learned, in whatsoever state I am, therewith to be content." He endured because of his profound hope and trust in Jesus Christ. In 2 Timothy 3:12, he stated, "All that will live godly in Christ Jesus shall suffer persecution." The truth of the trials on earth is just a taste of the joy to come in the next life, which "worketh for us a far more exceeding and eternal weight of glory" (2 Cor 4:17).

In conclusion, perseverance is an essential quality in life, enabling us to face life's challenges and obstacles. The Bible provides many examples of perseverance, including the stories of Job, Paul, Naomi, and Ruth, along with other Bible verses supporting perseverance's importance in our lives. As we face life's challenges, may we remember the importance of perseverance and have the courage to keep going, knowing that God is with us every step. The biblical principles of perseverance are essential for achieving our goals, overcoming adversity, and growing in our faith. Perseverance builds character, leads to growth and progress, and demonstrates our faith and trust in God. Therefore, we should persevere, even when faced with challenges, knowing that God is with us every step of the way. As the Bible teaches us, "Let us not become weary in doing good, for at the proper time we will reap a harvest if we do not give up" (Gal 6:9).

THOUGHT QUESTIONS FOR "PERSEVERANCE"

1. When you consider the topic of perseverance, which person in your life comes to mind? What experiences did he or she endure that you draw encouragement from?

2. What kinds of trials do women face throughout life? What have you yourself experienced that required an extra measure of perseverance?

3. How would you counsel a friend or sister who is facing hard times? What coping methods would you recommend to her?

4. Discuss ways we can encourage each other to prepare for future trials. What can most, if not all, women expect to deal with if they live long enough?

5. What Bible verses do you turn to when you are faced with challenges?

GROWING THROUGH ADVERSITY

Becky Barlar

We also exult in our tribulations, knowing that tribulation brings about perseverance, and perseverance, proven character, and proven character, hope.

Romans 5:3-4

My parents, Harold Nance and Freda (Bailey) Nance, were childless for 16 years when I was born. They immediately needed to relocate my dad's veterinary clinic so we would not have people and animals coming through our home day and night. He bought the building that became his clinic that year and practiced there until he retired. My mother was his secretary/surgical assistant. This was a complicated job requiring overseeing the front desk, packing surgery trays, and assisting with small animal surgery. Despite preferring to stay home after my birth, whenever my dad's assistant was ill or on vacation, she filled in for her. Whenever a new person was hired, my mom was responsible for training her, so I spent many days at my dad's office where I learned useful life skills like typing and filing.

I had an idyllic childhood growing up in the small town of Lawrenceburg, Tennessee. I lived four blocks from the stores on the town square and two blocks from my elementary school, my congregation's meeting place, and the movie theater, so I could walk to many places I wanted to go. Most of the young people in this town were from religious families, and many were Christians, so it was relatively easy to be a child of God there. My mother converted my father seven years after they married, and they were faithful Christians throughout their lives, attending every service of the church and teaching me the importance of God and His Word. They were involved in many professional and civic organizations, letting their lights shine in the community. They instilled in me the habits they learned in their early married years during the Depression and World War II, including working hard, serving others, and being frugal, hospitable, giving, and thankful.

My parents bought a Gulbransen spinet piano for my eighth birthday. I had a serious illness that summer, which caused me to be bedfast, but a few months later, I began piano lessons with a neighbor around the corner. In seventh grade, I began playing flute in the band. I was passionate about both instruments. I was drum major for the high school band in my senior year. When I was ready for college, I knew I wanted to major in music, but I was not sure which of these instruments I would emphasize. I briefly considered Florida College, but since they did not have a band, I decided instead to attend Middle Tennessee State University, where I had attended summer band camps.

My husband, Doug, and I married during our time at MTSU, where we both pursued music education degrees. While still playing flute in the band, I decided to concentrate on piano to teach music in my home when I had children. The Vietnam War was raging, and Doug had a low draft number, so he auditioned for the National Guard Band in Nashville. While I continued my classes, he took a semester off to complete Army basic training as part of his six-year commitment to the Tennessee National Guard. When we were expecting our first child, I was seriously ill for a few weeks, but a healthy daughter we named Jennifer was born during our senior year. I gave my senior piano recital six weeks before she was born, and Doug gave his senior tuba recital when she was three months old. Since I was his accompanist, we set Jennifer in her infant seat on stage beside us while we practiced.

After graduating from MTSU, we moved to Franklin, Tennessee. I had a home studio where I taught piano and flute while Doug worked on his master's in Tuba Performance in Nashville at Peabody College, which later became a part of Vanderbilt University. Doug played tuba professionally in the Dixieland band at the Opryland theme park during the summers, so we spent many fun hours there. During our third year in Franklin, Doug was hired as band director at Franklin Junior High while finishing his doctoral coursework in the evenings. We bought our first home and had our second daughter, Nancy, during this time. Nancy had a health crisis shortly after her birth. At six weeks old, she had life-saving surgery at Vanderbilt Hospital, followed by a five-day hospital stay. It took many months for her to regain her health and strength after that ordeal.

In 1976, Doug had the opportunity to move to Temple Terrace to begin a band program at Florida College. Considering this an interesting challenge, we packed up all our possessions and moved our two daughters 700 miles away from our families just in time for Jennifer to begin kindergarten. We knew almost no one in Tampa when we moved here, but we fortunately found a supportive church family at the University church. Those first years in Florida were difficult in many ways, but we gained much maturity and independence that has served us well ever since.

Three weeks after our move to Tampa, my parents were in an automobile accident. My dad went to the hospital in Tennessee, and my mom was sent for medical care in Birmingham, Alabama, to undergo open-heart surgery to repair a leaking thoracic aorta. The doctors gave her a five-percent chance of surviving the surgery. We immediately flew to Birmingham, where my in-laws met us and took our children home with them. When my mother stabilized, Doug returned to Tampa to begin his college duties. My mother was in the hospital for almost two weeks. This was an extremely stressful time for me and my family, but fortunately, my mom survived. Six years later, her aorta was replaced again and she ultimately lived another 21 years after the second surgery, thanks to God and a skillful surgeon.

During our first year at FC, I taught a piano class and accompanied some voice lessons for Joella Pickup. Joella and Harry had spearheaded hiring Doug to begin the band program.

College girls babysat our daughters in the dorm while I worked. From then on, they looked forward to when they would be FC students and live in the dorms. Since we lived down the road from the University of South Florida, I began to think about returning to school for graduate work. I was awarded a fellowship, which enabled me to spend the next two years working on my master's in Piano Performance/Pedagogy while also getting experience teaching class piano in their electronic piano laboratory. That degree qualified me to teach music theory classes part-time at FC while teaching private piano in my home studio. As an only child, I always wanted a large family, so in the early 80s, we added two sons, Jonathan and David. While I taught in the late afternoons, my girls learned responsibility by doing household chores and watching their little brothers. I have always been thankful I had a job that enabled me to stay home with my children during their early years.

Providing for a family of six was extremely challenging on a Florida College salary. It soon became obvious that I needed to earn more income, so in 1986, I was excited to join the full-time faculty at FC as a piano and music theory professor. Working while my children were in school was easier than teaching in the late afternoons when they were home and needed me to transport them to after-school activities. My schedule followed the school calendar, so I had holidays and summers off to spend with them. As a bonus, I earned my own salary, retirement, and health insurance. Despite our jobs, Doug and I tried never to miss the boys' soccer, baseball, and basketball games, the girls' cheerleading, and other activities in which they were involved.

Doug always had many night obligations at FC. Besides all the instrumental groups, Doug was responsible for setting up sound for every event on campus. Therefore, when their dad could not be home in the evenings, I took our family to Doug's events on campus. Our children spent many nights listening to concerts in the seats of Hutchinson or Puckett Auditoriums. They cheered for the Florida College basketball team in front of their dad's pep band at home games and with the visiting crowd when away. All four of our children were in FC musical productions as young children while their father directed or played in the pit orchestra. If I stayed on campus past three o'clock, they enjoyed playing on the riverbank with the children of other faculty and staff members. Our children grew up on the Florida College campus!

Doug got the band off to a good start and continued leading the instrumental music program for 25 years. He eventually added a wind ensemble, jazz ensemble, and string ensemble and worked with the popular music group "Friends" that did recruiting for the school. He also taught a band program at Florida College Academy for one hour every school day for 24 years. In the early 2000s, Doug and I were privileged to travel with the "Friends" on their May tours. We toured the eastern seaboard up to Canada, the Midwest, and the west coast from California to Washington. We are thankful for the hospitality and the many new friends we made during those travels.

I began teaching each of our children piano the summer before they started first grade. They all began band instruments at FCA in sixth grade under their dad's direction. Doug and I spent 12 enjoyable years as band parents at King High School, attending all the concerts, home and away football games, and marching contests. Two of our four children were King High Marching Lions drum majors. Doug served two years as president of the band boosters' organization and chaperoned some of their out-of-town trips. When our children became FC students, they participated in their dad's wind ensemble, jazz ensemble, and "Friends," and they worked with musical productions as actors or musicians in the pit orchestra. I am so thankful they had not only the Florida College experience but also these FC music experiences they enjoyed because of their dad's success in starting these programs.

Throughout Doug's time at the college, he has preached on a regular basis. Over 35 of those years were in St. Petersburg, where Doug also serves as an elder. We packed up the children and drove over for the entire day on Sunday and again on Wednesday evening. The time in the car was beneficial since our busy family often went in several different directions at other times. We made many friendships at these congregations that continue to this day.

It appears our children were influenced by growing up around an educational institution. Two of our children followed in our footsteps as educators. All four attended FC for their first two years, with Jonathan staying for his bachelor's degree. Jonathan spent 15 years as a teacher and principal in the Hillsborough County School District. He currently teaches at FC's education department and serves as the education department chair. He and his wife recently started a tutoring company called Foxtail Learning. Nancy was a music education major and spent over 10 years as a middle school band director. After finishing her doctorate, she taught online classes for several colleges and universities. Starting in 2015, she taught at Florida College full-time until she died in 2020. Jennifer married an educator and is a speech-language pathologist who has worked in various settings, including elementary schools, and as an adjunct clinical instructor for USF. After many years working in healthcare, she now has an administrative position as supervisor of rehabilitation at a hospital and three of their outpatient clinics. David, a graphic designer, lives near Nashville and owns an advertising agency. Although his field is not related to education, he is active in the teaching program at his local congregation. His wife is a speech/language pathologist who teaches in their children's elementary school.

Our youngest child, David, graduated from high school in 2000, the same year our oldest grandson, Ty, was born. Ty's brother Casey was born in 2002. Those first few years of the new century were difficult for me. My parents moved into an assisted living facility in 2002. My dad stayed there for a year and flourished, but my mother had to be moved to a rehab center after two months due to her rapid decline. As an only child, all the responsibility for them fell upon me. Caregiving from 700 miles away was very difficult. My mother died in December of 2003 at the age of 86. The following summer, our family spent several weeks cleaning out the home my parents had lived in for 60 years. My dad passed away the following April at the age of 94. I regret missing some of Ty and Casey's early years because I was preoccupied with my parents' care. However, during this time, I was able to arrange my schedule to keep Ty one morning a week while his mother worked. Despite stressful days, we spent many happy times with our family, traveling to visit my parents or to take care of their home.

In 2001, Doug changed jobs at the college when he was appointed Dean of Student Services, a position he held for eight years. The college was beginning to add four-year degrees, so under his leadership, the Bachelor of Arts in Music degree was approved in 2004 and added to the curriculum. During this time, Doug taught four music history classes and worked with the "Friends" group. In 2009, Doug returned to the music department, where he continued to serve as Chair. Under his leadership, the college received accreditation from the National Association of Schools of Music, making it easier for our music students to get accepted into graduate programs. He and Nancy also designed and received college and state approval for our Bachelor of Science in Music Education degree. We were also involved in the FC travel program and led student tours to Germany, Austria, Czech Republic, Hungary, Norway, France, and Italy.

My teaching became even more enjoyable and rewarding after we added the four-year music degrees. Previously, I worked with students just long enough to see them begin to blossom as pianists before transferring to another school, but now most stayed for four years, and I was able to guide them through their senior recitals. I also served as chair of the college's lecture/recital series, sponsored the college's future music educators' chapter, and served on the curriculum review committee. I was involved in the local music teachers' association, holding every office at some time. Since 2005, I have been on the Executive Board of the Florida State Music Teachers Association (FSMTA). Ultimately, I rose to the office of president of the Association and the Foundation. In 2022, FSMTA honored me with a Music Teachers National Association (MTNA) Foundation Fellow award. I taught full-time at Florida College for 30 years and part-time for another 10 years before retiring in 2016. Doug officially retired in 2021, although he still teaches an online class for the college's dual enrollment program. He also plays in a community band called Fanfare Concert Winds group and continues to preach on Sundays.

While carrying out my various life roles, I dealt with many health challenges. Most disturbing for my professional career, I had four hand and wrist surgeries and severe osteoarthritis in my hands and fingers that prevented me from performing and accompanying as I had done during my early years at FC. I also had five major surgeries, four serious infections requiring hospitalizations, and three different cancer diagnoses that required biopsies, surgeries, and/or cryoablation (but fortunately, no chemo or radiation). I still need frequent imaging and monitoring of my health, including surveillance on a thoracic aortic aneurysm that was discovered 14 years ago. More recently, I have had two knee replacements, two chronic illnesses, and diagnoses of Parkinson's Disease and macular degeneration. With the help of God, my excellent team of doctors, and medications, I am still doing well overall.

The most challenging time of my life did not involve my health but my daughter Nancy's health. In 2012, Nancy was diagnosed with invasive breast cancer. After they found lesions in her liver, her diagnosis upgraded to stage four. Seeking to fight the cancer aggressively, Nancy had chemotherapy and two major surgeries. The chemo was effective, and she spent a few years with "no evidence of disease," but as the doctors had always anticipated, the cancer returned, and she knew she would be on some kind of chemo for the rest of her life. Since Nancy was single, I was her primary caregiver. Nancy made a "living list" instead of a "bucket list," and she tried to see and do as much as possible while she still had the health to do so. We were fortunate to join her on several of her trips. We traveled together to Australia, New Zealand, South Africa, England, Scotland, and Canada. We cruised to Italy, Spain, the Greek Isles, Portugal, Morocco, and St. Petersburg, Russia. Nancy eventually passed away in May 2020 at the age of 45, almost eight years after her original cancer diagnosis. By the time of her passing, she had been to all 50 states and over 45 foreign countries, most while she was fighting this terrible disease. In my opinion, losing a child is the hardest thing a parent can go through, and I pray none of you are unfortunate enough to outlive your children.

Nancy had requested that we endow a scholarship in her name to benefit Florida College music education majors, and this scholarship is now fully endowed. The first recipient was her nephew, Ty Ackett. Ty participated in every musical group on campus at FC and graduated in 2022 with his Bachelor of Science in Music Education. Doug was pleased that he was a tuba major like his grandfather. He taught middle school band in Tampa for one semester before moving to Conway, Arkansas, where he teaches band and chorus at a Christian school. He married a young lady he met at FC in June of 2024 in Texas. Ty's brother Casey is a senior at FC. He plays saxophone in wind and jazz ensemble and sings and plays electric bass in "Unplugged," and he has recently decided to add a music minor to his Finance degree. Our other three grandchildren are still in elementary/middle school. Jonathan's son Drew has studied piano with me and sings in a community children's choir. David's children, Lylah and Mason, began piano lessons last year, and Lylah is playing flute in beginning band this year. Lylah also had a role in her school's recent musical production of "The Little Mermaid." I hope our grandchildren can attend Florida College and benefit from our legacy in the music department.

When coming to Florida College, Doug expected to stay for five years and use that as a stepping stone to a larger college or university job. However, we both loved the students we taught, the people we worked with, and the spiritual emphasis of FC. We found Temple Terrace to be a great place to raise our children. After almost 48 years, we have made many friends through Florida College, which has greatly enriched our lives. I hope we, in turn, have impacted the lives of the students we taught for the better. We have been and continue to be richly blessed by our decision to work at this little college by the Hillsborough River called Florida College, and I am grateful to God for leading us in this direction.

While working on this project and reflecting on my life, the one thing that stood out is that I have had more than my share of challenges and difficulties along the way. I have always considered myself to have had a happy and richly blessed life, but there have been many adversities I have faced throughout my life. Moving to Florida at age 26 to begin work at Florida College and leaving behind everybody and everything that was familiar to me was challenging but equally rewarding. Having sole care of my aging parents for the next 29 years while living 700 miles away from them was also difficult. I have faced many personal health problems, and I have lost a daughter to a hard-fought battle with cancer. Reflecting on how all these circumstances affected my life, I have realized that instead of defeating me, these challenges have caused me to grow into a much stronger person. This led me to study how God tells Christians to deal with adversity, and I will share some of my thoughts with you here.

Merriam-Webster defines the noun adversity as "a state of serious or continued difficulty or misfortune." [1]It goes on to say, "Adversity comes from Middle English adversite, meaning opposition, hostility, misfortune, or hardship, which itself is from Latin adversus, the source of adverse, which means bad or unfavorable."[2] There are many synonyms for adversity, but a few are trouble, disaster, suffering, affliction, sorrow, and misery. In the King James Version, nine verses in the Old Testament use the word adversity, and only one verse in the New Testament uses that word. The more modern translations use other familiar terms to talk about the concept of adversity, but there are many Scriptures we can go to for help in our struggles.

More simply put, adversity is any kind of challenge, difficulty, or hardship that affects a person's ability to attain their goals in life. Everyone who lives long on this earth will experience adversity. Adversity can take many forms, and different people have different types of misfortunes, many greater than anything I have ever experienced. Sometimes, we feel unequipped to deal with our afflictions or to help our family and friends through their difficulties, but we must remember God provides all the answers we need through the Spirit-inspired Scriptures. As the psalmist said in Psalms 28:7, "The Lord is my strength and my shield; My heart trusts in Him, and I am helped; Therefore my heart exults, And with my song I shall thank Him" (NASB).

Another scripture that helps me is Psalms 46:1-2, which says, "God is our refuge and strength. A very present help in trouble. Therefore we will not fear, though the earth

---

1 Merriam-Webster. s.v. "Adversity." accessed April 8, 2024, https://www.merriam-webster.com/dictionary/adversity

2 Merriam-Webster. s.v. "Adversity." accessed April 8, 2024, https://www.merriam-webster.com/dictionary/adversity

should change and though the mountains slip into the heart of the sea." Lately, our country has been plagued by what seems to be an unusual number of severe weather events like hurricanes, tornadoes, earthquakes, blizzards, fires, floods, and mudslides. Everyone is talking about "climate change." Living in Florida, we hover around the television to watch the hurricane symbol with its "cone of uncertainty" approaching our area. When we think we have everything under control, God shows us who is in charge and what is most important. Our possessions are temporal, but our souls are eternal. Paul says in Philippians 4:6-8, "Be anxious for nothing, but in everything by prayer and supplication with thanksgiving let your requests be made known to God. And the peace of God which surpasses all comprehension, will guard your hearts and minds in Christ Jesus."

When I am discouraged, I think of Job. Job lost all his children, all his property and possessions, and even his physical health. But what does the Bible say that Job did? Job 1:22 says, "Through all of this Job did not sin or blame God." When Job's wife encouraged him to curse God and die, he reprimanded his wife by saying in Job 2:10, "You speak as one of the foolish women speaks. Shall we indeed accept good from God and not accept adversity?" We often take the good in life for granted and then blame God when troubles come. However, we must remember we need His help every day, in good and bad times. Paul said it best in 1 Thessalonians 5:16-18 when he wrote, "Rejoice always; pray without ceasing; in everything give thanks, for this is God's will for you in Christ Jesus."

The Scriptures have many examples of biblical characters who overcame misfortune and trials. Despite his sin, David repented and is spoken of as a man after God's own heart. Esther dared to face the king and plead for her people. Noah spent many years building the ark, enduring ridicule from the people around him, but never once doubting God would save him and his family from the flood. You can draw more inspiration from reading about the heroes of faith in Hebrews 11. These people were just ordinary people like you and me, but they had extraordinary faith. James says in James 1:12, "Blessed is the man who perseveres under trial; for once he has been approved, he will receive the crown of life which the Lord has promised to those who love Him."

The apostle Paul endured more suffering than I can imagine. He said in 2 Corinthians 11:26-28, "I have been on frequent journeys, in dangers from rivers, dangers from robbers, dangers from my countrymen, dangers from the Gentiles, dangers in the city, dangers in the wilderness, dangers on the sea, dangers among false brethren; I have been in labor and hardship, through many sleepless nights, in hunger and thirst, often without food, in cold and exposure. Apart from such external things, there is the daily pressure on me of concern for all the churches."

As well as the physical dangers, Paul had daily worry and concern for the Christians he had converted. Through the inspiration of the Holy Spirit, he said in Romans 5:3-5, "We also exult in our tribulations, knowing that tribulation brings about perseverance, and perseverance, proven character, and proven character, hope; and hope does not disappoint, because the love of God has been poured out within our hearts through the Holy Spirit who was given to us." At the end of his life, Paul spent many months imprisoned in Rome. However, he never doubted his struggles would be worth it. In 2 Timothy 4:7-8, Paul says, "I have fought the good fight, I have finished the course, I have kept the faith; in the future there is laid up for me the crown of righteousness, which the Lord, the righteous Judge, will award to me on that day; and not only to me, but also to all who have loved His appearing."

The best way to handle adversity is to prepare before troubles arise. How can you be prepared? Read and study God's Word to know what God desires of you. Your faith will be strong when your trials come. Psalms 119:143 says, "Trouble and anguish have come upon me, yet Your commandments are my delight." Jesus says in John 16:33, "These things I have spoken to you, so that in Me you may have peace. In the world you have tribulation, but take courage; I have overcome the world." James 1:2-4 says, "Consider it all joy, my brethren, when you encounter various trials, knowing that the testing of your faith produces endurance. And let endurance have its perfect result, so you may be perfect and complete, lacking in nothing." Some translations use the word adequate instead of perfect. Knowing God's word will make us adequate for the task at hand. Psalms 46:10 says, "Cease striving and know that I am God. I will be exalted among the nations, I will be exalted in the earth." How often do we struggle to find our own solutions instead of listening to what God tells us to do to find true peace?

Remember, God is always there to help you. Pray to Him for perseverance and strength not only during trying times but at all times. James 4:7-8 says, "Submit yourself to God. Resist the devil and he will flee from you. Draw near to God and He will draw near to you." Proverbs 1:27-28 says, "When your dread comes like a storm, And your calamity comes like a whirlwind, when distress and anguish come upon you. Then you will call on Me, but I will not answer. They will seek Me diligently, but they will not find me. Because they hated knowledge and did not choose the fear of the Lord." Do not find yourself in a situation where your sins separate you from God. He is eager to help us if we approach him in prayer and make our requests known to Him.

Do you ever struggle to find the right words for your prayers? Paul says in Romans 8:26-28, "In the same way the Spirit also helps our weakness; for we do not know how to pray as we should, but the Spirit Himself intercedes for us with groanings too deep for words; and He who searches the hearts knows what the mind of the Spirit is, because he intercedes for the saints according to the will of God. And we know that God causes all things to work together for good to those who love God, to those who are called according to His purpose."

Remember that Philippians 4:13 says, "I can do all things through Him who strengthens me."

Before troubles come your way, nurture relationships with Christian friends who can give you advice based on God's word. Job's friends were not good counselors, but by staying faithful to God despite his tribulations, Job had his prosperity and family restored to him and the hope of heaven to look forward to in the future. In Proverbs 17:17, Solomon said, "A friend loves at all times. And a brother is born for adversity." When you face adversity, reach out to your Christian friends for strength and support. Do not isolate yourself and give in to the temptation to try to handle difficulties alone. Share your burdens with the saints and ask for their prayers. James said in James 5:16, "Therefore, confess your sins to one another, and pray for one another. The effective prayer of a righteous man can accomplish much." I saw the effect of prayers when our daughter was diagnosed with metastatic breast cancer at the age of 37. I will always believe that she was granted almost eight more years of life because of the many prayers sent to God's throne on her behalf.

The answer to every problem can be found in God's Word. When Satan tempted Jesus, he always answered, "It is written." If even Jesus was tempted during His time alone in the wilderness, we should not be surprised that we have troubles in this sinful world. We may not understand why things are happening, but we must remember God is in control and knows what is best for His children. One way to shine your light is to show others your faith by how you deal with times of adversity. Remember that when praying in the Garden of Gethsemane on the night He was betrayed, Jesus said in Luke 22:42, "Father, if You are willing, remove this cup from Me, yet not My will, but Yours be done." We must realize that God is our present comfort in all circumstances.

Peter said in 1 Peter 1:6-7, "In this you greatly rejoice, even though now for a little while, if necessary, you have been distressed by various trials, so that the proof of your faith, being more precious than gold which is perishable, even though tested by fire, may be found to result in praise and glory and honor at the revelation of Jesus Christ." We glorify God if we handle life's challenges appropriately, relying on Him for our strength. First Peter 5:9-10 says concerning our enemy the devil, "But resist him, firm in your faith, knowing that the same experiences of suffering are being accomplished by your brethren in the world. After you have suffered for a little while, the God of all grace, who called you to His eternal glory in Christ, will himself perfect, confirm, strengthen, and establish you."

I pray you will emerge from your adversities a stronger, more faithful Christian. Trials and struggles on earth make us yearn for our heavenly home, where there will be no sadness, pain, or tears and we will be in the presence of the Lord forever. If you stay faithful and righteous, if you are not able to overcome your time of hardship, your final destination, heaven, will be far better than anything we have ever known on this earth.

THOUGHT QUESTIONS FOR "GROWING THROUGH ADVERSITY"

1. What does Psalms 46:1-2 mean when it says believers "will not fear"? Is being afraid a sin? Does fear show a lack of faith in God?

2. Which Biblical character do you most admire? What character trait(s) did this person possess that provide(s) encouragement to you in times of trouble?

3. When someone you know blames God for their misfortune, what scripture(s) would you give them to refute their doubt?

4. Think of a Christian whom you know who is currently struggling? What can you do to encourage them and help them bear this burden?

5. How can you rejoice when you are in difficult circumstances?

6. How do you react if the answer to your prayers is "no?"

REJOICE IN THE CHOICE

Elizabeth Behle

Rejoice always, pray constantly, give thanks in everything;
for this is God's will for you in Christ Jesus.
1 Thessalonians 5:16-18

As children, our parents' choices direct our paths. Because I was raised in a family of teachers, my childhood was partially shaped by the world of education. My father taught high school English for 30 years and at the collegiate level for ten years, and my mother taught elementary school for 22 years. They had five children and worked incredibly hard to provide for us. While pregnant with me, my mother completed her master's degree, raised other children, and taught full-time. Though we never went without what we needed, the financial struggle of raising five children on the salaries of teachers caused them to make continual sacrifices for us. I witnessed the raw, unfiltered life of an educator and became intimately acquainted with this career path from a young age. My three older sisters became teachers, and many in my extended family were also educators. The profession seemed the natural choice for me, and I assumed I would follow in the footsteps of my family members, and in a roundabout way, this assumption was correct.

My family learned about Florida College camp when my oldest sister was a senior in high school. She attended camp for only one year but, following her experience, made plans to attend the college in the fall of 2000. From this point on, my family has been well acquainted with Florida College. My other siblings and I were able to attend camp for most of our childhoods; I went to camp for nine years. Since my four siblings and I all attended public school in the primarily Catholic town of St. Charles, Missouri, we often felt isolated in our faith from those in our age group though we tried to be good examples. That all changed for this one week each year. We were suddenly cut off from the distractions of the world and surrounded by more Christians our ages than we ever thought possible. This annual retreat to the Lake of the Ozarks was an integral part of our spiritual growth, and attending camp each summer was always the natural choice for each of us.

The most important choice any individual will make is the choice to follow Christ, a choice I made on August 7, 2007. This decision was the first critical choice of my life. Though I grew up attending church services with parents who were devout Christians, I wrestled with making this decision. I wanted to make sure the choice was mine and not one born out of the expectations of my family. After much hesitation and consideration, I made the decision after a discussion with my older sister when my extended family was vacationing in Arkansas. I was baptized in the pool, and I remember the sensations of overwhelming relief, joy, and freedom as I came out of the water to my entire family singing "O Happy Day." My sins were washed away, and my life was forever changed.

Four out of the five of my parents' children attended Florida College. My father encouraged this even when attending community college or the state school where he was a professor would have been free. My dad often lamented that he had not been able to attend FC himself. He went to a large state school where temptation was presented at every turn, and his own experience caused him to urge us to make the most of our time in the drastically different environment that FC had to offer at such a pivotal point in our lives. My parents never let on that attending FC would be a burden. Even after my parents retired, they continued to substitute teach to help my brother and I, the youngest children in the family, attend FC. They never suggested we seek a more cost-effective option. Because of their encouragement and my own experience at camp, the choice to attend FC was an easy decision.

Up to this point, my life had been characterized by relatively simple choices with little vacillation. In my first semester at FC, this trend continued as I promptly declared myself an elementary education major. However, I was soon placed in a bustling kindergarten classroom to observe, and as I sat cross-legged among these tiny rambunctious students, I realized with overwhelming feelings of alarm and consternation that this was not the path for me. I had never considered another major, and I suddenly felt paralyzed by the options before me. After weighty consideration, these feelings morphed into freedom and elation. I could choose whatever career path I wanted. I was not bound by what my family members had done, by what I thought was expected of me, or by my self-appointed limitations. This epiphany led me in a serpentine way to the glaringly obvious path of becoming an English major. I had always been an avid reader and writer, so I vanquished the misplaced compulsion to be an education major and made a choice I knew was better for me. I made this choice with the mindset that in all reality, I would be working in my chosen field five days a week for most of my life. Wanting to ensure that I would find joy in my work and be able to serve God through it, I approached this decision with caution. Once I did make this decision, however, there was no wavering.

The only downside to my plan was that Florida College did not yet offer an English degree, but as I was resolutely set on my new path, I began researching other schools. I was seriously considering transferring and had begun working on applications when an English degree program was added at Florida College. I am so grateful to have been able to stay at FC to study English. The biblical lens through which literature is examined provided me with a foundation that helped me stand strong in my faith through my master's studies, which approached literature from a drastically different worldview.

A voracious appetite overtook me as I devoured the material presented in my English courses that only served to confirm the choice I had made. Reading and discussing literature ignited a fire within me. My professors inspired me by being life-long learners themselves who possessed a true love of the subject. They encouraged and challenged me, pushing me beyond what I thought I was capable. While I enjoyed all my courses, I fell in love with British literature. I took a variety of enlightening classes, but I soon recognized the limitations of a bachelor's degree. I would not be able to learn all I wished about the subject in four years, and I began considering further educational opportunities.

After graduating with a Bachelor of Arts degree in English in 2015, I began teaching middle school language arts at a private school in Valrico, Florida. While working there was my choice, it was an unexpected choice born out of necessity. I had spent the summer job searching, and this position seemed almost to fall in my lap after several months of dead ends. Having no experience, I received an education by fire as I was tossed into a room of 11-year-olds. After fleeing from education four years previously, I was teaching. On a good day, these middle school students were only marginally more mature than the kindergarteners who had first frightened me away from the profession. Even though teaching middle school was not originally part of my professional goals, I grew to love those middle schoolers. I soaked up their enthusiasm and their delightful naïveté. Many of them were eager to learn, and I was learning much from my students. I discovered how to meet their needs and foster a love of reading and writing. In surprising ways, I was able to reach students who were self-proclaimed haters of language arts and witnessed remarkable mental, physical, spiritual, and emotional growth in them. In this role, I realized exactly how hard my parents had worked. I admire the choice that they and all others working in the field have made. Education is a service-oriented field that asks its teachers to give of themselves in a way unlike any other profession, but the intangible return can be endlessly rewarding. Spurring one student on to a love of the subject makes the difficulties worth it.

Teaching middle school had a profound impact on me, but the most life-changing opportunities that this position provided happened outside of the classroom where, for the first time in my life, I witnessed true adversity and learned the meaning of making difficult choices. In the summers between school years, I was given the chance to travel twice to Central America for humanitarian work with a group of teachers and students from my school. My first trip was to Costa Rica and Honduras. On this trip, I saw more tragic poverty than I thought possible. Several sights have stayed with me and haunted me. I witnessed a three-year-old child walking barefoot through the waste of a massive dump surrounded by vultures and scrawny pregnant dogs while women scavenged in piles of dirty diapers for semi-clean ones to take home for their babies. As we drove through the cities, I saw trash heaps polluting every corner, and both men and dogs digging through and eating out of those piles. I saw barbed wire, razor wire, electrical wire, glass bottle shards, and iron bars covering every wall and window. Families with seven or more children lived in houses the size of a storage shed. These homes were pieced together with whatever scraps they could find and had no electricity or running water. We visited hospitals, and I saw women in stained clothing clutching newborn babies while sitting on thin, stained mattresses in hospital rooms shared with five other new mothers. At local schools, students sat in desks that should have been thrown out long ago with only unstimulating bare classroom walls to view and an overwhelming absence of books. School libraries consisted of one shelf because of the difficulty and expense of acquiring books written in Spanish. When teachers went on strike in these countries, it was not for a pay raise, but for the simple necessity of being paid again.

In addition to witnessing these depths of poverty and human degradation, I also saw sights that challenged and changed me. I saw children happier and more loving than many U.S. children; they were often content just to sit and hold your hand and overjoyed to receive one cheap toy as a gift. I rarely heard a child issue a complaint or angry word, but I did hear children engaged in and excited about biblical teaching. After the completion of a house build, I saw families shed tears of happiness over receiving the small comfort that promised protection from both the elements and their fellow man. At the hospitals, the sick and their families were happy to join in a prayer. They accepted this comfort with gratitude. Driving around the cities, I saw "God Is Love" written on nearly every building. Compared to what I was used to, these countries were shockingly and beautifully open in their belief in God. Reconciling these opposing sights took me some time, but I soon came to recognize God's hand in the abundant joy and gratitude possible even in the depths of poverty. Though they were often unfairly limited by their circumstances, these people still chose belief and happiness in ways I had never witnessed. Most people in the United States have never had to make such a choice under such circumstances, and I was forced to confront the notion that if I had been plunged into such a desperate life situation, I do not know how I would react or what choices I would make.

A few years later, I returned to Central America for another opportunity to serve, this time in Guatemala. Our primary purpose was working with an organization called Street Kids Direct (SKD). Their mission is "to see a world where children and young people do not need to depend upon the streets in order to survive." In Guatemala there is a high percentage of children who either spend the majority of their time in the streets or who live there full time. Children who spend most of their time in the streets make this difficult choice because their home life means staying in a situation where violence is rampant. Father figures are regularly absent from their children's lives, and if they are present, they are often abusive. However, once a child makes the transition to living full time in the streets, their life expectancy drops to only four more years, and they become subject to a life filled with every kind of violence, crime, gang activity, hurt, and hunger imaginable. A cemetery near Antigua, Guatemala, is reserved specifically for kids who have died in the streets. The workers at SKD have personally known and wept over many children who have met this fate.

Some children, whether because of criminal activity or just not having a place to go, are placed in a "safe" house. These safe houses, I learned, are far from safe. They overflow with more than double their capacity of children, and many of the guards sell out the young girls and subject them to abuse for profit. In 2017, a group of 41 girls rioted and attempted to run away from one of these homes. To escape the room, they started a fire in hopes that the guards would open the door. No help came, and the children burned to death. For most, living in the streets is a choice preferable to this type of situation. SKD works to change the limited, dangerous options available to these children.

Every afternoon SKD provides a safe place for children to get away from their harsh lives for a little while, do their homework, spend time with friends, and just know that someone cares for them. SKD also has developed an impressive mentoring program where each child is assigned a mentor whom they meet with one-on-one for at least one hour per week. This program has radically changed the courses of many of these children's lives. SKD also provides medical assistance but not regular food, water, or money because they want to ensure that these children and their families do not get comfortable living on the streets and that they seek to better their circumstances. SKD assists with this by working side by side with their families to find work and better situations.

During my time in Guatemala, I worked closely with these children and the organization. We engaged with the children by offering them individualized attention. We also worked at their new center that was in the process of being renovated by painting the building and clearing out debris. We learned the names, ages, and situations of every child with whom SKD was partnering at the time. Some had special education needs, some worked in the dump to make a living, some were bullied at school, some had absentee parents, some had mothers who worked as prostitutes, some had parental figures struggling with illness, and nearly all lived in or around La Terminal, an extremely dangerous area of the city. After learning about the children individually, we took time to say a personal prayer for each one. I do not know where many of these kids are today, but I continue to pray they defeated the odds and are living happy, fulfilled lives.

Despite their trauma, these children exuded joy when we spent time with them. They chose to be happy when every aspect of their lives encouraged them to choose otherwise. As I was chatting with one child, he looked at me with a big smile on his face, pointed to himself, and simply said "happy." This child worked in the dump with his family to make ends meet and was partially deaf, but he found happiness through the impact of SKD's work and the love and care poured out to him. These children taught me that joy is a choice that depends on the One who is far more consistent than any surrounding circumstances, no matter how dire.

My trips to Costa Rica, Honduras, and Guatemala changed my life forever. Even though the people were living in scrap houses and struggling to find their next meals, I saw both God and joy in abundance in these impoverished countries. I built these people houses and gave them medicine, food, and water. I visited and prayed with the sick in hospitals and children in orphanages. I visited the local churches and engaged in conversations about Jesus. I tried to have an impact, but the people I encountered had a far greater impact on me. They changed my perspective and encouraged me never to stop choosing joy or helping the needy. They showed me what a blessing it is to be born in the United States without the constant struggle for food, shelter, and safety. They taught me ignoring the needy is a choice, one that I cannot afford to make, but they also taught me that drawing near to God is often easier in poverty than in abundance. When you have nothing, turning to the God who grants everything is an obvious conclusion.

Shortly after returning from my trip to Guatemala, I was given the opportunity to teach a high school creative writing elective, which rekindled a love for the art not lately exercised. At this point, my professional goals began to morph. I wanted to pursue creative writing, and though I enjoyed teaching middle school, I wanted the chance to teach literature to students at a higher level. I started taking classes toward a Master of Fine Arts in Creative Writing. Like in my undergraduate work, I devoured the material presented me. The reading, the discussions, and the creative writing assignments refueled the dwindling flame from lack of stoking. Completing my master's while teaching full-time was grueling, and by the time I completed my degree in 2020, I was burned out as a middle school teacher after working in the position for six years.

After encouragement from many, I applied to Florida College on two separate occasions. In the fall of 2021, I was offered a position and made a major career change. The material I taught provided a pleasing change of pace. We discussed topics at a deeper level than I could evoke in 11-year-olds. I also began teaching two literature courses in my second year: Major Figures in English Literature I and II. These literature students have been a delight; they are eager to read, discuss, and learn. They are excited about literature in a way that is eerily familiar to my own time in their position. I strive daily to promote a love for the subject in all the students I encounter and to be an example for good in their lives. I love to see the biblical connections students draw with the material and to have discussions that help bring us all closer to Christ. I came to Florida College with the intent of helping students learn and grow but am amazed at how much the students have done the same for me. I hope students can see that God has offered them many choices in life that can bring contentedness, opportunities, and abundant blessings. I hope they never allow their blessings to become distractions but strive to help the needy and to choose joy and God every time options are presented.

While in my second year of teaching at Florida College, I was faced with one of the most difficult times in my life, a time when choosing joy and contentment was a struggle. In the beginning of 2023, my mother was diagnosed with cancer. Our family does not have a history of cancer and had been abundantly blessed with good health, so this diagnosis hit us hard and unexpectedly. My mom asked her dentist about some suspicious places on her tongue, and when test results revealed them to be cancer, we were all shaken. The next few months were a whirlwind of appointments, tests, and intense surgery. After the surgery, my mother was not able to talk, smile, or eat normally for months. Even now, more than a year later, she still has to go to regular appointments as a precaution. One of the most encouraging aspects of this ordeal was watching how my mother dealt with it. Though she was the one most affected, she was constantly optimistic and bolstered us when it should have been the other way around. In addition, I was encouraged by how those around me, both at work and in my congregation, rallied around us. My students brought me cards and flowers, and my coworkers offered to cover my classes. Members of our congregation offered unceasing prayers and brought my parents meals, flowers, and gifts. We would not have made it through without God and the people He placed in our lives, but amid uncertainty and worry, choosing to cast our cares on Him was not always easy. Counting your blessings in times of anxiety is far more difficult but so necessary. By choosing to depend on Him, we were brought through this trying time, and my mother is now cancer free. As I examine the choices of my life, the natural and challenging ones, and admire the choices I have witnessed others make, I have learned to rejoice in the fact that God has given me many choices and continually pray that I make every decision with His glory in mind and that I continue to choose joy and contentment no matter the circumstance.

Since the beginning, God has endowed mankind with freewill and given him the choice between good and evil (Gen 2:16-17). God has provided His creation with every motivation, encouragement, and reward to choose the good (Pro 3:5-6). He has also revealed the consequences for choosing evil (Gal 6:7-8). The ultimate choice is clear, but it is still ours to make (Mat 7:13-14).

An essential tenet of the Church is unity (Gal 3:28). We are to be of one heart and mind (Act 4:32) and united in our love (Joh 13:35). Yet, another essential tenet is individuality, which is intimately connected with the choices we make (Rom 12:4-8). Daily, we see individuality causing brutal divisions among people in the world, which might cause some to believe unity and individuality to be opposed. However, in Christ, unity and individuality are not contrary, but compatible precepts. Our diverse capabilities allow us to expand the kingdom, and we can serve God more effectively because of our differences, rather than despite them. 1 Corinthians 12:14-20 equates individual Christians to the parts of the body as it emphasizes this point. Without our will to choose and our individuality, we may think we have achieved unity, but we would be united in nothing as we would not be a body of Christ's people. As Christians, we must make certain choices that help achieve unity in the Church, but in other areas, choices must be left to each individual. In all areas of life, we should rejoice in the choices God has given.

Christians must "choose the good portion" (Luk 10:41-42). The world presents many temptations that we know should be avoided, but beyond that, it provides distractions. Many of these are not inherently sinful but can be when they pull us away from our Lord. As Martha learned in Luke 10, if we do not have enough time to dedicate to God, we are too busy. We need to take a step back, examine our lives, and cut the excess. Choose the good portion above the busyness and meaningless distractions of life, no matter how pressing they may seem.

Christians must also choose to flee from temptation (1 Cor 6:18) and to imitate Christ (1 Cor 11:1). As Christians, we can no longer go on sinning (Heb 10:26). Fleeing temptation and sin is an active and continual decision. The first step is to not place ourselves in situations where sinning becomes the easy choice. Being careful about the company we keep (1 Cor 15:33), the places we frequent, and the thoughts we allow to linger (Phi 4:8) will help with this endeavor. But inevitably, when we find ourselves confronted with such a choice, we must choose to run from it, like Joseph in Genesis 39:12 when "He left his garment in her hand and ran out of the house." No matter the situation in which we find ourselves, seeking to imitate Christ will produce the proper outcome (Mat 4:1-11).

All Christians must choose contentment and rejoicing (Phi 4:4, 11-13). These states are more lasting than any fleeting feeling of happiness the world will encourage us to pursue, but they are more difficult to consistently achieve and maintain. Joy and contentment are states of mind to be trained and honed continually though they come more naturally to some than to others. These states are separate from a person's socioeconomic status, relationship status, or employment status. In fact, those born and raised in poverty often find joy and contentment more easily than those reared in wealth, privilege, and status as turning to God can come more simply when there is nothing in the way, nothing to falsely bolster our pride (Luk 16:13, Mat 19:21-24). No matter someone's life position, when we adopt these states and dwell in them, we gain everything. In Philippians, Paul said, "Not that I am speaking of being in need, for I have learned in whatever situation I am to be content. I know how to be brought low, and I know how to abound. In any and every circumstance, I have learned the secret of facing plenty and hunger, abundance and need. I can do all things through him who strengthens me" (4:11-13). We too have been made privy to the secret Paul learned; we just need to take advantage of the benefit of contentedness.

This unwavering joy and contentment will come about when we choose to seek and pursue opportunities of service (Mat 25:35-40). If we look for them, these opportunities are never in short supply. We cannot afford to ignore the spiritually and physically needy. If able, we as individuals should help monetarily, but we must also give of our time, our energy, and ourselves. Pour into others and receive the deep, abiding joy that only service to Christ can give (Eph 6:7-8) for "as you did it to one of the least of these my brothers, you did it to me" (Mat 25: 40).

For the sake of unity and the furtherance of the kingdom, all Christians should choose the good portion, choose to flee temptation, choose to imitate Christ, and choose joy and contentment in every circumstance. However, in maintaining our God-given individuality, some choices must be left to each Christian. God does not limit us by our life situations, and we must not place unnecessary limitations on ourselves or others either. Our choices are not anyone else's choices, and we must never impose upon others where God has not. We cannot rob others of their choices and resulting contentment by insinuating that they are less because of the choice they have made if it is a choice condoned by God.

One example of a choice that must be left up to individual Christians is the choice of relationship status, and this is a choice that must not be belittled. Marriage is one of the most important decisions an individual will ever make. Insisting that it is necessary, expected, and the preferred life path to young, impressionable Christians causes many to rush into marriages that end in disaster. Phrases like, "You'll find someone," "It'll happen when you least expect it," or "Your time will come" imply that a Christian's current state of singleness is inferior to one of marriage. These phrases should be eliminated from our vocabulary as they place expectations on young people for an event that may never occur. While emphasizing the blessings of marriage, we should likewise emphasize the blessings of singleness and how choosing to remain single is far better than being stuck in a destructive situation. We must keep in mind that marriage, as God intended it, is an irreversible choice. If we choose to spend our lives with another person, we need to make the decision with full individual confidence and not based on the comments and influences of others directing our paths. As both married and single Christians are equally valuable and worthy in God's eyes, presenting marriage as the only choice available or as the superior life choice strays from biblical teaching and causes much grief to individuals.

When everyone else seems to be choosing to get married, being the odd one out can be discouraging and isolating. To many, being single does not feel like a choice, but a burden. We must thank God, however, for each life situation and learn to replace our discouragement with contentment and the knowledge that abundant life is available to all Christians, no matter their state (Joh 10:10). If we all tried to serve God in the same life position, some tasks in His kingdom would be left undone. We would be lacking in the individuality and diversity spoken of in Scripture. Singleness is not a pitiable state but one filled with opportunities of a different kind of service than can be found in married life. Paul said to the single that "it is good for them to remain single, as I am" (1 Cor 7:8) because one who is unmarried "is anxious about the things of the Lord, how to please the Lord" (1 Corinthians 7:32). An unfair pressure to get married is placed on college-aged women in particular, and it often results in disappointment that young ladies are ill-equipped to handle. I encourage young women not to see their college education or future career as a "back-up" option. Family life is certainly a noble and worthy pursuit that can and does bring rich blessings to the lives of many Christians, but it is not the only choice in which a fulfilling life can be lived. You can also serve God as a single person working in your field, and you are no less worthy than someone who serves God as a wife and mother. If we look down on singleness as an undesirable state, we are robbing our youth of contentedness (Phi 4:11-13). We should teach and practice embracing the blessings of whatever state God has placed us in and refuse to waste time pining after a future that may never be. We must keep in mind that the choices others have made may not be the best choices for us.

Another example of a choice that Christians may unnecessarily criticize or belittle one another for is employment. There are some employment options that would be unwise for a Christian to pursue because of their conflict with Biblical teaching. However, in most instances, Christians are free to choose where they want to work. Too many parents encourage children to do what they (the parents) want them to do or encourage children to work in a certain field because of the money it will make them. These are both ways to steal choice, joy, and contentment from someone. Christians can work in many different fields and still please God, and being pleasing to God, not having money, (Heb 13:5) should be the determining factor of any part of our lives. Through our individuality of working in many different fields and places as we use the talents God has given us, the Gospel will reach more people. As long as Christians consider God's will in every choice they make, their freedom of choice should not be inhibited by other Christians.

Christians are united in their imitation of Christ, but Christians are not cookie-cutters of one another. We cannot use our talents and strengths (1 Pet 4:10, Rom 12:6) as effectively for service to God if they are stifled by those who would limit our choices and put restrictions on us where God does not. Be careful that you do not do this to others by word or example. Never disparage the choice of another if one may serve God in that choice.

Above all, make your choices with God's will in mind and excel still more (1 The 4:10). Rejoice in the choices God has blessed you with, but remember the impact that a single choice can have. As seen in the example of Esau selling his birthright (Gen 25:29-34), one decision has the power to change the course of a life. Do not give in to the passing pleasures of sin by making wrong choices. Make choices that glorify God and choose life (Deu 30:19-20).

THOUGHT QUESTIONS FOR "REJOICE IN THE CHOICE"

1. How do you reconcile the Christian tenets of unity and individuality?

2. Aside from those included, can you think of other choices that Christians must make?

3. In addition to the examples mentioned, can you think of any Bible characters who are known for their choices (either good or bad)?

4. What questions should be considered before making the choice to marry or the choice to work in a particular field?

5. A couple life choices were provided where Christians can demonstrate their individuality but are often challenged by other Christians. In what other areas do we try to influence or change another Christian's mind unnecessarily?

6. How do you differentiate between advising someone about their choice and belittling their choice? Where should the line be drawn?

KINGDOM CONTRIBUTIONS

Bonny Cable

Now may the God of peace... equip you with everything good that you may do his will, working in us that which is pleasing in his sight, through Jesus Christ, to whom be glory forever and ever. Amen.
Hebrews 13:20-21

I was born to be a teacher. From the first day I set foot in Kindergarten, I knew I was right where I belonged. The smell of the gently used books and freshly sharpened pencils comforted me. Mrs. Cook's soft smile, welcoming me at the door with a tender tone and kind eyes, set me at ease right away. I loved going every day. My love for school grew with each year, and my admiration for my teachers was consistent from year to year.

Even my toughest teachers taught me how to approach and overcome material and content that wasn't my strong suit. I appreciated them for their devotion to their subject and commitment to a job that was challenging. A love of learning kept me going and motivated me to give my all. From the front row, I would watch my teachers work and dream of being up there one day, taking mental notes on what worked well that I would implement in my own classroom and what changes I would make to have a powerful impact on student learning.

To go back further than my school days, I was set up for success from the beginning. Our home was a breeding ground for cultivating a love of learning. My father, Ralph Walker, often spent evenings reading aloud to us. Though my 5-year-old self may have been too young to comprehend the wonders of Tolkien's The Hobbit, I adored climbing through the wardrobe into the wonderland of Narnia. I also grasped my dad's message — that he valued reading and reading these texts as important enough to introduce them to us at early stages. Attending storytelling festivals and listening to read-alouds in the car emphasized the importance of our auditory skills and the benefit of literary experiences to further advance our cognitive development. Many Sunday mornings we spent time around the breakfast table before church hearing my dad read excerpts from the newspaper aloud, often from the Dave Barry column, while my sisters and I perused the Sunday comics, sharing quips from Family Circus or challenging each other in the Hocus Focus picture puzzle. My mom politely chuckled at his read-aloud from the kitchen while she busied herself fixing Sunday's roast and biscuits.

My mother, Paula Walker, is the unsung hero of my early years of learning. She spent hours with me going over the Alpha Phonics book she had used to teach us girls to read. We spent our summers with weekly visits to the children's library to check out books that helped us progress through our summer reading program. We would move our paper balloons across the wall of the children's section, signaling our increased number of books read. I volunteered at that library, called the Canon Memorial Library in downtown Concord, North Carolina, for two summers working with the children's librarian, Mrs. Leslie. She taught me how to check in/check out books and shelve them. Before we moved to Florida, her parting gift to me was a brand new copy of the children's classic by Roald Dahl, Matilda-which my boys have devoured to this day! At one point, I considered becoming a librarian but soon discovered when my report card behavior marks came back as 'talks too much' that perhaps a quiet zoned work environment may not suit me best for the way the Creator designed me.

Though our upbringing brought strong cognitive development, our physical abilities and athleticism were, to say the least, lacking. Carrie Ann, the brave, confident firstborn, tried hard for whatever team my parents signed her up for and survived each season. Amanda, the compliant peacemaker, also got onto whatever court, track, or field they put her on to play, sometimes even sharing shoes with Carrie Ann when we couldn't afford two pairs of basketball shoes at the same time. And me? Have I mentioned yet that I am the baby of us three girls? It is true in every sense of the word. I never played on a single team. Ever. The only class in school I dreaded was PE. When I asked my mom, the true athlete of the family, why she never signed me up for any team, she said, "Because you cried every time we even mentioned it! So we didn't bother!" That seems right; crybaby is a more accurate birth order title for me. I ended up doing community theater, which was quite fitting.

After the failed attempts at sports, our dad chose to put us on a different path- public speaking. He was right—1,000 times over. We all took the 4-H "Speak up" classes. Sidenote: I also helped my mom with her 4-H cake decorating class and took the baking classes. We'll see that pop up later in life!

With trembling voices and shaky hands, we all competed in speech contests, sometimes against each other, which meant the baby never won! My dad told us we would never regret the confidence this experience would give us, and he was right. We found strength in using our minds and mouths! Blame him if you invite us all to a social gathering and can't get a word in edgewise; Dad trained us to be this way! The training in public speaking has proven to serve us in each of our jobs and in service to the Lord's work. It was well worth it.

While my younger self discovered I was meant for a career in teaching, a mind and mouth career, my parents predestined me to attend Florida College. My sisters and I were born with Falcon blood coursing through our veins. My baby book revealed a newborn photo of me from January of 1982 wearing a fuzzy, yellow-footed pajama sleeper with the words Florida College class of 2000 printed on the left side. I never resisted this path. From all the stories I heard my parents tell about their time at Florida College and all the friends they had from their time there, it seemed like it would fit me just right. We poured over our parents' yearbooks, asking questions about all the courts, societies, and banquets. With eagerness, we planned out which dorms we would live in, what activities we planned to be a part of, and for me, which musical groups and plays I would try out for.

The first time I recall attending Florida College camp was when I was eight years old. That was the last year Florida Camp was held on campus. I had a blast and met friends there whom I have stayed in touch with and even roomed with at Florida College! I attended Florida camp for nine years and looked forward, with much anticipation, to that week in the summer, knowing it was a taste of what life at Florida College would be like. We came down for lectures for my dad to speak at an evening lecture in the gym, and I fondly recall the thrill in my soul upon hearing the basses boom, "He is everything to me," as we praised the Great Redeemer within the walls of the gym before I promptly fell asleep on the front row. I was only eight years old, mind you.

One year, we came down for lectures, staying with my grandparents in South Tampa, and I recall things felt different. My parents were gone several times that week, leaving us with Gran and Papa while they had meetings. I noticed more hushed conversations from them and my dad taking more phone calls in the other room than usual. Something was going on. I had spent all my life in Concord, North Carolina, always with a preacher father and mother who worked part-time jobs while managing a home of three girls. That was all about to change. Their love and support of Florida College, along with some recognized potential in my dad's tremendous people skills, had been called upon to be used to serve our dear FC.

I was busy using my public speaking training to write my speech for the Student Council secretary in the upcoming seventh-grade elections when my dad summoned us girls to join them in the living room. He announced that in August, we would be moving to Florida so that my dad could become the Public Relations Director of Florida College. My sisters sobbed in sadness. I sat quietly, stunned. As the baby of the family, this didn't hit me quite as hard as it did my sisters, who were going into 11th and 9th grade, a tough time for such a big transition. My dad went into more detail about how the plan would unfold while my sisters sniffled and sobbed about the huge upheaval about to occur in our lives. Tears wet our faces, but when the conversation ended, I slowly plodded down the hall and returned to the computer. I stared at the screen. Crestfallen, I highlighted the whole speech and hit the delete key. It was gone. This phase of life in North Carolina was coming to a close.

Concord was my home. That parsonage behind the church building was where we became the Ralph Walker family of five when I first came home from the hospital. We were leaving a church family that loved us so deeply that we felt part of their family trees with tightly connected roots. Our home on Wendover Road held all my childhood memories: late nights outside catching lightning bugs, roller skating routines under the carport set to tunes of the Monkees and Weird Al Yankovich, running through the sprinkler in the yard or hurling ourselves down the Crocodile Mile slip 'n slide; all three of us girls huddling around the kerosene heater in the kitchen during frozen winter mornings; and sharing more meals than I could ever count around a small oval dining room table that held up plates of visiting preachers, cake plates of all birthday celebrations, often surrounded by hands parting the pages of the Bible during studies, and folded in prayer. We were leaving the charming Carolinas, which flowed with Cherry Lemon SunDrop and Sweet Tea, and trading it for the orange groves and sandy coasts of Florida with humidity so thick you can taste it, destined to live in a constant state of fighting frizzy hair, brutal sunburns, and a plague of lizards.

It was a heartbreaking August day when our church family came and helped us load the U-haul. Pulling away from the only home I'd ever known physically and spiritually felt like a block of ice on my shoulders that even the Florida sun could not melt away. The tears and hugs spilled over, yet there was a tinge of excitement at what the future held for us in Florida. The sights of Busch Blvd and 56th Street didn't make for the most impressive welcome parade, but the excitement grew when we viewed the palms and lofty pines that dotted the campus of our dear FC on the gator-laden Hillsborough River.

Thankfully, I was able to begin my Florida student experience at Florida College Academy, which locked me in with some lifelong friends. This was a game-changer for me. I had never had so many faithful friends before! This proved to be invaluable in my high school years. Though we didn't all end up in high school or church together, because most of our dads worked at FC and were preachers, we convened on the FC campus for every talent show, faculty alumni showcase, basketball game, and as many events as possible. These people and the wholesome activities on campus gave us great memories and comfort in getting through high school, knowing what awaited us when we attended FC as students.

I attended King High, a public high school, and grew exponentially in my faith by being tested and questioned on who I was and why I was "this way." I knew what they meant. My sisters had gone ahead of me and helped pave the way with what could pass the time to make high school enjoyable until we could get to FC. There grew in our family a thrill for high school marching band! I followed their path and was quite involved in the band. I happily claim to be a band nerd as a foundational core memory of my high school years.

In my senior year, I stretched myself and tried out for drum major—the student conductor of the marching band. Along with two other peers, I made it! At the time, I thought it was fun to learn conducting patterns and wear go-go boots and a cape with a whistle! I now see that perhaps the Lord was building up this ability to be useful later in a way I could have never predicted. My band director urged me to go into music education, but I knew I belonged in an elementary school classroom. During slow days in high school classes, I would practice my handwriting for writing on the board one day in my own classroom. Knowing I had a desire to teach one day, some of my less inspirational teachers would take breaks in the hallway during class and leave me to administer tests or quizzes to my classmates. How did my unfriendly peers not beat me up for that?!

Finally, the time came to graduate and go to Florida College. We loaded up laundry baskets with all my things because that's how locals moved out and made the half-mile trek from our house to Glen Arven Ave. I was ecstatic. At last, I was sitting in the seats of Hutchinson as a student, not a 'campus brat.' The shows, plays, musical groups, chapel, and societal events were now mine. This was a FC Falcon-footed-pajama baby's destiny.

All my years of practice singing 80s diva power ballads into a can of hairspray paid off, and I was able to be in the Friends group for two years! Again, following in my sister's footsteps, I joined KO because I liked the color green on me. However, after attending the first society game, I promptly vowed never to attend another event for KO again lest they ever wrongly expect any type of athletic ability from me. My second year FC added two new societies, and I became the spirit leader of the newly formed Psi Beta Gamma. I was cast in the highly coveted role of 'townsperson' in the FC musicals while I was there. Then, in my junior year, Mr. Moore decided to do something quite amusing. He cast me as Snoopy in "You're a Good Man, Charlie Brown." My sisters could not have been happier to hear that their baby sister was going to play the DOG on stage in front of an audience. Thanks, community theater! To add insult to injury, that weekend of the play, my very good friend from FC, Joe Cable, happened to come down for a visit, having graduated with his AA in the spring. When I heard he was in the audience, it made me want to crawl into the literal dog house I was perched upon and stay there until it was over, but I was the only one who knew the choreography to "Suppertime" so I grabbed my dog bowl and the show went on. However, 'good friend Joe' came back to visit again and then made the move to Florida, which turned out to be a really good move for me and us. My good friend Joe became my Joe! He was my answer to prayer, and he was right there all along, Snoopy performance and all!

As I sat in my education classes at FC to earn my bachelor's degree in elementary education, I remember watching my teachers and thinking, "Now that's what I would like to do someday! Teach teachers!" This came from the realization that I could have a greater impact on more students by shaping strong teachers to go out into all the classrooms for years and years to come! The seed was planted. Straight out of my internship at Riverhills Elementary, I got a job offer to stay and teach 3rd grade. It was my calling coming to life.

I survived all the major life changes in three months—graduating college, moving out of my parents' home for the first time, getting married to my darling Joe, and starting a new job!

Having my name, Mrs. Cable, on a classroom door with 20 kids to call my own for 180 days was beautifully hard, complicated, and magical all at once! I loved everything about school all over again, but this time from the teacher's standpoint. Our school had little parent involvement then, so I stepped in to run the PTA (sans parents) and school advisory council and hosted interns from FC and USF to work in my classroom. At that point, I wanted a bigger role in helping schools. I completed my Master's Degree in Educational Leadership from USF, thinking I might be a principal one day. But the craft of teaching is the siren's song I can't ignore, and it kept beckoning me back to the classroom to teach. Until one day, my calling changed.

After 6 years at Riverhills, I packed up my resource teacher's office with a belly full of baby, submitted my final assignment to complete my endorsement in gifted education, and then headed to the hospital to become a mama when my baby Jack was born. Everything changed. A baby changes everything. A dog becomes a pet again when a baby is born. I still cared about my kids from my classes but now this one child mattered more than anyone! My life's work had changed from teaching a class full of students from a range of families to one child who got everything I could give! I stepped aside from teaching to stay home with Jack. Joe worked two jobs, the best firefighter paramedic there ever was at Temple Terrace Fire dept, and several different jobs at hospitals to afford me the chance to stay home. He is so good to me.

Staying home was a dream come true. But it was hard for me. Days where Joe was on shift for 24 hours, and I was alone with a baby or toddler were taxing. My parents lived close by, so I would often call them on those days by mid-afternoon to see their plans and my intuitive mother always swooped in before I could ask with an offer to join them at Cracker Barrel for dinner and some adult conversation. I loved staying home, but I knew deep in my heart that I would send Jack off to school one day and return to teaching. I had the itch to teach. When Dr. Crispell called and offered me an adjunct position to come back to FC when Jack was 2, I jumped at the chance! This was the perfect chance to see if what I thought I always wanted was all it was cracked up to be. Turns out it was. I loved teaching college classes! It was a great intellectual challenge, and using my teaching side of the brain again as a professional was invigorating! Adjunct teaching was great, but the schedule was still tricky, even for one or two classes, and my number one priority was still at home. So, when the Lord said yes to our fervent prayers to have another baby, I knew I would have to lay that dream to rest a bit longer.

Jett came along and made me an official boy mom with two boys to care for. God has a sense of humor. I never once pictured being a boy mom and practically had to google how to be a boy mom. You can look at my parenting bookshelf and the abundance of 'boy mom' books to know how inadequately prepared I felt for this job. The only thing I know how to do with LEGO is build a skyscraper, but a Barbie dreamhouse is full of a million more possibilities! But God called me to be a boy mom. So I am giving it my all and trying to shape Jack and Jett into disciples who can be strong workers in the church, maybe heads of households, pray-ers, song leaders, and able volunteers in whatever way God calls them. I stepped out of the classroom and into 'boyland' to do my best to fake it as a boy mom. I'm so grateful I could make that choice, thanks to Joe, but the daily work of being a stay-at-home mom is hard! Many tears were spilled – and the boys cried some, too! But the books we read, the songs we sang, and the Daniel Tiger episodes we watched are memories I will never trade. The motherhood tasks I dreamed of living were the summers spent at the rec center pool watching swim lessons and attending library storytime programs. The repeated watching of Read and Share Bible story DVDs and packing our church bag with The Busy Bible are moments sweetly etched in the hallows of my mind to hold that era frozen in time. But babies don't keep.

As the boys grew and ended up in school, I threw myself into being the best homeroom mom and PTA president I could imagine—all while fighting that nagging itch to be back in the classroom myself. It's who I am. I wove it into my mothering, but I liked the lines of mom and teacher not to be too blurred, which was part of our decision to go to school and not homeschool. I would not trade my 10 years at home for anything. It allowed me to share precious time with my boys and grow personally. My spiritual life grew exponentially in that decade by having much time on my hands to be in the word of God and discover study methods that worked best for me to draw closer to my Lord. I found I had a joy for celebrating and decorating for major (and minor) holidays. My National Days Calendar app is my best friend! I discovered my love for baking, thanks again to 4-H kid summer classes. I was able to spend time honing those baking skills with plenty of time to practice and share, mostly with the fire dept! The combination of these skills still allows me to pull together a quick baked good to share with others when a need arises and to have happy memories of sharing quirky holidays with others, like National Pi (Pie) Day and Christmas in July. However, I still felt like I had other skills to share with people outside our home.

The conflict of feeling like mothering and marriage were supposed to be all I ever wanted made me feel guilty for thinking of a profession outside of the home. I thanked God for the blessings of having both of these roles, but I knew He gave me things to do in addition to being a Mrs. and a Mama. What if I would have never become either of those? How would Bonny serve the Lord and magnify Him with who He made me to be? Teaching was my calling.

I also see teaching as a powerful mission field. Being in school with colleagues and families who weren't in my usual circle was a great way to tell people about Jesus, which is more of the reason why we decided to send the boys to public school. When Jett was in 1st grade, I knew the trajectory of parent involvement would be slowing down in the years to come. I found myself feeling less useful at home during the day. Was it finally time? Would the Lord say yes to my prayer of the right timing to go back and teach? Would there even be a job opening that I could fill? People said, "You know there just aren't openings at FC right now to teach. Those are hard to come by." But I prayed. Oh, I prayed and scribbled those fervent prayers in my prayer journal for the Lord to put me where He wanted me. Then it happened. The door creaked open. I reached out to see if there was a need for adjunct help in the Education Department at Florida College–my happiest place on earth. In God's kindness, the answer was yes! After talking to Joe, he lovingly said, "You've supported me and my dream for nearly 20 years. It's time for me to support you with yours!" I RAN back to the classroom!

For two years, I eased back into work with part-time teaching. Then, the full-time position I had dreamed about became available. The Lord saw fit to make me wait for it, but the answer was YES! Ever my biggest cheerleader, Joe said he would help me in any way that he could to make this leap work out for our family. Boy, has he ever! Amidst his busy work as Captain Cable at the fire department, he partners with me to coordinate school drop-offs and pickups, grocery shopping, and cooking, not to mention the social and mentorship opportunities that the college provides. He has stayed by my side through it all, reminding me that we are a team, "Team Cable WOO!"-as we say in our household. Some days, Jack and Jett don't even know I went to work because the schedule allows me to be present for them before and after school. Our family has been so blessed by this work. Outside of the home, I feel I am doing the Lord's work by preparing more of His people to reach and teach children in education settings. I am privileged to help guide our students through this big phase of life, provide prayers and support, and point them to Jesus in their paths. Inside our home, we have shared life and fellowship with students from FC who provide examples for my boys as to how they can be strong men of faith into adulthood.

Through my teaching career, I have seen how the art and craft of teaching can be applied to the most important teaching–sharing and learning God's word! From teaching children's Bible classes to ladies' adult classes, facilitating women's workshops and planning ladies' Bible study events, even to writing camp Bible class material, all that I have learned through teaching can be used for good and for God! In his deacon's role, my husband Joe is currently in charge of the middle and high school curriculum, which means I get to totally nerd out creating a scope and sequence of the three and four-year cycles of teaching content to precious young souls!

Those 4H 'Speak Up' classes prepared me to be able to teach and speak at ladies' studies, sometimes alongside my mom and sisters, but they're still better than me! Remember those drum major skills I learned from being a high school drum major? Even that skill has afforded me the chance to lead singing at women's events. At the time, only God knew what He could do with that opportunity! He has never left me and has guided me all along the way. He was equipping me all along the way, even without me knowing it!

The family tree of God's people has many branches with abundant fruit, all nourished from the same deep roots. His plan for His people is perfect, and I have seen that His plan for me individually is perfect, too. Each step I take, I can see who He made me to be and how He has called me to hone those skills and use them to strengthen work in His kingdom and for His kingdom. I'm grateful He cares about me enough to shine a light on the paths He has wanted me to walk. As I often pray, I hope He is pleased with how I am using my time and talents from Him.

God always has a plan for His people. Sometimes, He has a plan for a whole nation, a community, or a region. Sometimes it is for an individual. The people God has plans for can work to help further His purpose. Through scripture, He has revealed the aspect of His nature that is meticulous in planning.

Some of the figures in scripture have big stories of ways God used them since birth or gave them grand gestures of enlightenment intended to alter their course. Other times, we see small ways that He has moved people along a path that He knows is best for them and brings about a greater good. His plans are perfect. There are plenty of cases of people who went against what God intended, and He found a way to use them anyway! Men, women, and children are all important to God, and He gives them paths and purposes that can be their contribution to the kingdom.

Exodus contains some of the most powerful stories of God's mighty hand at work to bring His people out of Egypt, but in His mercy, He includes them in the process. God makes waves by doing things never before seen and displays His power to do anything He wants without limit. This should give us trust in the God we follow and His complete control over the forces on this earth and the people within it. We also see a God who invites His people to participate in the process. The Israelites demonstrate faith by participating in the first Passover. Their feet must step into the bed of the Red Sea and cross through to the other side. They must choose to follow the cloud by day and fire by night. Through this plan, He reveals who He is and what it means to be His. He is the master builder. He is looking at the blueprint, but we are on the building team. We get to contribute to the work of the kingdom in special ways.

He has created within mankind certain abilities to work. He expects us to use the time to be workers in His vineyard. What that means, then, is that He has made us capable of doing the work. Not all our skill sets are the same, yet He can use all of us in special ways that grow His kingdom.

Let us camp with the Israelites in the wilderness in Exodus 35 and see how God prepared them to participate in His grander plans. On Mount Sinai, God and Moses had quite a productive meeting. God gave Moses the blueprints for the Tabernacle. Now that Egypt is behind them, God is ready to be among His people and establish a deeper relationship with them. In the middle of this wilderness wasteland, God asks for a great work to begin. He asks them to construct the Tabernacle exactly and carefully.

A swath of land dotted with tents as far as the eye can see now becomes the boot camp for God's people. Surrounded by sand, mountainous terrain, and only the resources they carried out of Egypt, He calls upon these nomads to seemingly make something from nothing - "ex nihilo." How can they do that? This was going to require manual labor. They were used to that. The conditions for building in Egypt were oppressive, but they did have taskmasters directing their every move. The output and products of their work were consistent, regular, and redundant. Showing up for work for the last 400 years was an unchanging routine. No decisions had to be made. Until Moses came along and disrupted the norm by challenging Pharaoh, the day-to-day life was predictable. They need to meet quotas and maintain the status quo. They knew what they were supposed to do and what they would do it with, for the expectations were clear. Work or die.

Now, that changed. Praise God for the rescue! But the God who brought them out of Egypt wants to set up camp in their hearts and dwell among them by way of a place of worship. He has left no question about how it would be constructed. Much like Noah's ark, He took the guesswork out of the end product. But how are they going to build this? They have left a land of abundant resources. They already used some of what they had to make an abominable calf as the centerpiece of their profane worship. Has God asked the impossible of them? Completing this task will demand great skill along with tedious, meticulous care to adhere to every measurement, material, and specification that Yahweh requested and deserves.

Who God calls, He equips. Who God equips, He calls. Oh to have the panoramic view that God has! He knew exactly what He was doing. He is beginning a new work by putting them to work using skills they may not even realize could be used for good for God!

Read Exodus 35:4-29 and pay attention to how many times the people brought something and what the condition of their hearts was to be. How many times did you count an offering or contribution being named? At least seven times (what a great number of completeness) in the ESV, the phrase "brought or made a contribution" is referenced here. There is also a link between their contribution and the Lord's contribution. They are starting to see that what they had all along was theirs to give because the Lord gave it to them. He gave to them so they could have something to give Him. God loves to display such beauty in the symbiotic relationship for us! While they are giving physical offerings, there is also a matter of the heart that is important to note. What did you notice about their hearts? Their hearts were to be "stirred and moved by their spirit within" in bringing their contributions. What a contrast from how they were used to building in Egypt! This was a choice. This was a chance to build for someone in power above them who loved them, who freed them! How could they not want to give back to the God who parted the waters for them? Now, they had a chance to show this almighty God how much His love meant and how much they loved him. Finally, a building project that meant something. A labor of love.

According to Exodus 35:25-26, what work were the women doing to contribute to this Tabernacle effort? They were skilled in this work of spinning with their hands. These women with sore hands, weary from their toil, retired to their homes every evening after spinning all day for Pharaoh, but they now happily spun without tire because what they were spinning mattered! God put their skills to use for His purpose. Yahweh deserved for their talents to be useful to bring glory to Him rather than to the glory of Egypt. Gathering bundles of blue, purple, and scarlet yarns was joyful work! Imagine their joy when they discovered more rich purple in the back of a pile of belongings in their tents to add to the collection of materials needed for God's Tent. Perhaps a shout of jubilation erupted with a fist emerging from a tent flap when they discovered more crimson yarn. Add it to the pile! Hooray for more goat's hair! It is easy to imagine the growing heap of supplies is not so heavy to carry when the purpose is so powerful. Did the women sing praises or chit-chat while spinning, remarking how this was such a rewarding way to use their skills? How important they must have felt using their craft to help contribute to this big work of making a place of worship for their God.

Where do you think they learned this skill of spinning? Could it be that the Egyptians taught them to make them more useful in mass-producing tapestries for their gods and places of worship while enslaved in Egypt? The perfect picture of irony is that God then used those skills taught by the oppressors to bring about His purpose later, a purpose in His time. Thanks be to Egypt for the time put into training them, but God takes it from here to further His plans instead of theirs. This recalls Joseph's statement, "You planned to harm me, but God planned it for good" (Gen 50:20). Perhaps their ancestors passed these skills down to them. This would link it back to being from the time of the patriarchs, who also can show God's hand in their history all along. Knowing He would call upon them to use these skills, the hands of the family members of Abraham, Isaac, and Jacob, including those women in the genealogy of Sarah, Rebekah, Leah, and Rachel, were possibly taught this as part of their family heritage, tradition, and skills. Now they can see why those skills were preserved within their family tree, that God might be able to use them to show His people how He is fulfilling His promise to Abraham to bless and establish their newly formed nation. Whichever way the skills came about, the conversations surrounding the spinners must have been reflective.

Can you imagine the righteous pride they felt in their hearts each time the priests assembled the Tabernacle again, draped in those fabrics they helped weave? They did that! They helped! They used their skill for the work of the Lord! Their hands gave to that work! Their hearts were in it just as much as their hands.

The scriptures also mention that those who used their skills were stirred in their hearts to do so. They felt called, compelled, and capable of using their talents to help complete God's plan. These ladies did not just sit in their tents and wait to arrive in the promised land before serving the Lord. They did not say, "We have big plans for our lives once we reach the promised land. We have expectations. We will just wait to do the work once we have this or become that.... " Not at all. They got to work. In the middle of the wilderness. In the waiting. They worked. They got busy. They realized what they had to offer, and their hearts were stirred to contribute. What a great example not to wait. We are not to wait until God has given what He promised or what we asked for but to realize what He has already given us, done for us, and wants from us. Do the work in the waiting. The skill of spinning was not dependent upon reaching the promised land. They had that skill while caravanning in the desert, so they used it well. Think about what skills and talents you possess. God has given you abilities right now. Name them. Then, decide how you can use those to further God's plan. Don't wait. Do it while you wait — while you wait for what is next, for the promised land. Stir your hearts to do the work as unto the Lord because He brought you up out of Egypt, too. Your Egypt was the life that once enslaved you, and He saved you! He has called you to do something. He has given you skills. Use them. For Him. This shows Him that you honor Him and want to create a dwelling for Him in the temple of your heart.

Go a little further into Exodus 35:30-36:2. We see the Lord called Bezalel of the tribe of Judah. He called him, and He equipped him. What does it say God gave him? He filled him with the Spirit of God, with skill, intelligence, knowledge, and craftsmanship. He inspired Bezalel to teach others the skills God gave him. There is no doubt this ability was imprinted on him by God. Scripture repeats this fact. God did this so that Bezalel could teach others the skill and use it to complete the Tabernacle and its elements. Exodus 36:2 reiterates that God put skills in the craftsmen and those willing felt stirred to do the work as their offering. When they put their efforts and skills together, they had all the workers needed to follow God's plan.

The parallel to us is crystal clear. God has made you with skills, intelligence, and knowledge. He can use you. Right now. Where you are with what you have. He needs you to have a heart moved to jump in and carry the load of doing the work that you can do. You have a place and a purpose that contributes to the work being done here on earth to further God's plan. What a gift to be a worker for Him! While we wander in this wilderness, awaiting the Promised Land, consider what your kingdom contribution can be. God has a plan. God always has a plan for His people. Like the Israelites, bring your free will offering to the Master Builder, and let His work come to completion by using who you are to magnify who He is.

THOUGHT QUESTIONS FOR "KINGDOM CONTRIBUTIONS"

1. What other Bible characters can you think of that had skills that they used for good and for God? Find their stories in scripture and share the outcome of their skills being put to use.

2. Can you think of Bible characters who did not want to use their skills for God, but He brought it about for His purposes anyway?

3. Think of other Christians you know in your life who have abilities that you can see are useful to God's work. Share their story! How have they used their skills in growing and strengthening the kingdom?

4. Name 3 skills you have right now. How can you turn those skills into contributions to the kingdom of God and His work?

5. What aspirations do you have for work you can do with your skills? How can that be used for God?

Pray to God thanking Him for the stories of skilled workers. Express to Him how you want to use your skills for Him. If you need clarity on your skills, ask Him to reveal those to you. If you need to see how you can be useful to Him right now, ask Him- He will show you! He's the God that will see you through the wilderness and lead you all the way to the Promised Land.

EXCELLING STILL MORE

Hope Chandler

Finally then, brothers and sisters, we request and urge
you in the Lord Jesus, that as you received instruction
from us as to how you ought to walk and please God
(just as you actually do walk),
that you excel even more.
1 Thessalonians 4:1

I planned to attend Florida College for almost as long as I can remember. Before my father earned his chemical engineering degree from Vanderbilt, he and my mother had attended Freed-Hardeman College, and they wanted an education among Christians for their children, as well. As a Board member, he received copies of FC's yearbook, The Royal Palm, and I often leafed through those pages and imagined myself as a student there.

Perhaps I looked forward to FC more than some because my high school experiences were unusually challenging, at least to me at the time. When I was a sophomore, my dad's company, Procter and Gamble, assigned him to the international division. We moved to P&G's headquarters in Cincinnati for eighteen months and then to Hamilton, Ontario, for my senior year, uprooting me twice, leaving friends behind, and requiring me to make new ones as a senior, in a foreign country. Anticipating FC felt like the constant in my life.

I later came to realize I had learned a valuable skill from all that moving around--flexibility. Life does not always fit perfectly with our expectations, and the unexpected often requires rethinking our plans. I came to know that happiness is a choice, as Paul taught: "I have learned to be content in whatever circumstances I am" (Phi 4:11 *NASB*). Living that lesson early has served me well through a life full of changes.

On a hot August day in 1966, I arrived at FC with my parents and friend-roommate Carol Gunter to move into "A Dorm," which stood where Boswell Hall now stands. After settling us into the dorm, my dad gave us some wonderful advice. He offered the usual "study hard" but also urged us to take advantage of the secular opportunities available in FC's God-focused environment. In other words, he urged us to seek balance. He then added advice I did not fully grasp until I myself was a professor at FC. He urged us not to be judgmental of professors if they sometimes disappointed us. He reminded us they were well-educated, sacrificial Christians, serving out of love for God and for us. He explained that some worked second, part-time jobs to help support their families since FC's pay scale was below that of professors elsewhere, and he urged us to be grateful that they cared about educating our hearts as well as our minds. Using that filter, I came to respect many professors very highly, and I remain grateful to them.

I dated several fine young men in high school, but, like many, I found my true love at Florida College. Royce and I savored our two years there. (Bachelor's degrees were not yet offered.) We intentionally soaked up as many experiences as we could and then married August 30, 1968, two years to the day from when he first caught my eye as he led a song at a Sutton Hall singing. We enrolled at Western Kentucky University in Bowling

Green as I had always planned because my grandparents B.G. and Lena Hope lived there, where he preached for the Twelfth Street church (now the Lost River church). Surprisingly, several of our classmates transferred with us. That was the beginning of the FC to WKU migration that has continued, giving birth years ago to the nickname "Florida College North." WKU administrator and fellow Christian Dr. Paul Cook took notice and worked to make transferring as smooth as possible, encouraging Florida College graduates and transfer students to attend there.

While attending WKU, we lived happily in a small preacher's house in Auburn, Kentucky, eighteen miles away. Royce preached for that little country church, following in the footsteps of Robert Jackson, Louis Garrett, Ferrell Jenkins, and others who also began their preaching careers in Auburn. We finished our bachelor's degrees just before the Par Street church in Orlando, Florida, invited Royce to work with them for a time alongside Roy Cogdill. Our first child Luke was born there in 1971, the year Disney World opened a few miles from our home.

We next moved to Danville, Kentucky, a lovely little city near Lexington, and stayed eight years, long enough to remain Kentucky Wildcat fans even now. Our son Todd and daughter Laura were born there. During our stay, Royce, along with Bible scholar and elder Kelly Ellis, offered college-level Bible classes for those who could not attend FC. Royce had offers to work with other churches but declined them, finding fulfillment and purpose in the work he was doing.

When our oldest son was a toddler, Dean Louis Garrett first invited us to teach at FC. My degree was in French, English, and education, and Royce's was in speech communication and religious studies. We declined; Royce loved his work, and I knew the timing was wrong if I were to meet my own personal goals in marriage and motherhood. We continued to get invitations from the College -- and continued to say no. Still, I tucked the possibility in the "ideas for the future" file in my head and continued rearing our children in the Lord and serving as a Christian beside my husband. As the children grew older, I began occasional substitute language teaching in local high schools to stay somewhat involved in education, and I enrolled in a few classes offered in our community through a nearby university.

As a young wife and mother, I learned firsthand that living comfortably, if carefully, on a preacher's salary is possible. Looking back, I have no regrets for my decision to be a full time homemaker in that season of my life, Betty Friedan's recent '60's book The Feminine Mystique notwithstanding. Children all too soon are grown, and the time for bonding and molding in the image of Christ is over. If I were to rear my own children again, I would spend even more time with them. I was grateful to have the option of "... making the most of (my) time, because the days are evil," offering my children my best, not my leftovers, in teaching them "what the will of the Lord is" (Eph 5:16-17 *NASB*). I treasure those memories.

In 1973 when our sons were two years old and newborn, the elders, at Royce's suggestion, invited a young man who aspired to preach to work as a "summer intern" with the church. Interns are common now, but this was a new idea then. We continued this work with other churches, as well, for fourteen summers. Through the years, some amazing young men lived in our home: Barry Hudson, Rick Lanning, Jamie Hinds, David Banning, Jerry Crolius, and Australian Steve Wilson, among others. We felt living with our family helped them learn some important realities of a dedicated preacher's life; for example, Royce has always been very diligent to maintain "office hours," both to help dispel the idea that "preachers work only on weekends" as well as to stay productive. He expected the same from these young men.

Our children also benefitted greatly from these "big brothers" in their lives every summer. In addition to spiritual modeling, each young man brought something special to them. For example, Jerry Crolius was a University of Miami National Champion pitcher and coached our young son Todd. The extra work for me was worth every minute those men blessed our family.

In 1976 life took a surprising turn when we were drawn, I believe providentially, to take the gospel to Colombia, South America. We were naively unaware of what changes were about to affect our lives when a young Colombian in a Missouri state prison requested the Bible correspondence course Royce offered in our weekly, local newspaper — in Kentucky. It remains a mystery as to how that newspaper ended up in that prison, but the man eventually was baptized. He was released and sent home a few months later, but finding no New Testament Christians, he wrote a very moving letter asking Royce to come teach him more about the gospel so that he could teach his family and countrymen. By faith, my non-Spanish-speaking husband invited Wayne Partain, known for his lifelong work in Mexico, to go with him, along with the elders' blessings, and soon the first New Testament church was born in Colombia. That phenomenally successful work has become an integral part of our lives with surprising connections to Florida College, as well.

As that work grew, Royce was seeking a way to learn Spanish while maintaining a full-time job and a family when the Franklin Road church (now the Woodland Hills church) in

Nashville invited him to work there. The elders agreed he could also study Spanish, so he accepted the job and enrolled in a Berlitz "total immersion" course rather than college, hoping to "jump-start" his mastery of Spanish. That study, his natural talent for language, and his intense desire to learn enabled him after those two weeks to write out sermons and read them aloud.

Three years later, however, it was clear he needed far more exposure to Spanish, so we moved to San Antonio, Texas, to work with Wayne Partain and a Spanish-speaking church. Royce enrolled in more classes, as well. Eighteen months later, he felt he had reached his goal, so when the church in Mason, Ohio, offered him a job, we accepted. Those elders were, thankfully, very supportive of the Colombian work and the need to travel there often. During our six years in Mason, we both also earned master's degrees from the University of Cincinnati.

Royce (often with others or me) has made more than 60 trips to Colombia and other Spanish-speaking countries for 47 years. Over 100 churches have been established in Colombia. We have witnessed, "Blessed are those who hunger…for righteousness…" (Mat 5:6 *NASB*) in live action. The earliest Christians were mostly university students seeking the truth in their Catholic culture, and as they grew in the faith, they married and had children. When those children became teenagers, we told them about FC. Like many around the world, they had studied English in school but had not mastered it. We found that in addition to the strenuous legal and financial requirements to obtain a visa to study in the States, students also had to prove mastery of English by passing the TOEFL, a "Test of English as a Foreign Language." The exam is difficult and expensive, but a few began studying English intensely, hoping to attend FC.

In 1996, Maria Mantilla (now Mrs. Nathan Collier) was a pioneer, the first Colombian to try to attend FC. When we invited her to live with us a few months to prepare for the TOEFL, we had no idea we were beginning a long journey with our "Colombian children" that continues today. Her tuition was also a roadblock. Non-U.S. citizens are usually ineligible for scholarships or grants, and Colombian brethren rarely can contribute much, if anything, so Royce made the first of many requests for funds to help a Colombian study at F.C.

This work has manifested many wondrous examples of God's providence and our brethren's generosity. Twenty-two Colombians have attended FC; sadly, others have been inexplicably denied even a visitor's visa by our embassy or have been unable to pass the TOEFL. The successful ones have typically spent several months in our home to work on

English although more recently they have come in "multiples," too many to accommodate for long. I serve many roles: chauffeur, maid, nurse, confidante, wedding dress consultant, dorm set-up shopper, English coach — in short, as their mom! The earlier students called me "Mom," but recently I have become "Grandma-ma," very apropos since we have fourteen grandchildren.

In 1989, before the "Colombia/F.C. Connection," FC President Bob Owen hired us to teach. We felt the timing was finally right. I first worked part-time but later began full-time teaching that also required serving on committees and sponsoring a campus organization. Usually, I worked with the Young Women's Training Organization (YWTO). We had weekly devotions but also sponsored enriching events. We prepared dinners for Sower's Club men. We held Ladies' Days. We offered homemakers' workshops, learning to make a great pie crust from Wanda Dickey, sewing tips from Judy Sheehan, and more. We invited speakers to discuss relevant topics such as "Dating Etiquette" and "Christians and Finances." More recently, the club (under a new name) has held devotions-by-the-pool/sleepovers at my home even though I am retired.

My FC service took an unexpected turn early on when chorus director "Dudy" Walker asked me to be the piano accompanist. The chorus met daily, culminating in an annual tour over spring break. "Dudy" always provided two-part concerts: sacred music, of course, and a secular section, complete with costumes and staging. Royce and I traveled with them; he managed the staging and set-up, and I was accompanist for the secular half, as well as "chorus mom," helping solve issues that arose and serving as liaison with the hosts who housed us at each stop. When "Dudy" retired, we continued working with directors Clark Dugger and then Scott Wyatt for several more years. I learned that preparing oneself in a secular area such as playing the piano can open the door for unexpected opportunities to serve.

Like many FC professors, Royce has also preached in Tampa. About twenty years ago, Spanish speakers occasionally visited our congregation, and our bilingual men began announcing song numbers in both languages. That small beginning has evolved into efficient, bilingual services. English and Spanish speakers meet as one body. We sing both English and Spanish songs, as well as some specially arranged bilingual hymns, using Power Point translations. Non-English speakers wear audio devices, and proficient, bilingual men provide simultaneous, live translations of the worship service for them. I am very grateful for our dedicated translators and for my Hispanic brethren.

We know Christians need each other, especially students who daily face the world at school, but we must also be lights in the world, showing we are "a people for God's own possession" (1 Pet 2:9 *NASB*). Being Christians should show. A favorite example is when our daughter Laura was in marching band at Tampa's big, culturally diverse King High School. One Friday, we planned a birthday party for her and some band friends after the football game, and dozens more came than were invited. As they joyfully piled into our house, I was counting heads to see if we had enough paper plates when a young man yelled something like this: "Hey, it's time to eat! We're at the Chandlers', so let's pray! Bow your heads!" He then prayed a most unusual prayer — but sincerely. He had likely noticed our Laura and other Christians in the band behaving as "sheep of His pasture" (Psa 100:3 *NASB*). Perhaps he became more aware of their faith when F.C. music professor Doug Barlar and I served as chaperones on the band trips to provide a way for Christian students to worship on Sundays in one of our motel rooms. In any case, I appreciated what that birthday moment confirmed: we are meant to be lights in this dark world, and sometimes the lights we shine reach unexpected places with surprising results.

A big part of our lives has always included hospitality. Our mothers (and my grandmothers) regularly practiced it, so it is a very natural habit for us. Years ago, dear friend Carol (Gunter) Gaines nicknamed our home "Chandler Inn" and even had a pack of note cards printed for me that said, "Chandler Inn, where nice people stay." Being part of both the Lord's family and the Florida College family brings us many opportunities. Usually, we have "no vacancies" during lectures and at graduation, and sometimes we house brethren we have not met but whose children we have come to know. We are blessed.

The last five years during FC's annual Lectureship, we have hosted "The Golden Grads" reception for alumni who graduated 50 or more years ago. Occasionally, someone attends whom we have not seen since our graduation, but it is equally exciting to see the same friends from the past every year. Our record crowd so far is 82. I always ask my granddaughters to help so I can visit instead of be "Martha," but the more important reason is to help them learn how to serve. They could likely manage the whole evening by themselves now.

We have always tried to nurture young people, so another focus in our lives has been camps. Our first experience was in 1983 when we were invited to counsel at FC's Ohio camp. The next year we were asked to direct it. We agreed and learned a great deal about people and camp organization that year. The camp grew, finally serving 421 campers, plus staff, our last year. At that time, we had more campers than FC had students. We worked hard to persuade every senior to attend F.C., and not many slipped away. FC music professor Doug Barlar and future professors Nancy Barlar, Julie Gant, and Matt Johnson were on our staff. We began directing the Florida camp, as well. To help campers recognize FC as college rather than camp, we moved it from the campus to a campsite near Ocala. In our fourteen years as directors, the camp grew to over 400 campers, plus staff. Several in the FC family served with us: Thaxter Dickey, Donald MacLendon and Dan Petty counseled boys, and Loretta Atherton, Wanda Dickey, Cathi Lykins, and Kathy Petty served girls. We also recruited Board member Wally Hayes and his wife Sandy. He always said camp was the one week in the year when he was not tempted to sin.

In 2008, we took our experiences to Colombia and held a camp in the Andes mountains, funded largely by generous American Christians. Some of the campers had never even slept in a bed. Our resourceful Colombian brethren took notes and for years now have rented a school campus for their own "Encuentro" every year. Royce usually serves as the Bible teacher.

We began a very different camping adventure in 2012 that we call "Broadway Comes to Camp." We are a musical and dramatic family, so we decided to try a project our whole family and others could enjoy together: putting on a Broadway musical, in nine days from start to finish. We have now presented twelve summer shows. About 100 very talented Christians come from several states to participate, including some entire families. Our focus is the Lord, using the talents He gave us to present a "cleaned up," professional-level production. Because we rent FC's campus, we also promote the College. I can affirm that Christians are very talented.

Some years ago, we started "Paque and Grandma-ma Camp" for our fourteen grandchildren. (First grandchild Tim coined the "Paque" name when he tried to say, "Padre," Royce's chosen grandpa name.) They all live nearby except for the two married ones, and they are often in our home, but we have one week each summer when the available ones stay with us for "camp." We plan special activities, have daily devotions they themselves lead, and take a little trip for the grand finale. Several have "aged out" now, but we treasure the time and the memories.

We are a family with generations of faithful Christians and FC connections who believe Florida College is unique among colleges in her stand for God's truth. My father Fred Pollock served as an elder and on the FC Board of Directors. Royce's mother Pauline was an elder's wife and a dorm mother for many years. Royce preached for decades and serves as an elder; we both have been F.C. professors. Our daughter Laura is an elder's wife, a dedicated Bible class organizer and teacher and a homeschool leader. Our son Todd is a deacon and a beloved FC biology professor, who often preaches. He led a Galapagos Islands trip in 2024, emphasizing anti-evolution evidence. Son Luke is an elder, historian, preacher, and FC Bible professor who leads world tours, including excavations in Israel. Our three children met their spouses, all dedicated Christians, through FC. Our three oldest grandchildren are Christians and FC alumni; two are now married to wonderful FC-graduate Christians. The next three are Christians and current FC students. Four more are also baptized believers who eagerly anticipate FC, and our youngest four, we pray, are "waiting in the wings" to follow in those footsteps.

We often find F.C. and "Christian" connections in surprising places: for example, on the Tube in London (their sons attended Ohio camp) and on a train to Versailles (a seatmate's roommate was an alumna). Worshipping on vacation, we frequently meet someone who knows us or who has a mutual acquaintance. Years ago, French student Lindsay Wolfgang and I realized we had relatives married to each other, and she joked that someday Christians would not be able to marry at all because we would all be related! I am blessed to have served in both the Florida College family and in the Lord's family, His church.

We who know and love the Lord are blessed. As we journey toward heaven, God's Word gives the faithful not only abiding hope but also challenging duties as we await our glorious eternity. In the early days of the church, Paul felt such concern for the Thessalonian babes in Christ that he sent Timothy to encourage them and was delighted to learn they had remained steadfast in their faith and love. However, after expressing his thankfulness for them, Paul offered an extra little push: he told them to "excel still more" (1 The 4:1,10 NASB).

How do we reflect excelling still more in our walk today? Paul tells us we begin by seeking "the things above" rather than earthly things, removing the sins of our old selves, such as malice and lying, and adding godly attributes to our new selves, for example, humility, and patience. (Col 3:8-10). Our old selves were buried in baptism, and we are sanctified through Christ's blood. He now lives in us. Therefore, we are to "abound with greater care and fidelity" on the road we have entered.[1] To excel still more day by day, we must sift each thought and action through the filter of an ever-deepening understanding that our redemption is possible only through our Savior's sacrifice.

We must also excel still more in love for our brethren with the "special affection" believers have for each other.[2] In our busy lives, do we make time for this? Do we truly care about fellow Christians?? Do they know we care about them? Do our interactions indicate our love for them? Are we aware when they need guidance? For example, are we close enough to a young sister that we can lovingly warn her when she is "playing with fire" in her choice of a boyfriend? Do we notice when a brother is falling into the habit of missing worship? These examples indicate how strong our "special affection" truly is.

Additionally, we must excel still more in love for unbelievers. This begins by living honorably before them (1 The 4:11-12). Because Christ lives in us, unbelievers can see Him manifested even in life's trivial moments. We must not only love them; we must also conduct ourselves "with wisdom toward unbelievers, making the most of the opportunity" to show them the Way (Col 4:5). We infuse spiritual wisdom into our hearts by reading and meditating on the Word of God, and this wisdom not only enables us to see when a door of opportunity is open for teaching another but also guides us in our approach. Of course, there must first be an attraction—a wise, godly Christian. Have you experienced an unbeliever, perhaps a work colleague or a neighbor, asking what makes you "different"? Searching hearts notice when our very lives "proclaim the excellences of Him who has called us out of darkness into His marvelous light" (1 Pet 2:9). Do our characters and conduct in daily life attract others to seek the Lord? Manifesting spiritual wisdom toward unbelievers is a part of excelling still more.

In Philippians 1, Paul expressed great joy and thankfulness for those Christians whose sincerity, when "examined by the brightest light," was found "pure and without fault."[3]

---

1 I The 4:10, Pulpit Commentary, vol. 21, p.74

2 Ibid., 75

3 MacKnight on the Epistles, vol. III-IV, p. 405

He prayed that their love "abound still more ... in real knowledge and all discernment" (Phi 1:9). Wuest believes this "real knowledge" is limited not only to what has been taught but also to what has been gained from experience, coupled with "all discernment" that he describes as "a sensitive and moral, ethical tact."[4] Thus, spiritual wisdom gained from God's Word along with our empirical knowledge, when used carefully and honestly, will enable us to "abound still more, far beyond the everyday, easily understood spiritual obligations." We will grow in "the finer points of Christian conduct,"[5] leading us to "approve what is excellent" (Phi 1:10). Do we examine Scripture carefully enough to feel confident it is Truth? Do we treasure its excellence? Do we hunger for it? We must have this attitude if we are to be "sincere and blameless until the day of Christ; having been filled with the fruit of righteousness which comes through Christ" (Phi 1:11).

How are we "filled with the fruit of righteousness" through Christ? John 15:1-2 tells us Christ is the Vine, and we are the branches, a beautiful metaphor that helps us understand our total dependence on our Savior. As the branch lives by the vine, so we Christians, as branches, live by our Vine, the life of Christ.[6] Christ is also the Word (Joh 1:1, 14). The grafting of our lives into the Word, the Vine, brings forth fruit, the "fruit of righteousness," and the wonderful result of this is supreme excellence, to "the glory and praise of God" (Phi 1:11).

The Bible often refers to excellence. Ruth's future husband Boaz cited her reputation: that everyone in the city knew her to be "a woman of excellence." Most certainly this was a factor in his choosing her as his wife. Proverbs 12:4 discusses the excellence of a godly wife, who is a crown to her husband. Proverbs 17:7 approaches the idea of excellence from a negative perspective, saying, "Excellent speech is not fitting for a fool." Philippians 4:8 includes "excellence" along with "worthy of praise" as the kinds of things we should dwell upon. We are a "chosen race, a royal priesthood, a holy nation, a people for God's own possession," put here to "proclaim the excellencies of Him ... who called us into His marvelous light" (1 Pet 2:9). First Corinthians 12:31 introduces the beautiful chapter on love, describing it as a "still more excellent way." Our Father surely desires excellence from His children.

---

4 Wuest, Word Studies in the Greek New Testament, vol. II, pp. 36-37

5 Ibid, p.37

6 Pulpit Commentary, Vol. 20, The Epistle to the Philippians, p.4

How is "excelling still more" seen in our lives today? Imagining a large, spiritual umbrella labeled "excel still more" over our entire existence is a good reminder that God has expectations for each of us, not only as Christians, but also as wives, mothers, employees, homemakers, and neighbors. How do we "excel still more," pleasing God in all our roles?

Besides our becoming Christians, there may be no factor more important for excelling in our walk than choosing our spouses. If a man does not love God more than he loves you, he is not a good choice for a husband. Period. (Some things are clearly black and white.) If he grows to the point of loving God more than he loves you, and you love him, marry him -- but settle for nothing less if your intention is to excel still more on your road to heaven.

Women are increasingly working outside of traditional roles for women. If you are a young woman choosing a career (and wisdom dictates we prepare ourselves to be independent), and you also want a family, please choose wisely. Some careers are so demanding that you cannot have much time with your family or to serve the Lord and others; go a different direction. Some careers are difficult to step back into if you want some years off to rear children; perhaps choose another. However, the most important consideration is this: no one can fill three or four (Or five? Or more?) ongoing, demanding roles excellently, all at once. Is this not true?

My advice as a professor and academic advisor for young women was this: "You can do everything you want to do in your life—but not all at the same time." Imagine yourself as a wife, a mother, a Christian in a local church, and a woman with a full-time job. Even if you get home when your children get home, even if you work from home, even if your husband cooks dinner or does the grocery shopping, and so on … something critically important will slip in your efforts to excel still more in all your roles. You may feel too busy to teach children's classes at church, to take a meal to a sick family, to help host a baby shower, or even to read your Bible daily. You may have very little (or often even no?) time or energy to chat with your children about their concerns, to share their happy moments, to notice when they are struggling spiritually, or even to feed little souls with nightly Bible stories and songs and to hear bedtime prayers. You may be stressed and feel guilty because the household duties are never really finished, so you do not invite others in for a meal or a Bible study. Perhaps you are so exhausted from being mom, wife, employee, maid, nurse, cook, chauffeur, etc., that you and your husband find little time or energy to nurture your marriage spiritually, physically, and communicatively. Not one of us is Superwoman. So, if you feel discouraged staying home with your children, make this your mantra: I can do everything I want to do in my life—just not all at the same time.

Consider, as well, being mostly available during the critical years when your teen's growing independence needs loving supervision. Let your home be "the happening place" for her and her friends. Of course, you must be there, too, but I assure you the sacrifice is worth it. We can always work, but we have no second chances to train a child to love the Lord with all her "heart, soul, strength, and mind" (Luk 10:27). Spiritual excellence does not just happen; it must be purposely cultivated and demonstrated in every facet of our lives.

Our attitudes also affect excelling still more. Are we easily dissatisfied, or are we joyful, having learned from Paul's example to be content in any circumstance? (Phi 4:10-11). Do we feel justified when we react poorly to stress or misfortune? All of us have disappointments or sometimes even devastating obstacles in our walk. When this happens, we must work even harder on our attitudes. (Reading Philippians 4 is wonderful therapy.) When my young children were very tired and became grumpy, I told them they could be sad or even cry—but that being tired was not a reason to be grumpy. It just meant they had to try harder to be pleasant. Do we adults sometimes need that advice? We cannot control all situations, but we Christians can and should learn to control our reactions to them.

Christians must excel as servants, as well. Jesus taught that serving is a great blessing when He said, "It is more blessed to give than to receive" (Act 20:35). He Himself served His disciples by washing their feet. Serving "as for the Lord" (Col 3:23) is the epitome of excelling still more, and we must seek opportunities to serve, as our Lord did. In Matthew 25, Jesus spoke about the judgment when the King commended the righteous for clothing, feeding, and tending to Him. This puzzled His hearers because they had not done those things for Him. Jesus' point for them and for all believers is that serving others is also serving Him. Is this not wonderful motivation to excel still more in our service to others?

How can we ensure personal excellence in the Lord in our daily lives? We are so busy. Stress is our "24/7" companion! -- and we seem not to mind so much since we often do nothing to change our situations. Do we sometimes ignore or resist doing what can offer relief and peace? We can petition our Father for help. We can feed on His Word every single day. That Word is our lamp; we need not remain in darkness. We can find direction in a crisis by asking ourselves, "What would Jesus do?" We can remember that God gave us each other and can choose to spend time with a trusted Christian, drawing strength from her love and wisdom. We can examine our priorities to see if they are in line with the Lord's expectations or if we need to rethink how we fill our days. Perhaps we feel overwhelmed, unappreciated, or even bitter, and we pray for the Lord to take it all away. Yet, resolving issues takes time and deliberate effort with the Father's mercy and His Word as our guide. Of course, we often stumble in our efforts to excel, and we humbly seek forgiveness. Then, Jesus' blood cleanses us, again and again, so that we can begin anew, and, blessedly, those failings are remembered no more.

No one attains excellence without setting goals. Athletes set benchmarks toward being stronger, faster, or more accurate scorers. Performers work hard to learn and interpret lines or to perfect music. Setting goals is just as necessary to ensure spiritual excellence. Besides working toward conquering our weaknesses and using our strengths in His service, we must set goals in family relationships, especially with our spouses, as well as with our spiritual families.

We can study Scripture and pray together as a couple; we can meet regularly with fellow Christians to study, to serve others, or just to enjoy faith-building fellowship. Goals can even be quite simple. For example, when I was a young mother, four of us homemakers joined a weekly bowling league. Our goal was just to spend time together. We were not great bowlers, but we enjoyed those weekly moments. Afterwards, we often shared lunch, visited a shut-in, or took a lonely person out to eat. Those brief moments together strengthened our bond as sisters in Christ even as we served others.

Excellence is always a choice. Furthermore, achieving spiritual excellence is a lifelong quest. We are sometimes lazy, ill-tempered, indifferent, or selfish, so we do not always demonstrate or even strive for excellence. However, this wonderful passage in Proverbs can serve as a compass in helping us to seek excellence as we walk this life's path:

> "Let your eyes look directly ahead, and let your gaze be fixed straight in front of you. Watch the path of your feet, and all your ways will be established. Do not turn to the right nor to the left; turn your foot from evil." (Pro 4:25-27)

THOUGHT QUESTIONS FOR "EXCELLING STILL MORE"

1. What "tools" were available to the Thessalonian Christians to enable them to "excel still more"? What "tools" are available to us today?

2. What things would have been a hindrance to the Thessalonian Christians in their intentions to "excel still more"? Discuss what they might have done to overcome them. What things are a hindrance to us today? How can we overcome them?

3. What are your goals as a wife? As a mother? As an employee or worker? As a Christian? What will your life look like when these are the goals?

4. In what ways does attitude affect one's spiritual walk? Create several different life scenarios, real or imagined, that are challenging for Christians, that make it easy to sin. Describe how we might typically react in the moment, without careful thought or concern for God. Then, describe the reaction of one who has a "mind of Christ attitude" in these same situations.

5. In setting goals for ourselves as women who want to follow Christ in all things, what are some realistic expectations in our busy, everyday lives? Considering your life as it is now, what adjustments must you make to meet these expectations?

6. What do you think would be on God's list of goals He wants us to have in our everyday lives? (Be specific. For example, do not say, "Read the Bible" and stop there!)

DEDICATED AND PURE:
LIVING BY THE BOOK AMONG A PECULIAR PEOPLE

Julie Gant

"But you are a chosen people, a royal priesthood,
a holy nation, a people belonging to God,
that you may declare the praises of him who called you
out of darkness into his wonderful light."
1 Peter 2:9

I am privileged to serve in the English department of Florida College. In addition to composition courses, I teach great literature, the classics. Wherever appropriate, I have the happy task of connecting biblical and spiritual themes to our authors' essays, poetry, short stories, and novels. I celebrate with my students the most influential, enduring works of art—other people's stories. When asked to write a personal narrative, however, I face an unfamiliar and daunting task. I view my life as a long process of contributing to other people's life stories—that of my parents, husband, children, students, and brethren.

What, then, what is my own story? Whatever it is, it involves books.

Anyone acquainted with my extended family knows that we have a penchant for books that borders on obsession. In a clan full of preachers and teachers, professors, physicists, engineers, musicians, artists, and researchers, books are the default gift of choice. We read for information. We read to improve ourselves. We read for pleasure. We read when we should be doing other things. Many of us wait impatiently for the next good library sale. We cannot resist even the smallest used bookstore (especially when we know the proprietor keeps a cat). And when we discover in our haunts a worn but well-loved tome copiously annotated by an intelligent former reader, we cherish this peculiar, great treasure. We agree with Mortimer J. Adler that "marking up a book is not an act of mutilation but of love."[1]

The most treasured tome in the family is my father's heavily annotated ASV Bible. When my sister called with the dreadful news that Dad had lost the beloved Book, I cried. While helping our mother into the car, he had mistakenly left his Bible on the hood. They had retraced in vain the lengthy journey from the driveway to the church parking lot, scanning every ditch and bend in the road. Seventy years of marginal notes on every page in Dad's beautiful hand—outlines, sermons, teaching notes—gone forever. Here was a lost future inheritance more valuable than the house, piano, telescopes, books, or antiques could ever be. When a delivery van arrived the next day with Dad's Bible, only slightly scuffed, imagine our joy! We praised God and asked his special blessing on the kind soul who had retrieved and returned it anonymously.

My parents' decades of dedication to God's Word serves as context for my own story. I am blessed to have grown up among a peculiar people, if I may borrow the quaint wording of the King James Bible: "But ye are a chosen generation, a royal priesthood, an holy nation, a peculiar people..." (1 Pet 2:9). "Peculiar" has come to connote quirkiness and oddity,

---

1 Mortimer J. Adler, "How to Mark a Book," Modern English Readings (New York: Farrar and Rinehart, 1945, Fourth Edition) 268.

and, certainly, this more modern usage describes some of our clan more closely than we care to admit. But if I lean into the 1611 concept of a special, treasured people of the Lord's own possession, I realize that at every stage of my life the Lord has surrounded me with consecrated people who have modeled the dedicated life. I have always had everything I needed for life and godliness.

I had "peculiar" parents who came from equally "peculiar" grandparents. They in turn descended from generations of "peculiar" forebears who came to the truth at various stages of the Restoration Movement and dedicated themselves to first century, New Testament worship and practice. My aunts, uncles, and cousins share our "peculiar" bond, and we pray that we will continue to reap the blessings of the legacy through our children and grandchildren. We know we are not saved on the group plan, so we are ever in prayer for each other. Some of our number became "peculiar" by a different route, coming to the Lord with searching hearts and encountering the gospel through friends. Scattered now from coast to coast, we are blessed to worship in congregations alongside beautifully "peculiar" brethren.

My own quirkiness emerged early. Batman and Robin taught me to read, I often joke. In our little yellow house in Akron, Ohio, I remember donning my Batman slippers before each episode of the campy Adam West TV series. I followed the exploits of the Dynamic Duo with solemn and devoted interest. When the inevitable fisticuffs broke out with villains, the screen would be splattered with the colorful graphics which accompanied the melee—WHAMM! ZOWIE! KRUNCH! What did the splatters say? I had to know! Only a person skilled in the mysterious martial art of phonics could decode those delightful interjections, but I was a willing apprentice.

My dear parents, David and Mary Koltenbah, were busy people in the 1960s. Our family consisted of a gospel preacher who was finishing his PhD in physics, a schoolteacher who was finalizing her MA in music, and the towheaded, caped crusaders who came in rapid succession. Mom gave birth to three kids in three years, bless her, and those were the days of cloth diapers. We soon moved our chaos to Muncie, Indiana, where Dad began to "make tents" as a professor at Ball State University while offering his preaching and teaching talents to a fledging congregation of the Lord's people.

Life in Muncie, or "Middletown USA" as it was dubbed by sociologists Robert and Helen Lynd,[2] was as close to idyllic as city kids could ever hope for. Muncie had grown from its

2 Renowned sociologists Robert and Helen Lynd published the first of their Middletown studies in 1929, selecting

Native American and pioneer roots to a prosperous and cultured town. Home of the historic Ball Family and their world-famous canning jars, Muncie boasted other large businesses and factories, a university with a sports complex, planetarium, and an art museum, multiple symphonies and orchestras, theatres, parks, and historic mansions repurposed for public use. Orchard Lawn, our neighborhood, had sprung up next to the university, and I and my sister Betsy (now Sarah Hersey), my brother Ben, and our young neighbors claimed the adjacent, undeveloped campus property as our own personal Meadow, Woods, Creek, and Duck Pond. For many happy years, we flew kites, built tree forts, dug up arrowheads, built rock bridges, and gathered blackberries and wildflowers. Eventually, Ball State broke our hearts by plowing up the Meadow for campus development. When architects and engineers came with their blueprints and mallets, we wept aloud with each wooden boundary stake they planted. Childhood was not over for us, but it had taken a serious hit.

Orchard Lawn was a place designed to nurture family life. For a few happy years, our family of five lived in the same neighborhood as our grandparents and our uncle, aunt, and four cousins. Our clan, along with a handful of others, formed the nucleus of a new congregation planted in Muncie in the 1960s as a scriptural alternative to the many area churches of Christ which had strayed into digression. Our Pawpaw, E. C. Koltenbah, a studious and dedicated gospel preacher, and our Grandmama Sarah, his devoted wife, moved to the neighborhood soon after the Ledfords, our dad's sister and family, had done the same. They lived in cul-de-sacs a short walk or bike ride away. Our schools were also within walking distance, allowing Kiki, our old orange tabby cat and self-appointed nanny, to walk us as far as the crossing guard in the morning and to accompany us home in the afternoon. Dad rode his basket-rigged bicycle to campus every day, and Mom's piano students came to our house each afternoon. Though the branch library was too far away for us to bike to, the Bookmobile came almost to our door. Our world, though compact, was large in the things children need to be able to flourish.

Life was a happy rhythm of worship, school, and play. When I visited my grandparents around the corner, I would be set to work with my "indoor grandmother," watering the rosebushes, helping cut cookie dough, or running a dust rag across the antiques. I spent many a happy hour sprawled on the floor with scrap paper and crayons behind

---

Muncie, Indiana, as the basis for their field research on the cultural, social, and economic changes of a typical population in the 20th century American experience. "Robert Lynd and Helen Lynd." Encyclopedia Britannica, March 22, 2024. https://www.britannica.com/biography/Robert-Lynd-and-Helen-Lynd.

my grandfather's chair. I watched him prepare his sermons at his book-laden desk by the picture window, which was surrounded by a great band of yellow *National Geographics*.

I learned later that these elderly people had once been young and brave, fleeing the rising waters of the 1937 Ohio River flood with their two small children. Pawpaw, a preacher in Lawrenceburg, Indiana, lost his library and the family's possessions in the disaster. Because my grandfather had been studying issues of authority and had concluded that some of the congregation's practices were unscriptural, he decided to cut his ties with the group even though this meant he would be without income. It was the middle of the Depression, and my grandparents were homeless. But God rewarded their resolve to begin afresh in their application of biblical principles. Brothers Robert Turner, James Cope, and other generous brethren housed the young family and helped my grandfather find preaching opportunities. The Lord blessed my Pawpaw and Grandmama's courage and dedication to the truth, and He set our clan on a new path of service. Eventually, that path led us to Muncie, Indiana, to the fledgling church, and our life in Orchard Lawn.

Given the number of teachers and professors in our clan, I took to learning like ducks to the water in the Ball State Pond. And I was eager to pass on that learning. I have a toddler memory of lining up my dolls, lecturing them from my board books, and administering corporal punishment to the unruly. My Christmas and birthday presents were nearly always educational—a microscope, an ant farm, the Invisible Man and Woman kits, paint-by-number projects, a chemistry set, a child-sized typewriter, and, of course, books.

Reading was as essential to me as breathing. On a few tantalizingly rare occasions, I experienced fleeting pangs of intense joy which came to me unexpectedly while absorbed in my books. I could not explain these moments to anyone and felt alone in them. While reading *Surprised by Joy*[3] as a young adult, however, I was thrilled to discover that C. S. Lewis had also been struck by these sudden and tantalizingly brief flashes on three occasions as a child, two of which came as he was reading. He describes this phenomenon as "that of an unsatisfied desire which is itself more desirable than any other satisfaction. I call it Joy...I doubt whether anyone who has tasted it would ever...exchange it for all the pleasures in the world."[4] Like the great author, I found that the "stabs of Joy" hinted at a higher, more enduring delight in the One who is the source of all joy.

3 Lewis drew his title from a line by William Wordsworth: "Surprised by joy—impatient as the wind" (from Sonnet XXIX).

4 C.S. Lewis, *Surprised by Joy: The Shape of My Early Life* (London: Harvest/Harcourt Brace, 1955) 17-18.

Reading and writing stories are best done in trees, so I spent my afternoons and summers up in the leaves. My treehouse was in the Meadow beyond our fence, but the best reading tree was the tall, supple poplar in our backyard. The neighbor lady would call my mother when a storm was coming to report that, once again, I was lost in a book up there in the branches, whipped about violently by the winds and heedless of danger. I was communing with the Pevensies, Jim Hawkins, Meg Murry, and Anne Shirley and could not be bothered to climb down. What storm?

Anne of Green Gables had been a gift from Grandmother Armistead, my mother's mother. She was my "outdoor grandmother," having begun her teaching career at age 16 in a one room schoolhouse. In the early years, Granddaddy went from farm to farm to pick up students in his horsedrawn wagon. Grandmother enjoyed a long career, teaching in successively larger schools until the state of Tennessee forced her to retire at age 70. Born in 1897 and 1900, my grandparents worked a sizeable farm, raised six children, buried three of them, and met faithfully with their local congregation. I remember country breakfasts cooked before dawn, an open Bible on the piano bench, a bookshelf near a woodstove, two pairs of wrinkled hands bowed in prayer, and my stout little grandmother walking across the fields to carry dinner to an ailing neighbor. Education, hard work, and dedication to God—these are the captions I affix to my mental snapshots.

Back in Muncie, my dad's parents continued to labor with the church throughout the 1960s and 1970s. Life rolled along beautifully for me until Uncle Jim, a college English professor, and my Aunt Mimi moved their family to Fort Lauderdale, Florida. The heartache when the cousins were separated only served to make them dearer to us. After my "indoor" grandmother and my grandfather passed away, my father tried to shoulder the responsibilities of preaching and teaching while "making tents" as a full-time physics and astronomy prof. When this load became too much for Dad, the brethren searched for a preacher to move to Muncie who could commit to fulltime work. My sister and I were baptized on June 27, 1979, three weeks before Darrel and Jean Haub and their four children moved to help us.

My high school years were happy. I was blessed with a group of spiritually-minded friends who held high standards for themselves. I am also grateful to God for those teachers and mentors who did not share my faith but who nevertheless influenced me by their expertise, discipline, and high character. My piano teacher was a martinet, but my Bach Inventions progressed. I feared the English teacher who dressed entirely in black and frowned through pince-nez glasses, but only once did she have to cast my essay in the wastebasket for me to mend my shoddy ways. I served as a writer and editor for the school newspaper, played cello in the orchestra, took four years of German, and enjoyed advanced biology, zoology, and Greek and Latin derivatives class. When a paper route and babysitting ceased to hold charm, I got a job among the ghosts at the Carnegie Library downtown. Reshelving books in the poorly lit, ironwork loft, stamping piles of checkout cards in a shadowed corner, and manning the paperback room in the dank basement cured me of reading murder mysteries for a few years.

My siblings and I went with the Haub kids to Florida College camps, one in West Virginia, and the other at Camp Kern in Cincinnati. It was at the Ohio FC Camp that I decided I had to go to Florida College. Fellow camper Terry Rogol (now Teresa Bunting) became my dear friend and pen pal, and we betrothed ourselves to be college roommates. Though my father had attended "FCC" (as it was called in the early 1950s), he did not have FC on the radar for us. As Ball State faculty offspring, we would have our tuition waived for us. I am eternally grateful that Dad yielded and allowed me, and later my sister, to go to Florida College for one year. It was important to me to graduate from FC with my AA to call myself an alumna, so I sat for several CLEP tests and took course overloads to achieve that goal.

What a wonderful decision! My whirlwind year of 1982-1983 was formative in more ways than I can describe. I knew I had a one-year shot at the FC merry-go-round, so I grabbed hold of the ring and rode with intention. To help with expenses, I took a campus job as piano accompanist for some of Mrs. Pickup's voice students. I sang alto in Dudy Walker's chorus, took piano lessons, played in piano duo and quartet, and enjoyed YWTO (Young Women's Training Organization, now called Woven). Every class I took was valuable. The experience of sitting at the feet of scholars from many fields—all of them brethren—was thrilling. My Bible classes were excellent. I still cherish my notes from Phil Roberts, Robert Turner, James Cope, Melvin Curry, Colly Caldwell, Brent Hunter, and others. With my dear friend Vicki Dvorak (now Copeland), I took what, that year at least, were otherwise all-male classes for Bible majors. I left at the end of the school year with my diploma, a buoyed heart, a long list of lifelong friends, and a greater resolve to serve God.

Our congregation in Muncie grew numerically and eventually moved from a converted dwelling house at the edge of town to an historic church building on Calvert Avenue, adjacent to the Ball State campus. After I came home from my year at Florida College in 1983, I met Kathleen Pamer, now Trigg, who had been baptized a short time before. We were soon separated by time and distance during the intervening decades that we did our graduate work, built our early careers, got married, and raised our children, but, happily, our timelines converged again in 2013 when my family moved to Temple Terrace. My friend is now a beloved colleague, right down the hall in Dicus.

A year after FC, my classmate and designated "big brother" Rich Gant followed me to Indiana where he interned for the summer at a congregation in the Indianapolis area. Rich had been converted by friends in Fort Lauderdale, worshiping at the same congregation where my Ledford cousins had moved and where my uncle served as an elder. After studying music at Florida State and working in the construction field a few years, Rich had come to FC to take upper division Bible, befriending my roommate and me and taking the role of our protective big brother. After I returned to Indiana, Rich had stayed another year to complete the Bible program certificate.

When Brother Haub and his family had to move away, the Lord helped Rich raise enough support that he could come to preach in Muncie. He lived in a little apartment at the corner of campus, right down the alley from our church building. Rich was a busy bachelor, traveling around the state to study with older preachers, preparing sermons, teaching classes, leading campus studies, and beginning to assist in prison work. At Ball State, Rich and I took New Testament Greek together, and went with other young people to area gospel meetings. Gradually, the brother/sister relationship grew into much more. Willing to take on a harried college senior with years of coursework ahead, Rich proposed, and we were married in August 1985 at a mansion that one of the Ball Brothers had donated to the college. Next year in 2025, if the Lord wills, we will celebrate 40 years.

My undergraduate years were in overdrive, even before I took on the role of a preacher's wife. I was an Honors College student and an English education major with a double minor in humanities and classical studies, so my reading list and writing load were incredibly challenging. But I had come away from Florida College with a greater incentive to achieve academically, having absorbed some of that standard of excellence that characterized my professors there. Because I had free tuition at BSU through Dad, I piled on many extra electives offered in my major and minors, a menu far beyond the requirements. I found other professors to admire, many of them published authors and recognized experts in their fields. I had the privilege of writing the featured student essay for the shorter *MLA Handbook* the year one of my professors served as its editor. My neighbor and sister in Christ, librarian Veva McCoskey, offered me a campus job as her student assistant in the interlibrary loan department, and I taught library instruction workshops. After I was no longer the dependent of my faculty father, I was grateful I could help Rich cover my college bills. When I graduated *summa cum laude*, I gave my sweet husband much of the credit for the emotional support he had shown, his patience with my subpar cooking, and the long hours he had spent in the library to keep me company.

In the nine years before Betsy and David were born, Rich's preaching and the work of the church were my primary focus as I finished my degrees and, later, began to teach a full load at Ball State. I arranged to teach all my courses on Tuesdays and Thursdays so that I could be more available to serve the brethren. We hosted many guests in our little apartments—those in town for gospel meetings, family, friends, and strangers with whom we had Bible studies. I began to write lessons and to speak at events for women in other congregations, and I also edited for preachers who were writing and publishing in our area. Rich and nearby classmates—Tom Hamilton, Doug Raymer, and Jerry Crolius—got together frequently to study and prepare sermons. Their wives and I took turns hosting, and Rich and I learned much about child rearing from observing their parenting. These were the years when we were proud just to keep dog Waldo and our houseplants alive, so we benefited greatly from our friends' examples.

During my years in graduate school and early college teaching, Rich and I began to volunteer our limited vacation time as counselors for the Florida College Camp in Cincinnati. Royce and Hope Chandler were the directors and welcomed us with open arms. Their son Todd was still in high school and quickly became our favorite camper. What an honor to worship and to work with him on campus these many years later. Royce and Hope ran their large camp like a well-oiled machine, and we remember fondly their talents, leadership, and dedication. When the Chandlers gave Linda Wessel and me a creative writing class to teach, and in an airconditioned cabin no less, I was in camp counselor heaven.

Rich and I moved from Muncie in 1990 to join the Southport congregation in Indianapolis where the Lord granted us wonderful growing years. In those days, the church owned the preacher's house and allowed us to use the back property for a large garden, so we grew a lot of our food, and I learned to can. The Lord favored us by growing our family when our Mary Elizabeth "Betsy" was born in 1994. I was grateful that I could leave the world of academia to focus on motherhood. The beautiful examples set for us by many older Christians helped us to grow spiritually, and the lessons we learned still guide us. In these years we increased our teaching skills, observed firsthand how saints show courage in adversity, and received nurturing as new parents who were juggling church work and hospitality. The Dickeys, the Roses, the Millers, the Joneses, the Stewarts, Rhonda McCort, Judy and Jonell—I could go on and on. May the Lord bless them for the grace and love they showed us. I will never forget dear sister Iva, who took me on a brisk autumn walk through old town Franklin, Indiana. We talked about the Psalms as we walked because that was what she had been reading. She handed me a sack to pick up trash as we went. "Always leave it better than you found it," Iva said. That sums up the life of a "peculiar" Christian quite well.

My earliest and most enduring example of someone who leaves it better than she found it has been my mother, Mary Koltenbah. She has modeled dedication and service consistently throughout her life. Mom served as a tender caregiver to all four of our grandparents, her twin brother, the widowed neighbor next door, and our sister in Christ, Veva, the unmarried librarian who had no relatives to care for her. Mom's hands have always been busy with good works. In her nineties, she still crochets blankets for the many babies in her life.

We moved to Columbus, Indiana, in January 1996 when the elders there asked Rich to come work with the 10th Street Church of Christ. We had not considered moving, but their invitation gave us an opportunity to worship with friends we had made at FC Camp, and we could now buy our first house. We enjoyed nearly 18 years of happy service there. Treelined, cultured Columbus with its renowned architecture was an ideal place to raise Betsy and her little brother David Benjamin, born in 1997. Eastridge Manor had the feel of my childhood Orchard Lawn, and we enjoyed a happy caravan of cars on the Lord's Day when our brethren who were also neighbors streamed to worship.

Our wall calendar was completely covered over with duties and events during those many full years in Columbus. The congregation grew steadily, requiring a move from our old landlocked meeting house to a new location, and our church family was renamed Lakeview Church of Christ. Because of Rich's past experiences in construction management and cost estimation, he was helpful to the elders in the planning and careful budgeting of the new building project. While preaching and teaching in Columbus, Rich also began to make trips overseas, first to China, and then to Sierra Leone in Africa to assist preaching friends in those works. We housed visiting evangelists multiple times a year as the church hosted spring and fall meetings, men's and ladies' days, county fair outreach, VBS, and other events.

For my part, I taught actively in children's and ladies' Bible classes and spoke for area workshops for women. I continued to bloom where I was planted by my blessed association with the sisters at Lakeview. Wherever I turned, I found talented, godly ladies to model hospitality, marriage, parenting, Bible class teaching, and homemaking. Loretta Brock, Mary Ann Grant, Pat Tharp, the Lancaster ladies—again, too many to list or to thank. My friend Nancy Churchill and I, along with our sisters, created a first-rate resource room for the teachers. At the elders' request, Nancy and I revamped lessons and wrote a three-year Bible curriculum that the congregation used for years. I wrote and taught semester-long ladies' curricula and one for junior high girls. What would I have done without my many teaching partners—Lori, Diane, Joy, Sue Beth, Betsy, and others? They are still a core part of me, friends for whom I cannot praise the Lord enough.

The years in Columbus, Indiana, flew by like leaves from a tree. Our days were happily filled with the work of the church and my home schooling of Betsy and David. Piano, violin, and art lessons, 4-H projects for the county and state fair, volunteer work—we were always stretching ourselves. When my kids' high school years loomed ahead, God sent me talented sisters to help me navigate subjects I had less confidence to teach. My friend Allison Walker, who has lately gone to be with the Lord, was a pharmacist who could teach chemistry, and my friend Teri White shared her talents in speech and debate, college prep, and Dave Ramsey skills. I pulled my weight by offering literature and composition instruction. Our little co-op and our many opportunities were as enriching for me as for my children. Museums, trips, competitions, plays, projects, concerts—we were never bored.

Florida College Camps became even more important to us as parents. When our kids were old enough to attend, Rich and I began to volunteer at the Indiana Camp as kitchen cooks and as teachers, often writing the camp's Bible lessons, which were then shared with other FC camps. For many years, Rich took David each summer to Russellville, Alabama, to help friends Sewell Hall and Paul Earnhart with their boys' camp. Betsy and I discovered the newly formed Daughters of Virtue (DOV) Camp, and I went as a teacher during her camper years. We have been repaid abundantly for these years of happy toil and dedication to young people.

We moved to Tampa in early 2013. Here we were, coming back full circle with our high schoolers, unwittingly following our Future Falcons to Florida College! After thirty years of preaching, Rich decided that real estate was a better fit for this stage of our lives, so he applied his construction knowledge and broker's license in a new direction. We live in a book-filled house in Rolling Terrace, or "Christian Acres," as it is affectionately called, once again in a neighborhood that feels like home with its Lord's Day caravan. Rich serves as a shepherd for the brethren at Livingston Avenue in Lutz, continuing to teach Bible classes and private studies. We are blessed continually by our association with our beloved brethren, some of whom are neighbors and colleagues. When we look around from pew to pew at our worship services, meet with smaller groups at our house-to-house studies, and work shoulder to shoulder on teaching projects or service opportunities, we are overwhelmed by the way God continues to provide vivid examples of the consecrated life. Elderly folks, new converts, little children, our deacons and their families, young parents—a beautifully "peculiar" people who radiate the Lord's love.

For nearly ten years, I have been honored to teach in the English department of our dear FC among the beloved and dedicated faculty, staff, and administration. I endeavor to rise to the standards set by the gifted professors who preceded me. Though the work is challenging, I am borne along by our common devotion to the world's First and Greatest Author, whose Holy Book continues to influence and inform my appreciation of every other literary work worth reading and teaching.

In a few weeks, I will welcome a new set of students to campus and help them craft chapters in the books of their own lives. I will be, as ever, a minor character in other people's stories.

"Dedication" is a word we associate with works of great importance. When a building or bridge is erected, a scholarship is established, or a charitable organization is formed, there is often a public ceremony to mark the occasion. A book may have a dedication page to honor someone who inspired or encouraged the author. Living a dedicated life, however, may be a private affair, one in which good works are performed quietly by a steadfast saint as part of her everyday devotion.

We are women of the royal priesthood. We women set the tone in our congregations, our families, and in our social groups. We have unique God-given opportunities to serve as royal priests and as channels of His love and holiness (1 Pet 2:9). We know that our devotion and purity have purpose, making us effective as teachers and models of God's blessings to others.

If we are already familiar with God and His Word, we know His high standards for purity. We know His expectation that we are to maintain a pure heart, pure speech, and pure behavior. We teach our young ladies and sons that God has strict standards concerning sexual purity, laws given by a loving Father for the protection of His beloved children. Perhaps if we could more fully appreciate the "why" behind God's demand for our purity, we might find it easier to live and to teach this subject.

GOD'S CALL FOR THE ROYAL PRIESTHOOD

The Bible is filled with beautiful metaphors that lead us to appreciate more fully the awesome nature of our God and how we stand in relationship to Him. Meditation on each beautiful word picture yields insight into the divine character of the Almighty as He reveals Himself to the inspired writers of His Word. When we read of the Good Shepherd and His sheep, the Vine and the branches, or the Potter and the clay, for example, we are enriched by each metaphor with fresh appreciation of our utter dependence upon our Lord. New Testament writers often revisit Old Testament metaphors in the light of our life in Christ.

The apostles and other inspired writers draw heavily upon imagery and types from the Old Testament Jewish system of worship to explain Christ's ultimate fulfillment and superiority to the former. The Book of Hebrews presents Christ as High Priest forever as well as the sacrificial Lamb of offering, a glorious paradox with great implications for our salvation and service (ch. 8-9). Paul presents God's people as the temple wherein His Spirit dwells (1 Cor 3:16-17), a holy temple which is being built upon the chief cornerstone (Eph 2:19-22). Peter's first epistle describes "living stones" that are being built into a "spiritual house to be a holy priesthood, offering spiritual sacrifices acceptable to God through Jesus Christ"[1] (1 Pet 2:4-8).

Peter further extends this word picture of the priesthood as he applies it to the Christian's high order of service. Peter connects the concept of Christ's Kingship with his role as High Priest to enhance our understanding of the great honor the Lord bestows on us as His

1 Unless otherwise noted, all quotations of scripture are from the NIV/1984.

subjects and servants. Referencing Old Testament scripture addressed to the children of Israel through Moses, Peter describes a privileged and exclusive calling that is extended to followers of Christ (Exo 19:5-6). In First Peter 2, the apostle describes God's special people as members of a "royal priesthood," a phrase accompanied by other descriptors that illustrate the consecrated life: "But you are a chosen people, a royal priesthood, a holy nation, a people for God's own possession, so that you may proclaim the excellencies of Him who has called you out of darkness into His marvelous light..." (1 Pet 2:9 *NASB*). This beautiful passage, written to Jewish Christians as well as to their Gentile brethren, highlights the elevated status of those belonging to Christ. The apostle's message proclaims that through the blood of Jesus we are all granted entrance to His courts to serve our Priestly King.

The Book of Leviticus sets forth in detail the work of the Levitical priests, their special duties to be performed first in the Tabernacle and later in His more permanent house, the Temple. When the sons of Levi were scattered to live in cities among the other tribes, God in His wisdom planned for the priestly influence to permeate every corner of the land of promise. God's purpose was to promote the practice of holiness and blessing so that all His children would remain devoted to Him. Whether leading in worship, teaching God's law, or ministering to the sick and suffering, priests were commissioned to perform tasks which required special preparation. God specified their dress for His work and worship. He held priests to stricter standards of marriage, limiting their choices of marriage partners. God required that they purify themselves first before offering sacrifices and purifying their brethren. Though to the Levites in particular God had said, "I am giving you the service of the priesthood as a gift" (Num 18:7), He had intended that all the people of Israel would serve Him in consecration and holiness.

In his gospel account, Luke records that early in His ministry Jesus stood up to read in the synagogue in Nazareth and was handed the scroll of Isaiah. Choosing a passage in which the prophet foretells the coming of the Messiah, Jesus read aloud, "The Spirit of the Sovereign Lord is on me, because the Lord has anointed me to preach good news to the poor." Jesus read further that God's Anointed would come to heal the brokenhearted, bring freedom to captives, and "proclaim the Year of the Lord's favor." Jesus cited this very passage as a declaration of His mission statement, concluding his reading with the simple but profound words: "Today this scripture is fulfilled in your hearing" (Isa 61:1-2; Luk 2:14-22). When we go back to Isaiah 61 and read four verses beyond the passage that

Jesus highlighted, we encounter God's invitation for His people to partner in the Messiah's restoration: "And you will be called priests of the Lord, you will be named ministers of our God" (Isa 61:6). In context, Jesus' reading from Isaiah indicates His role as the High Priest who leads His priestly people in joyous service.

When we as women who profess Christ reflect upon our own duties, we do well to study the Old Testament to learn what principles apply to our special status as a "peculiar" people, a people set apart as holy (1 Pet 2:9 *KJV*). Let us imagine, if we will, our heavenly resumes, on which each of our names is written next to our profession--"royal priest." That is our job description, sisters! In fact, it is our vocation, our calling by God. We may have a reluctance to accept this assignment because we are women, and we know that priests under the Old Law were exclusively male. There were no priestesses in the worship of God, but women did serve in supporting roles in the temple worship. Their talents and skills were valuable to God (Exo 35:25-26; 38:8; 1 Sam 2:22; Luk 2:27). Like their male counterparts, holy Jewish women devoted themselves to worship and service. Attempts in the modern denominational world to promote women as priests violate scripture in multiple ways by misinterpreting or ignoring biblical teaching on church leadership, authority, submission, and the role of women in the church.

However, we need not allow others' false doctrine and practice to cause us to devalue our proper place as women in the "royal priesthood." All Christians, male and female, serve together symbolically as priests with a little "p" under the direction of Jesus our High Priest. We are not high priests. We do not wear the Urim and Thummin on a breastplate. That honor belongs exclusively to the One and Only High Priest forever. The metaphor and imagery of the royal priesthood under the New Covenant is radically different from the Old, which was nailed to the cross when Jesus died. Though as females we have been elevated in status to serve in the role of priests under the headship of Christ, this in no way negates the scriptures that dictate our roles of submission in the home and in the church (Eph 5:22-24; 1 Pet 3:1-6; 1 Cor 14:33-35; 1 Tim 2:9-15). Peter presents no conflict when he includes all believers—Jew, Gentile, male, and female—as sanctified and beloved in the "royal priesthood" of the Lord (1 Pet 2:9). Our worship and work may differ from that of our brothers in Christ in important aspects, but our priestly service is no less valuable to God.

We women should never doubt our value in the eyes of our Heavenly King. Those of us who have had loving earthly fathers know a little of what it is like to be treated as royalty. Many a girl can boast that that she is called "Daddy's little princess" in her home. If we remember that God was the One who gave our fathers the capacity to love us so tenderly, we realize that God Himself loves us infinitely more. As our first and perfect Parent, God created us in His image, and we who have been redeemed from sin are now re-created in Christ. We are doubly the beloved daughters of our King. If a Christian can come to appreciate fully her status as a royal priestess, she will see herself as someone of great importance and value in His Kingdom. When we embrace our favored relationship with Him, we become available to do great work for Him.

PURITY IS GOD'S GIFT TO US

Our dedication and devotion to God must include a commitment to purity if we are to be pleasing to Him at all. This teaching is central to the gospel message. Jesus addresses His audience on the mount with His beautiful encouragement that "blessed are the pure in heart, for they will see God" (Mat 5:8). The Hebrew writer echoes Jesus' beatitude when he writes, "Make every effort to live in peace with all men and to be holy; without holiness no one will see the Lord" (Heb 12:14). Paul instructs the church at Ephesus to avoid even the hint of immorality, greed, or obscene or foolish speech, "which are out of place" for the Christian (Eph 5:3-5). In the Book of Revelation, the heavenly city, lit by God's glory through the Lamb who is the lamp, is the antithesis of sin and darkness: "Nothing impure will ever enter it, nor will anyone who does what is shameful or deceitful..." (Rev 21:23, 27).

Just as we cannot get through security at the airport gate with anything dangerous or destructive, we cannot hope to enter through the Heavenly gates and go into the King's presence if we are lugging a backpack full of impurities. The alarm at the gate will go off every time. We must be careful to follow the rules and to cast aside whatever hinders us from approaching.

In the eyes of modern society, purity of mind, speech, body and soul seems a quaint, outgrown quality from a bygone era, much like yellowed lace and faded flowers stored in the trunk of a Victorian lady. When a modern bride and groom keep themselves pure until marriage, for example, some consider it a sweet but naïve custom. Worldly people are inconsistent, however. They value pure drinking water, pure communications ("Can you hear me now?"), and pure blood for transfusions. The best things are said to be pure, as in diamonds, gold, and silver. Outside of a religious context, purity is considered a good thing and a practical quality to be applied everywhere, perhaps, but where it matters most–in our character and conduct.

We must be vigilant to protect ourselves and our families from that which is impure and unholy. The prophet Habakuk acknowledges that his God is like none other: "Your eyes are too pure to look on evil; you cannot tolerate wrong" (Hab 1:13). "Be holy, for I am holy," God has commanded us (Lev 11:44-45; 1 Pet 1:15-16). Our Father demands our entire selves in devotion to Him—mind, body, and soul, attitude, speech and behavior (1 Cor 6:18-20; Eph 4:19-24; Phil4:8; 1 The 4:3-8; 5:21). We can live consecrated lives set apart for God or else our impurity will set us apart from Him.

God knows we can never achieve purity or maintain it without His divine intervention. We come into the world pure and sinless, formed in the womb by our Creator. Jesus valued little ones and exhorted His disciples to become like them in their purity and humility. But Satan enters our lives at some point and tempts us to sin. Separated from God, we forfeit our innocence and become enslaved to the evil one. When we surrender our lives in baptism, God redeems us, restores us in His image, and cleanses us from our impurity. Paul tells Titus that the grace of God that brings salvation instructs us to live in self-control and godliness as we await the glorious return of Christ, "who gave Himself for us to redeem us from all wickedness and to purity for Himself a people that are His very own, eager to do what is good" (2:11).

Our attitude should be one of a continual yearning for cleansing. A royal priestess cries out to the Lord when she becomes weak, fearing separation from Him more than any other calamity that could befall her. She devotes herself to her King and Father in prayer. Like David, who cried out to the Lord for cleansing and restoration, she appeals to God continually to help her remain devoted and pure that her worship and influence might not wane (Psa 51).

The Lord grants access to His presence only to those who are holy and pure (Lev 19:1; 1 Cor 7:1). The Jews worshiped Him at His House, but within there was a Most Holy Place, a forbidden, innermost sanctuary where the Almighty alone dwelled. As New Testament Christians and priests in a royal priesthood, we draw near not once a year as the high priest did, but daily "with a sincere heart in full assurance of faith, having our hearts sprinkled to cleanse us from a guilty conscience and having our bodies washed with pure water" (Heb 10:22). This powerful image in Hebrews conveys the blessed thought that we do not merely peek into the sanctuary through a little crack, nor do we sneak in, slink in, or intrude. We enter boldly into that Most Holy Place by the blood of Jesus, "by a new and living way opened for us through the curtain, that is, his body" (Heb 10:20). The curtain was torn from top to bottom on the day Jesus died so that we could not miss the seismic change that has occurred in our status. He suffered pain, disgrace, and shame, though He was the Lamb without blemish and the perfect High Priest—though He was God Himself. The gift of purity came at an enormous price. How humbling!

That love was shown at its ultimate, most poignant moment when the Father sacrificed His Only Begotten Son on the cross. Jesus not only makes us holy through His suffering and death, but He purifies us so that we can be joined into God's family in a close, intimate bond (Heb 2:11). Citing several Old Testament scriptures, Paul urges the Corinthians to keep themselves sanctified to God and set apart from the idolatrous world: "Therefore come out from them and be separate…Touch no unclean thing…I will be a Father to you, and you will be my sons and daughters, says the Lord Almighty." Paul concludes his exhortation by a call to purity: "Dear friends, let us purify ourselves from everything that contaminates body and spirit, perfecting holiness out of reverence for God" (2 Cor 6:14-7:1).

PURITY AS PREPARATION FOR SERVICE

Just as the priests of old were taught to purify themselves before engaging in Temple worship and work, so we too need to purify ourselves before presenting our own sacrifices and offerings of service. This requires the Christian to learn to distinguish between the pure and the impure. How do I know what is defiling me? How do I come to recognize impurity?

One of my favorite bits of wisdom comes from Susanna Wesley (1669-1742), the mother of the famous English reformers, who wrote a letter to her young son John who was living away from her motherly watchfulness. She wrote,

> If you would judge the lawfulness of pleasure, take this rule—
>
> Whatever weakens your reason…
>
> Whatever impairs the tenderness of your conscience…
>
> Whatever obscures your sense of God…
>
> Whatever increases the authority of your body over your mind…
>
> Whatever takes away your relish for things spiritual…
>
> This is SIN, no matter how innocent it seems in and of itself!
>
> (Letter, June 8, 1725).[2]

Mrs. Wesley's wise words are based on biblical principles and are useful for meditation.

---

2 James W. Lee, et al. The Illustrated History of Methodism (St. Louis and New York: The Methodist Magazine Publishing Co., 1900) 44-46.

God will answer the humble prayer that asks for wisdom to recognize what is pure or impure. We need to pray for the wisdom to become women who are "mature, who by constant use have trained themselves to distinguish good from evil" (Heb 5:14). A trained and tender conscience is vital when it comes to purity (Rom 14:14). When the Father disciplines us through His word, we repent and obey, knowing He does so as a loving Father for our own good. The Hebrew writer tells us this correction allows us to "share in his holiness" (Heb 12:4-11).

We are not missing out on anything when we give up worldly thoughts and practices. Because we are following God's commandments, we are turned loose, given wings to our feet, and released to a greater joy and freedom than we could ever have imagined apart from God. The Psalmist declares, "I run in the path of your commands, for you have set my heart free" (Psa 119:32).

Our purity becomes a dynamic, powerful force in the plan of God. If our perception of the dedicated woman is that she is a passive, cloistered, wilting violet locked up in a tower, we must amend our thinking. Purity that never sees the light of day, that never rolls up its sleeves to work, is like a buried treasure of no use to anyone. Think of the foolish servant in Jesus' story who hid his one talent rather than investing it on his master's behalf. Instead, we are purified by Him and go out to put our holiness to action.

We are not cleansed merely for ceremony. Why do surgeons go through such meticulous washing, masking, and gloving routines? People in the medical field view purity as best practice for themselves and for their vulnerable patients. Doctors purify themselves as preparation for service. If our purity does not lead to better, higher sercie for God and others, Satan will snatch it away and replace it with his own impurities (Mat 12:43). If we do not "glove up" to serve, the devil can easily distort our "purity" into self-righteousness and judgmentalism. We must nurture the holiness God grants us so that it manifests itself in our behavior and conduct.

THE POWER OF A WOMAN'S PURITY

Everyone is called to live a life of purity. The scriptures are replete with instruction for both genders, adults and children alike (1 Tim 5:2; 2 Tim 2:22; Pro 20:11). Directing his letter to female readers, Paul gives detailed instruction to women that they are to live in reverence and holiness, being self-controlled and pure, "so that no one will malign the word of God" (Tit 2:3-5).

Peter taught that there was a tremendous power in women's purity, so much so that he suggests it can save their unbelieving husbands (1 Pet 3:1-6). All women, whether single or married, can put this principle into their lives. They have potential to benefit others in eternally significant ways.

Throughout the history of His people, God has set apart or sanctified for Himself women from all walks of life to serve His purpose of restoring the fallen race to fellowship with Him. Central to a woman's usefulness in God's plan is her purity. When God needed to find the right young woman to give birth to and raise His beloved Son Jesus, He looked for one who was prepared—mind, spirit, and body. Just as Mary's purity was instrumental to God in His scheme of redemption, so also our own purity as Christian women is a powerful channel for God's plan to save our sinful world.

There is great transforming power in the sacrifices of a dedicated woman. Paul instructs his readers that "in view of God's mercy, to offer your bodies as living sacrifices, holy and pleasing to God—this is your spiritual act of worship" (Rom 12:1). We daily lay down the entirety of ourselves upon the altar. Our purity is a gift that we willingly and lovingly present to God before His throne. Paul urges us to purify ourselves from all that contaminates body and spirit, "perfecting holiness out of reverence for God" (2 Cor 7:1).

Becoming pure may seem like an unattainable goal. Are we on our own when it comes to maintaining a pure mind, body, and heart? Is this merely a self-improvement, self-help process? No! Our Father knows our frailties. He is our compassionate Ally in our quest for purity and holiness (Isa 57:15). Peter reminds us that God's "divine power has given us everything we need for life and godliness through our knowledge of Him who called us by His own glory and goodness. Through these He has given us His very great and precious promises, so that through them you may participate in the divine nature and escape the corruption in the world caused by evil desires" (2 Pet 1:3-4).

A ROYAL PRIESTESS PURIFIES HERSELF TO WORSHIP A HOLY GOD

Paul's focus on women's reverence for God leads us to consider our first and highest duty as women of the royal priesthood. In Numbers 8, the Lord told Moses, "After you have purified the Levites and presented them as a wave offering, they are to come to do their work at the Tent of Meeting. They are the Israelites who are to be given wholly to me" (Num 8:15-16). Worship is work. It takes effort and concentration. Like the priests of old, we women are purified, set apart so that we can "proclaim his excellencies" and be equipped "to test and approve what God's will is—His good, pleasing and perfect will" (1 Pet 2:9; Rom 12:1). That phrase "test and approve" carries with it the same idea as "discerning good and evil." Growing in our ability to worship God in reverence is a learning process. You have heard of a vicious cycle? In Romans 12 we encounter a precious cycle. We see the relationship between true sacrificial worship and purity: true worship leads to greater purity...and purity leads us to greater worship.

A ROYAL PRIESTESS PURIFIES HERSELF TO HELP OTHERS BECOME PURE

We can glean another principle from the Old Testament priests: an unclean person needs the aid of a clean person to become pure again. Sinful people cannot become pure again entirely by their own efforts. Moses gives instructions about the role of the priests in cleansing themselves so that they could administer purifying rites to the unclean so that no one would be "cut off from the community, because he has defiled the sanctuary of the LORD" (Num 19:19-20). This concept is borne out in the New Testament as well. To the Galatians Paul explains our role in God's saving grace to our erring friends: "Brothers, if someone is caught in a sin, you who are spiritual should restore him gently. But watch yourself, or you also may be tempted" (Gal 6:1). "Be merciful to those who doubt," Jude tells us; "Snatch others from the fire and save them; to others show mercy, mixed with fear—hating even the clothing stained by corrupted flesh" (Jud 22-23).

Think of those around us who cannot enjoy God's blessing in their lives because they are burdened by their sins. We are not ourselves the Great High Priest, but we are little priests who represent Him to others. In a time of plague, those who survive and are healed turn to those who are still sick and nurse them back to health. On an airplane the flight attendants instruct us to secure our own oxygen masks before we assist our seatmates. We have been delivered and purified so that we can direct others to wholeness in the Lord.

A ROYAL PRIESTESS PURIFIES HERSELF TO TEACH AND MODEL GOD'S LAW

Daughters of the King represent Him when they engage in devotion and duty on His behalf. Jesus included women among His disciples and valued the supporting role they played in His ministry. The scriptures teach that women serve as teachers in a different capacity than men do, but that does not mean that we are any less valuable in the kingdom. We are vital to the church when we use our talents to share God's word with other women and with children and when we live godly lives that serve as walking sermons to our neighbors and friends.

Like Levitical priests, we teach and model purity, helping bring peace between people and leading others to worship God in holiness. We ask the Lord to cleanse us so that He can use us in His plan. We distinguish between the holy and the common, knowing the grave consequences of confusing the two (Eze 44:23).

Of course, priests of old did not always live up to the expectations God had set for them. But in their good days, when things were ideal and the people were obedient as God had designed, priests were beacons of truth among God's people, as was Ezra during the time of restoration and the rebuilding of the Temple. The Lord's description of the ideal priest through the prophet Malachi should encourage us to reverence God and share His covenant of life and peace, "for the lips of a priest ought to preserve knowledge, and from his mouth men should seek instruction because he is the messenger of the LORD Almighty" (Mal 2:5-7).

Why does our purity matter so much? Souls are at stake. We strive to remain "blameless and pure, children of God without fault…as [we] hold out the word of life" (Phi 2:12). Like stars in the cosmos, we shine the light of our glorious Savior that those lost in darkness might find their way to Him.

A ROYAL PRIESTESS PURIFIES HERSELF TO SERVE OTHERS

Priests were servants of the people. They served as judges and peacemakers when there were disputes, they examined and advised people with illnesses, and they took care of the poor and needy (Deu 17:8-13). Priests bore the responsibility of being actively involved with the people, engaged in direct personal contact so that they could advise and lead them to sound health and spiritual purity (Deu 24:8-9).

Just as Old Testament priests received special instructions about their clothing, we women are to dress modestly, not lavishly, clothed "with good deeds, appropriate for women who profess to worship God" (1 Tim 2:9; Mat 5:16). When a woman wears clothing that is too tight or too revealing, she is a distraction and not suitably dressed to worship a holy God and to do His work. Instead, we women are called to high and holy service, clad in good works, wearing garments of holy labor that point others to the Lord rather than to ourselves.

Jesus calls His own priestly people to join Him in this work of service. Knowing we are part of a holy nation and a royal priesthood, we women look continually for fresh opportunities to fulfill that calling with our time and talents (Tit 2:11-14; 3:14).

A ROYAL PRIESTESS BLESSES OTHERS THROUGH HER KINDNESS

Remember the priestly blessing that God taught Aaron and his sons to speak over the Israelites? "The LORD bless you and keep you; the LORD make his face shine upon you and be gracious to you; the LORD turn his face toward you and give you peace" (Num 6:24-27).

Although we do not go around every day uttering these words over the heads of our friends, as royal princesses and priests of our Father and King we should be thinking about practical ways that we can call down God's blessings on them. We follow the example of Jesus, who "went around doing good and healing all who were under the power of the devil, because God was with Him" (Act 10:36). We practice harmony, compassion, and humility as we counteract insult with blessing (1 Pet 3:8). Like the Proverbs 31 woman, "the law of kindness" is on our tongues.

We have heard the saying, "Before people care what you know, they first need to know that you care." Author Elisabeth Elliot suggests that we should not underestimate the importance of our daily service. "We are not often called to great sacrifice," she writes, "but daily we are presented with the chance to make small ones — a chance to make someone cheerful, a chance to do some small thing to make someone comfortable or contented."[3] Elizabeth George explains that habits of holiness are essential for the priestess,[4] which include acts of kindness. Using her monthly planner, she identifies at least one act of kindness each week and then transfers her plans to her daily calendar. "What a joy it's been to plan for kindness," she shares. "The woman who is good dispenses what is good and beneficial. Just as a pharmacist dispenses medicines that will heal, so we plan to dispense the medicines that promote the lives of others."[5]

God is both a great planner and a great doer, a God of peace and not of disorder. If we want to be like Him, we will plan for kindness and put our purity into action (1 Pet 4:10; 1 Tim 5:9; 2 Thess 1:11-12). We can sanctify our "to-do" lists and daily plans by appealing to our High Priest for His guidance: "Commit to the Lord whatever you do, and your plans will succeed" (Pro 16:3).

---

3 Elisabeth Elliot, A Path Through Suffering: Discovering the Relationship between God's Mercy and Our Pain (Vine/Servant Publications, 1990) 67.

4 Elizabeth George, A Woman's High Calling: 10 Essentials for Godly Living (Eugene, Oregon: Harvest House Publishers, 2001) 21.

5 Ibid, 279.

Let us look around us with intention. Whom has God placed in our lives? If God has given us family, friends, and coworkers, He has already made our duties clear. Let us rejoice that He has looked on us with favor. To whatever degree we have ability to serve in our individual seasons of life, we have the joyous privilege of being channels of His grace: "The Lord bless you and keep you!"

Royal daughters, your Father esteems you highly and values your worship and work. "Brighten the corner where you are," as the old hymn encourages us. Just as the priests of the Old Testament shared rotations of service at the Temple and a variety of tasks in their own priestly cities, you have a beautifully unique sphere of influence. Pray to Him that you might fulfill the work He has apportioned to you. Proclaim His excellencies as you bask in His "marvelous light" (1 Pet 2:9 *NASB*).

THOUGHT QUESTIONS FOR "DEDICATED AND PURE"

1. How do you define dedication? Who is the most dedicated person you know?

2. "God wants your holiness, not your happiness." Respond to that statement. Do you agree or disagree?

3. How do you prepare for church services on the Lord's Day? Describe the ways you focus your mind and heart for worship.

4. How do you determine standards of purity for yourself, for your family, and for those you influence in the following areas: dress, dating, social media, and pop culture?

5. How have you been blessed by others? How do you plan to "pay it forward"?

INTENTIONALITY IN CHRISTIAN LIVING

Annetta Hastings, PhD

Be very careful, then, how you live—not as unwise but as
wise, making the most of every opportunity,
because the days are evil.
Ephesians 5.15-16

My story begins almost six decades ago (December 1965) in a small, rural community in southern Indiana known as Floyds Knobs. I grew up in a Christian home and was the youngest of three children. My maternal grandparents, Frank and Vashti Purkhiser, were Christians. They owned an Oldsmobile car dealership in Corydon, Indiana, and I have fond memories of Sunday lunches after church at their apartment above the dealership. As a kid, the dealership was my playground – just imagine a game of hide-and-seek among the cars. My paternal grandparents, Gurvase and Ida Mauck, were Methodists. They lived and worked as farmers, so my other playground was in their pasture with chickens and pigs. My mom converted my dad before they married in 1959. They fondly recalled how their first dates were to church.

My dad served in the Army before he married and then worked most of his 30-year career for Public Service Indiana. He worked as a shift supervisor, equivalent to a Human Resources position today. My mom was a high school business teacher (e.g., typing, shorthand, accounting) for thirty years, and she served as a varsity volleyball and tennis coach for many of those years. In my early years, my siblings and I had sitters who watched us while my parents worked; a few sitters lived in our home during the week and helped my mom with meals and laundry. However, it was common for my family to eat breakfast and dinner together daily.

My parents were actively involved in the Silver Street Church of Christ in New Albany, Indiana. My dad served as an elder at the church for a decade. My parents were "given to hospitality" and regularly hosted Christians in our home. For instance, my mom often fixed Sunday lunch and several families from church would join us. My parents hosted annual Halloween costume parties and New Year's Eve celebrations, inviting the entire congregation to attend.

My parents opened our home for weeks at a time to Gospel preachers who were holding meetings in the local area. I learned the Bible from Robert Jackson, Colly Caldwell, Johnnie Edwards, Gary Henry, Ken Green, Ron Mosby, and Bill Cavender. Hence, I spent many formative years surrounded by strong Christian role models; preachers were my heroes. I thank God continually for giving me godly parents.

EARLY CHILDHOOD.

I attended public school and, early on, realized that I had a proclivity for mathematics. I would often finish my math assignment in class before others, and my classmates would ask me to help them with the assignment. In the fourth grade, I won the county-wide mathematics competition at Lafayette Elementary School. This was the beginning of my journey to learning and teaching mathematics. I participated in school sports like volleyball, basketball, and cross country.

In the summers and on weekends, I lived outdoors. My brother and I played with all the neighbors. We created trails in the woods for our bicycles and minibikes and played hide-n-seek and all other games that young kids could dream up. We played nerf football, basketball, wiffle ball, and badminton. I have such fond memories of my childhood on Flemar Drive. My family watched shows like "The Waltons," "Leave it to Beaver," "The Partridge Family," "The Brady Bunch," and "Happy Days." This was a time when families had few choices for entertainment, so we watched television together. We took annual vacations to different cities and regions across the US. I thought my life was practically perfect - my family was a source of strength and comfort, and I felt safe and secure.

MIDDLE YEARS.

I learned mathematics in the "Back-to-Basics" era of mathematics education, which meant teachers used rules, drills, and practice to promote mastery of a topic. Mathematics students practiced algorithms repeatedly, rather than seeing applications to understand a concept. My eighth grade Algebra One teacher, Mrs. Beverly Howard, fostered my love for mathematics. She was a no-nonsense, classy woman who dressed to perfection and who was articulate in her lessons. I admired her rigorous approach to teaching algebra; she made me believe in myself as a student. She was my only female mathematics teacher until much later in my college career, and I blossomed under her tutelage. I realized a great instructor significantly impacted my opportunity to learn mathematics.

During these years, the church at Silver Street hired Don Truex as the full-time evangelist. Don had recently graduated from Florida College, had married Vickie King, and was in the early years of his ministry. He and Vickie brought positivity and energy into the congregation, and they took an active interest in the young people. I was fortunate to begin Don's high school class while I was still in junior high. I recall him giving us exams at the end of a quarter, and I would feel the pressure to excel above my older classmates.

In addition to their respective roles at church, Don and Vickie organized social gatherings outside of church for the young people and were fantastic role models for our young lives. I sat by Vickie on the second row at church from the time I was twelve years old until I graduated from high school. I will never forget the Sunday evening on December 31,

1978, when Don baptized me into Christ at the conclusion of the Sunday evening worship service. Don's impact on my life would go much deeper than I ever realized.

My parents and another couple decided to invest in an ice cream shop called the Gayla Dairy Bar in 1978. Our family had been introduced to Florida College, and my parents wanted to send me and my siblings. This investment was a means to fund college education for their three children. In fact, Mom and Dad told us they would only pay for our education if we attended FC. My older sister, Mandy, was the first to attend FC in the fall of 1979.

My entire family was very busy operating the Dairy Bar in the summers, as we all worked, even though I was still in middle school. I learned the value of hard work and sacrifice. My parents had full-time jobs, so this summer business required many nights and weekends. However, I do not remember us missing a single worship service. It was one of the highlights of my young life, as I was able to create my own ice cream concoctions free of charge.

SECONDARY YEARS.

In 1980, I started high school at Floyd Central and took Geometry in ninth grade with a veteran teacher. It seemed that he believed mathematics belonged in the domain of the elite, which, in his mind, consisted of my male peers. The then-current patriarchal modes of teaching set an inequitable bar. I remember raising my hand to ask a question and the teacher throwing an eraser at me, asking me if I was stupid. I left the class defeated, questioning my ability to learn mathematics. I was placed on a learning trajectory to take Calculus my senior year but opted out.

However, during those years, I began running with my neighbor, Roger Moody, the middle school principal at Floyd Central. He was a former Science teacher and was extremely passionate about education, specifically learning styles. Roger profoundly influenced me because he cared about me and encouraged me to think about a career in teaching. He also fostered a passion for running that has stayed with me my entire life. Although Roger proclaimed atheism, we had many interesting conversations about religion during that time.

In 1981, my parents sold the ice cream shop, and my older brother, Tony, attended FC in the fall. The following summers, I worked three different jobs. First, I worked for the local school district, transferring media from film to cassettes. It was monotonous, but I gained skills in time management and organization. Then, I worked for the Green Valley Nursing Home, helping residents who could not feed themselves. It was sobering to observe death on such a personal level. Finally, I worked for McDonalds, flipping burgers and making fries. The manager approached me about management training at the end of the summer, but I quickly declined. From these experiences in menial labor, I learned a deep appreciation for higher education, and I could not wait to arrive at Florida College.

As my older siblings left home to attend Florida College, I remained at home with my parents. Many of my school friends were starting to dabble in worldly pleasures on the weekends. I had no interest in drinking, dancing, or partying, so I spent quality time with Mom and Dad, their friends, and the teenagers at church. I filled the gap with my passion for sports. I played volleyball, basketball, and tennis. I had an opportunity to attend an NAIA college in Indiana and play tennis on a college scholarship, but I would not dream of missing Florida College. By then, I had already visited the campus on numerous occasions. I was ready to be surrounded by Christians my age, to learn from Christian faculty, and to live in Tampa, Florida.

Don and Vickie, as alumni, were big supporters of Florida College, as they had met and married after their two years. Don gave me good advice before I left home. He said many other freshmen would be out having a good time, but it was critical to focus on academics. He recommended the first semester to sit up front in my classes and to spend extra hours studying. He believed that if you aced your first semester and learned how to succeed, the rest of your college career would be a breeze. Additionally, he said the teachers would take you seriously, and you would align yourself with other great students. It was some of the best advice I ever received.

COLLEGE YEARS.

I attended Florida College in 1984 to pursue a degree in accounting. In the 1980s, most Christian women who went to college pursued nursing or education degrees. David Hammontree taught my accounting class at Florida College, and it was one of my favorites. However, during that time, my priorities started to change. I remembered my strong roots in education and concluded that I wanted to pursue a degree where I could influence the greatest number of people, but also be at home with children. Besides, I was active and could not imagine sitting at a desk crunching numbers.

I took two mathematics courses at Florida College – College Algebra and Trigonometry - to satisfy the requirement for an Associate Degree in Liberal Arts. Florida College only had a four-year Bible program at the time. My mathematics professor, Dr. Curtis Byers, helped me rediscover my love for mathematics. He was a superb teacher, and mathematics was easy for me to learn. I assisted others with homework and gave tutorials before exams. After two semesters, Dr. Byers asked me why I was not pursuing a career path in mathematics. His belief in me was transformative. I realized the importance of confidence in one's ability to succeed if they wanted to learn mathematics.

Florida College changed my life! I cannot overstate the magnitude of this proclamation. In my freshman year, I sat at the feet of Brent Hunter and learned Old and New Testament History. His energy and passion for teaching God's word were evident, and even though my class was at 8:15 am every morning, he managed to spark my passion to learn more. We laugh about it now because he claims he was not an "early morning person" then. Still, Mr. Hunter managed to captivate me with his lessons from the Bible.

I also learned from the other greats of my era – Norene MacDonald, Darlene Anderson Walker, Almon Williams, Melvin Curry, Charlie Rice, Colly Caldwell, and Thaxter Dickey. Although Dr. Dickey was the most difficult professor I ever had, I thrived in his classes every semester – macroeconomics, microeconomics, psychology, and sociology. Dr. Dickey demonstrated all the best attributes of a distinguished professor, and he became a great role model for me.

Another influential person was Kenny Moorer, the Director of Admissions. There were 10-12 camps across the country, and Kenny traveled with groups of students - camp friends - to the camps every summer. I never attended a Florida College camp, but Kenny asked me during the spring of 1985 if I was interested in being a camp friend. The next thing I knew, I was traversing the country in a school van with Kenny and three other FC students to ten camps for ten weeks. It was one of the most transformative experiences of my life. I cried when we left each camp that summer! I met the greatest people on God's earth at FC camps. My love for the Florida College family was indelibly printed on my heart.

My sophomore year at FC was even better, as I took on leadership roles wherever possible. I was in Alpha Club, Omega President, and PTK President. I loved society sports and dorm life and took every opportunity to learn about my professors. I fondly recall going to President Owen's home on several occasions. The following summer, I traveled on a more limited tour with Kenny Moorer and one other student as a camp friend.

I gained so much confidence and strength during those years because I was surrounded by Christians who shared my faith. At graduation, Bob Owen presented me with the President's Award, previously designated for preachers. It was an honor that I will always cherish. I was devastated to leave FC after I graduated in 1986; I wondered how anything in my life would ever compare to such an experience.

I pursued my Bachelor of Science Degree in Mathematics Education at a small satellite campus of Indiana University. IU Southeast was small in 1986 but was known for its strong education program. The campus was one mile from my parents' new home in New Albany. I was encouraged to walk on as an athlete in the NAIA program, so I played collegiate volleyball and basketball for two years while I completed my secondary education degree. My coach, Gayle Horstman, a former University of Louisville basketball player, became a good friend and helped me adjust to life after FC. She hired me to work at the front desk in the gym which allowed me to get involved with the athletes in all the athletic programs.

Although I loved my education courses at IU Southeast, I was not enlightened or engaged by the advanced mathematics courses. However, there were sweeping reforms in K-12 education in the 1980s, especially related to the quality of science and mathematics instruction. As a result of this reform movement, mathematics teachers were to make problem-solving the focus of school mathematics. My epistemology of mathematics was beginning to change with the advent of the new reform: a problem-solving approach to teaching mathematics and the use of technology (i.e., calculators) in the classroom.

During this turbulent time in mathematics reform, I started my student teaching experience at Clarksville High School in 1988, paired with Mr. Ray Lewis, a veteran mathematics teacher, who became my mentor for many years. Not only was his quality of instruction masterful and his love for problem-solving contagious, but he also had compassion for his students, even those challenged in learning. The most important thing I gained from Mr. Lewis was his belief that every student could learn mathematics. I realized the opportunity to learn mathematics was a privilege and should be equitable for students with differing levels of ability. Mr. Lewis and his wife became life-long friends. I was fortunate to visit with him in Indiana shortly before he died of cancer.

TEACHING YEARS.

After my student teaching experience, I was hired by Floyd Central High School, my alma mater, to teach mathematics. I was one of two females in the department. Since no one wanted to teach calculus, I stepped up to the challenge in my first year. Additionally, I coached volleyball and basketball with my former high school coach, Paul Maymon. I taught a wide range of classes, from Algebra to Calculus. I could not imagine a better job or the fact that I received a paycheck while having fun. Unfortunately, Indiana was in a budget crunch in 1990, and the state eliminated my new teaching position due to statewide teaching cuts.

My brother was then preaching in Beaumont, Texas, so I decided to relocate to Houston, Texas. Through my FC network, I was friends with the Murff family in Crosby, Texas. Bill Murff, a member of the FC board of directors, was also on the school board of Crosby High School. That year, he convinced the superintendent to hire me as a mathematics teacher and tennis coach. I lived with the Murffs over the summer as I made plans to move. They were some of the finest people I have ever known. Since the Eastside congregation was 30 minutes from Crosby, I often rode to church with Mr. Bill and Mrs. Elaine. They were great mentors for me during those impressionable years and stressed the importance of marrying a Christian from a godly family.

In the Spring of 1991, Kenny Moorer called to tell me about an open position in the admissions department at FC. I decided to change my life and career to become a student recruiter at Florida College. To increase my salary, Dr. Colly Caldwell, the current president, suggested I teach at the Florida College Academy part-time during the day since much of student recruiting involved making phone calls during evening hours. The following year, I began teaching remedial mathematics classes at the college.

I continued to grow in my profession. While teaching developmental mathematics, I remembered something I had learned in student teaching: I became a champion for the underdog. The influence of Mr. Lewis would continue to echo in my heart. Learning mathematics is challenging for most students, especially at the college level. I wanted my passion for teaching and my compassion for students to impact the success of every single student in my classroom. I began to take an interdisciplinary approach to teaching mathematics. I realized the opportunity to learn mathematics was enhanced when it was relevant to all students. During this time, I completed a Master's Degree in Mathematics Education at the University of South Florida to further my education.

In the spring of 1992, Kenny Moorer asked me to lead a group of FC students around the country to work camps. There had never been a female ambassador to fulfill that role. There was some discussion among the administration about the wisdom in that decision, and I am forever grateful to Dr. Caldwell for blessing me with the opportunity. I guided a summer camp tour with four incredible FC friends through Texas, Arizona, California, and Missouri. It was a summer to remember!

Dr. Buddy Payne moved to Romania the following summer to preach the Gospel. His absence in the math department created an opening for me to step in full-time to teach mathematics at FC. I left the recruiting position and concentrated on teaching and finishing my program at USF. After the FC lectures in 1994, Kenny Moorer and I had a conversation that would redirect my life again. He wanted to introduce me to a former FC student (1980) and friend. Kenny initiated a blind date between me and Lee Hastings from Dyersburg, Tennessee.

FAMILY YEARS.

When I met Lee on Saturday, May 21, it was magical. He was everything that I was not and in all the good ways. I was 28 years old, and some had accused me of being too picky, but after my first date with Lee, I knew he was the answer to my prayers. We had a whirlwind romance. We were engaged after one month and married three months later. Dr. Colly Caldwell was gracious to let me out of my teaching contract for the fall, so we married on September 24, 1994. To this very day, Lee has inspired me to be the best version of myself. He is my best friend and spiritual partner. I thank God continually for bringing Lee into my life.

After Lee and I married, I moved to Lee's hometown of Dyersburg. We lived one block from Lee's parents, Walter and Vivian, and I learned how to love another family like my own. They were wonderful Christian people, and they treated me like a daughter. I could not have asked for more.

We worshipped at Central Church of Christ, a small congregation of about sixty people, where I met Scott and Cecil Owen. Scott, Bob Owen's son, was the minister at Central. Cecil helped me acclimate to life in a small town where I did not know a soul. I had many opportunities to teach children and ladies Bible classes at Central. I was an adjunct mathematics teacher at the local community college until Lee and I started a family. My son, Sloan, was born in October 1996, and my daughter, Olivia, was born in January 1999.

I was blessed to be a stay-at-home mom during those early years with my children. Lee worked in the banking business with his dad while buying and managing his own real estate. Our kids played YMCA sports, which provided opportunities to cultivate many friendships in the community. I volunteered at the primary school and served on an advisory board for the public schools. I still thank God for allowing me to have healthy children. Motherhood was my greatest dream, and my children brought me immense joy. Even though small towns can present challenges, I fondly remember my time in West Tennessee.

In 2006, I received a phone call from Dr. Buddy Payne, who had returned to FC as the Academic Dean. He asked me to consider a move to Florida to accept a full-time tenure track teaching position in mathematics. At the time, Lee's business had gone through some changes, and Lee decided he could work remotely. We moved to Temple Terrace on December 26, 2006, and our lives were forever changed.

Our kids attended Florida College Academy, and we placed membership at the Temple Terrace Church, where Don Truex was the minister. To this day, my whole family agrees that the Christian community at the church and Don's lessons from the pulpit grounded us deeply in the faith. I was thrilled to be back at my alma mater and threw myself into the new teaching position. I was honored to meet so many wonderful students during that era. I wish I could name them here because so many touched my heart and took an interest in my family. To this day, I enjoy traveling and seeing my former students around the country. I was privileged to work beside an amazing group of fellow teachers and servants in the kingdom.

After we moved to Florida, I began teaching Bible classes at Temple Terrace Church. All K-6 classes used the Our Spiritual Heritage curriculum. During that time, I reconnected with my humanities teacher from Florida College, Darlene Walker, who was now the church secretary. She taught me the curriculum and advised me how to teach it. At 40, I had an epiphany as I studied this Bible material. I understood more completely about the chronological story of God's plan, and it ignited my passion as a Bible student. I am grateful to Darlene for this spiritual awakening and the rich spiritual discussions that ensued.

EMPTY NEST.

By 2014, I was tenured and appointed the first coordinator of the mathematics department. My passion for education and mathematics was rooted in my long history in the field, and my love for the students motivated me to improve my teaching every year! Yet, after my children finished high school, I began to get restless and a little burned out. I needed to recharge and find other ways to grow. I realized that I desired a new challenge.

Sloan started FC in the fall of 2015. He finished his bachelor's degree in Liberal Studies in three years and had a wonderful experience. He completed a law degree at Vanderbilt in Nashville, TN. Olivia started FC in the fall of 2017 and completed her AA degree after one year. Olivia then moved to Bowling Green and acquired a Nursing degree at Western Kentucky University.

CAREER YEARS.

Meanwhile, I took a leap of faith and enrolled in a PhD mathematics education program at the University of South Florida. I also applied for a mathematics instructor position in the English Language Program (ELP) for INTO USF. The assistant director, Jordan Walters, interviewed me and asked me if I had any experience teaching mathematics to diverse learners. It was a pivotal moment in my teaching career, as I perceived how little I knew about language learning or cultural diversity in mathematics. I had taught very few international students throughout my entire career thus far!

Nevertheless, Jordan realized I was eager to learn. I taught mathematics workshops to students in the Academic English (AE) program. The AE program was designed for international students to take advantage of intensive language training before the university would admit them. This program gave me the freedom to create the mathematics content. I discovered that international students face cultural and linguistic challenges in learning mathematics in English for the first time. It inspired me to research the role of language and culture in learning mathematics for my dissertation.

In May 2021, my family hosted a graduation celebration – Olivia with her BSN, Sloan with his Juris Doctorate, and me with a PhD - at the Temple Terrace Country Club with about one hundred of our dearest friends and family. That night is one of my most cherished memories, as I specifically recall the joy of my parents as we recognized these milestones. I spoke that night of my gratitude to have such amazing parents who loved the Lord, who supported my family so well, and who inspired all my endeavors.

Little did I know that two months later (July), both of my parents would perish from Covid just a week apart. The only thing that saved me from such a despairing time was God and my Christian family. I am eager to see my parents again in heaven and share all they have missed with them.

In February 2022, Dr. John Weaver was elected the fifth president of Florida College. He approached me about a new position as his Chief of Staff and asked me to join his leadership team. It was the chance of a lifetime to reconnect with the college that I loved so much. Dr. Weaver's vision for the school mirrored my own. I was honored to work at the executive level to move the college forward.

In January 2023, however, Lee and I had the chance to fulfill a lifelong dream to live at the beach. After much prayer and deliberation, we decided to seize the moment! I was sad to resign from my position in May 2023, but I am forever indebted to Dr. Weaver for bringing me back to my Florida College roots.

My family continues to be my biggest blessing in life. Sloan lives in Nashville and is in his third year as a real estate attorney at Holland & Knight. Olivia completed two and a half years as an ICU nurse and is now a student at the Middle Tennessee School of Anesthesia as a CRNA student . They live three miles apart, and since neither are married, we continue to take annual family trips and spend as much time together as possible. Lee continues to build his real estate portfolio and is fortunate to have good partners in Dyersburg.

My children inspire me and make me want to be the best version of myself. Lee is simply God's answer to my prayer. Even though I never needed to work outside the home, Lee understood my yearning for career, community, and impact, and he graciously extended this privilege into my life. Lee still returns to his hometown monthly to manage his business, yet we spend much time together and enjoy many of the same interests. We read and talk about the Bible daily and challenge each other to think deeply about our faith. We pray that God will use us to spread His word to our neighbors and friends.

I never knew where the next chapter of my life would lead me, but I continued to dream of new ideas. I pray that God will place me in situations where I can best use the gifts He has given me to fulfill His ministry. Recently, I accepted another full-time position at Florida College with the Advancement team as a Major Gifts Officer. I am eager for this new role. I can only dream of what lies ahead.

I strongly believe in family first, and I have tried earnestly to keep that my top priority. But I also believe in forward progress. I hope to see my children marry, have grandchildren, grow old with Lee, and shine my light in the kingdom, but I understand that God holds the key to my future.

I wish I could name every person who influenced my path. I am only a by-product of all those "touches" that kept me focused on my future hope. I want to pay it forward and be an encourager to others. Do not misunderstand me - I made mistakes along the way. I suffered loss. I journeyed through valleys at times, just like we all do. We lost Lee's brother to cancer in September 2002, Lee's dad to Alzheimer's in March 2010, my parents to Covid in July 2021, Lee's mom to Alzheimer's in December 2022, and my brother to cancer in September 2023. God helped us overcome. I reached mountain tops at other times. I hope I have adequately thanked God for those great moments.

I am eternally grateful that a place like Florida College exists! I am convinced that through my pilgrimage at this institution I have been surrounded by the salt of the earth and the lights of the world. Nothing is perfect in this world. Yet, this once-in-a-lifetime experience brought more joy to my family than I could ever imagine. Thank you for reading my story. I hope that my journey will help you in some way.

What is intentionality? When I reflect on my life, I would say intentionality was an important aspect of my spiritual, professional, and personal development. I was goal-oriented from an early age and always worked to achieve something more in life. I can see intentionality as I pursued my education, my family, and my career. I spent my life creating short and long-term goals and continue to do so. I plan to achieve the goals I set. After I began my teaching career, I knew I would inevitably want to seek an advanced degree. That goal did not become a reality until much later in my life, at the age of 50. I also waited a long time to get married because I needed time to figure out who I was and what I wanted. I searched for someone who could help me reach my goals and ultimately go to heaven. I found my husband by God's grace and in accordance with my desires.

During some phases of my life, I was more productive in the Kingdom than in others. I was unsettled during the "quiet" times and struggled with frustration; sometimes, I found myself asking God to help me be more useful. I grew up with working parents who set a wonderful example of industry for me—my family was about productivity and service in God's Kingdom. My parents taught classes at church, practiced hospitality, entertained preachers, and constantly served others. It is definitely in my genes to work in the Kingdom! With this thought in mind, I want to address the topic of intentionality.

A sermon delivered by Russ Bowman inspired this idea. In the sermon, he asked, "Do you wake up every day with intentionality about your service to God?" Ouch! This one hit a little too close to home. I wondered if I consciously thought of how I was going to serve God every day. I started thinking about how my spiritual life also needed to be more intentional. Moving from there, I looked to God's word to help focus my attention on spiritual service and individual growth.

Intentionality is a noun defined as "the fact or quality of being done on purpose or with intent."[1] It also refers to "an attitude of purposefulness, with a commitment to deliberate action."[2] Intentionality is the consciousness (e.g., thoughts, beliefs, desires, hopes) directed toward an object or situation, a purposeful first step toward a goal. When intentionality is aligned with goals, mindfulness and motivation will be directed to match the goals. A few synonyms for the root word, intentional, are planned, deliberate, and premeditated.[3] For the context of our study, I will use intentionality to refer to thinking ahead and making choices based on your personal values, beliefs, and goals.

The Christian journey toward heaven indeed demands persistence and endurance. Scripture encourages us to focus on the present day, as we are not promised tomorrow. Paul's admonition in Ephesians 5:16 reminds us to "redeem the time because the days are evil." This call to make the most of our time reflects the urgency and importance of living faithfully and purposefully each day amidst life's challenges and uncertainties.

WHERE ARE WE INTENTIONAL?

The New Year is often when most people hit the restart button, and it is a common practice in our country to speak about New Year's resolutions. Most resolutions center around physical and mental exercise, increased productivity at work/job promotions, good spending practices, and eliminating bad habits. Consider some areas where many are intentional:

Health. Maybe we went to the doctor for an annual wellness visit and were reminded that our cholesterol was high or we needed to lose weight. We decide to get healthier because Timothy says, "For bodily exercise is slightly beneficial" (1 Tim 4:8). While exercise holds profit for us, Timothy's emphasis is that spirituality precedes physical appearance. Elsewhere, Paul reminds us to "honor God with your bodies" (1 Cor 6:19-20). Taking care of our bodies is essential to shining our light in God's Kingdom.

Wealth. We are to be good stewards of our money and to store treasures in heaven rather than on earth. We do this by guarding our hearts against the deceitfulness of riches

---

1 "Intentionality," Dictionary.com, Accessed August 2, 2024, https://www.dictionary.com/browse/intentionality

2 Ibid.

3 "Intentional." Thesaurus.com. Accessed August 2, 2024. https://www.thesaurus.com/browse/intentional.

(Mat 6:19-21). The Hebrew writer said to "be free from the love of money" (Heb 13:5). Timothy reminds us "not to put our hope in wealth" (1 Tim 6:17). We should reflect on whether we are self-indulgent or sacrificial in our stewardship. Being able to share for the sake of the Kingdom is the true measure of a man (Luk 3:11).

Relationship. There will always be people in our lives who are difficult to handle, whether on the job, in our home, or in the church. Some people can rub us the wrong way or create a stumbling block for our happiness. Every year, we might hit the restart button, try to reconcile with those people, and be more accommodating in our behavior toward them. God's word is full of examples that remind us to "love our enemies" (Mat 5:43), to "live peaceably with all men" (Rom 12:18), and to "love the brotherhood" (1 Pet 2:17).

Family. We all realize the importance and value of a good family. We find ways to stay connected and to encourage those who know us best. We might set goals to enhance those relationships or even to share the gospel with those who are unbelievers. It is an honorable thing to maintain loving relationships (Joh 13:34-35; 15:12,17; Rom 13:8). God's word is clear about our obligation to honor our parents (Eph 6:2), to not provoke our children (Eph 6:4), and to respect and to submit to our husbands (Eph 5:33; Col 3:18).

Spiritually. Paul reminds us to pursue spiritual growth and to "press on toward the mark" (Phi 3:14). In fact, many New Testament passages use verbs or action words to describe our daily walk with God. Although we tend to have the cultural mindset to "Live for the moment. Enjoy what you have. Don't worry about tomorrow," we are called to something more as God's children. If we continue to live every day, every week, every year the same, how boring life would be! God expected us to be productive, to grow our individual gifts, and to abound more and more (Phi 1:9-11). Teach us, Lord, to increase our faith (Luk 17:5)!

How will the premeditation I have described help us? It should elevate our lives beyond the norm to create a better version of ourselves rather than seeking the proverbial "greener pastures." Instead of focusing on what others have, what others are doing, what others have achieved, or how others are blessed, the mindset becomes one of improving ourselves to reach our greatest potential. I believe you can expect to gain four wonderful benefits from such an exercise:

1. Greater focus on what is most important in life.
2. A clearer mindset to enjoy the present rather than placing all hope in the future.

3. Increased commitment to bring more purpose and meaning to your life.
4. Heightened awareness of what you do, say, and think.

WHY IS INTENTIONALITY IMPORTANT?

Consider the parable of the talents in the New Testament gospels of Matthew and Luke, excerpted below. The parable highlights how ordinary people can make the most of God's blessings and demonstrates the role of opportunity, hard work, and accountability in daily life. God's judgment was based on our ability to increase our talent, that is, to put considerable effort into bettering our lives and the lives of our neighbors.

> For it is just like a man about to go on a journey, who called his own slaves and entrusted his possessions to them. To one he gave five talents, to another, two, and to another, one, each according to his own ability; and he went on his journey. The one who had received the five talents immediately went and did business with them, and earned five more talents. In the same way the one who had received the two talents earned two more. But he who received the one talent went away and dug a hole in the ground, and hid his master's money.
>
> Now after a long time the master of those slaves came and settled accounts with them. The one who had received the five talents came up and brought five more talents, saying 'Master, you entrusted five talents to me. See, I have earned five more talents.' His master said to him, 'Well done, good and faithful slave. You were faithful with a few things, I will put you in charge of many things; enter the joy of your master.'
>
> Also the one who had received the two talents came up and said, 'Master, you entrusted two talents to me. See, I have earned two more talents.' His master said to him, 'Well done, good and faithful slave. You were faithful with a few things, I will put you in charge of many things; enter the joy of your master.'
>
> Also the one who had received the two talents came up and said, 'Master, you entrusted two talents to me. See, I have earned two more talents.' His master said to him, 'Well done, good and faithful slave. You were faithful with a few things, I will put you in charge of many things; enter the joy of your master.'
>
> Now the one who had received the one talent also came up and said, 'Master, I knew you to be a hard man, reaping where you did not sow, and gathering where you did not scatter seed. And

> I was afraid, so I went away and hid your talent in the ground. See, you still have what is yours.' But his master answered and said to him, 'You worthless, lazy slave! Did you know that I reap where I did not sow, and gather where I did not scatter seed? Then you ought to have put my money in the bank, and on my arrival I would have received my money back with interest. Therefore, take the talent away from him, and give it to the one who has the ten talents.'
>
> For to everyone who has, more shall be given, and he will have an abundance; but from the one who does not have, even what he does have shall be taken away. And throw the worthless slave into the outer darkness; in that place there will be weeping and gnashing of teeth. (Mat 25:14-30 *NASB*)

The main lesson from this parable is that we must cultivate our unique, God-given skills and abilities to grow and produce spiritually. We must increase our talents to serve God and to take risks for the sake of the Kingdom of God. What is the risk? When we get out of our comfort zones, we run the risk of potential failure or disappointment. However, we should never be discouraged because if "God is for us, who can be against us" (Rom 8:31).

Some key takeaways include the following:

1. Success in life is a product of work.
2. God provides everything we need to complete His mission for us.
3. Every person has a unique set of gifts.
4. Our work should bring glory to the Father.
5. The stewardship of our gifts will result in eternal accountability.

WHERE DOES THE BIBLE SPEAK ABOUT INTENTIONALITY?

Intentionality and foresight take us to the core of the human experience. The Bible has much to say about it. Solomon reminds us, "God has set eternity in the human heart" (Ecc 3:11). In another passage, the Lord says, "For I know the plans I have for you" (Jer 29:11). Let us consider some Bible characters who understood the necessity of increasing their faith and the importance of fulfilling God's mission for their life.

Characters who were intentional in their actions and decisions fill the pages of the Scripture, leaving a legacy for the people around them. They displayed strong faith, courage, and determination as they followed God's plan for their lives.

1. Abraham demonstrated unwavering trust in God's promise through his intentional obedience to God.

2. Daniel illustrated intentionality in his daily prayers and devotion to God, even though his life was in danger.
3. David remained intentional in his pursuit of God's will to become a king.
4. Deborah exhibited intentionality in her leadership, led the nation to victory in battle, and inspired others to follow God's plan.
5. Esther risked her life and displayed great courage and intentionality in approaching the king to plead for the lives of her people.
6. Joseph exemplified the power of God's grace and redemption through his intentional forgiveness and reconciliation with his family.
7. Mary remained intentional in her obedience to God to give birth to Jesus despite the stigma she faced as an unwed mother.
8. Moses became intentional in his role as a leader in guiding God's people through the wilderness, despite his initial reluctance.
9. Paul displayed intentional dedication to spread the gospel after his conversion despite the possibility of persecution.
10. Ruth showed intentional loyalty and dedication to her mother-in-law and became a key figure in Christ's lineage.

These heroes of faith had premeditated in their hearts and minds that they would be faithful to God and complete His will for their lives. The supreme example was Jesus Christ. He knew He would endure the cross but intentionally stepped into dangerous situations to fulfill His ministry.

God expects us to work hard and find joy through that work. Recall Solomon's words: "Behold, what I have seen to be good and fitting is to eat and drink and find enjoyment in all the toil with which one toils under the sun" (Ecc 5:18). Further, Solomon emphasizes these blessings are "from the hand of God" (Ecc 2:24). David said, "You make known to me the path of life; in your presence there is fullness of joy; at your right hand are pleasures forevermore" (Psa 16:11). Timothy reminds us that God "richly provides us with everything we enjoy" (1 Tim 6:17).

The Bible is full of admonitions about our walk with God. Paul said, "Be very careful, then, how you live—not as unwise but as wise, making the most of every opportunity, because the days are evil" (Eph 5:15-16). Additionally, Paul advised, "Whatever you do, work at it with all your heart, as working for the Lord, not for human masters" (Col 3:23).

HOW COULD WE BE MORE INTENTIONAL ABOUT OUR SPIRITUAL LIFE?

Intentionality starts with how we approach each day. Growth requires good planning and execution. This good planning also requires some incremental steps or daily habits to make it happen and to grow our faith.

First, engage in a mental exercise—focus on five things to start each day. Spending time in mindful meditation before our day gets busy will center our minds on how we can serve God that day.

1. Begin your day in prayer (Col 4:2)
2. Rely on God's strength (Eph 3:20)
3. Count your blessings (Eph 5:20)
4. Set your mind on things above (Col 3:2)
5. Let peace rule your heart (Col 3:15)

Second, consider how you might increase your talents in daily life. Although we each have our own unique skills and abilities, we could all start this journey with four areas of spiritual growth: communication with the Father, relationships with other believers, attention to the lost, and knowledge of the Bible.

Communication with the Father. Remember, nothing is impossible with God (Luk 1:37). Talking to God frequently throughout the day will change your life. Although it is important to seek His favor first thing in the morning (Psa 63:1), the last thing at night (Psa 4:8), and before our meals (Mar 8:6), we should never undervalue constant communication with God throughout the day: "Draw near to God, and He will draw near to you" (Jam 4:7). One of my favorite verses is, "You will seek Me and find Me when you seek Me with all your heart" (Jer 29:13). Another result of this constant communication is "so that you may receive mercy and find grace to help in time of need" (Heb 4:16). Finally, our confidence comes after we have approached God because "if we ask anything according to His will, He hears us" (1 Joh 5:14).

Relationships with other believers. God did not intend for Christians to live in isolation. The early Christians "devoted themselves to the apostles' teaching and to fellowship, to the breaking of bread and to prayer" (Act 2:42). Christ instituted the church to bring believers together for admonition and encouragement (Col 3:16). In other words, we need fellow Christians to stir us up "to love and good works" (Heb 10:24). Spending time with other believers gives us the opportunity to learn, to grow, and to serve. This fellowship allows us "to bear each other's burdens" (Gal 6:2). Paul strongly warns about relationships with unbelievers by offering the following words: "What fellowship can light have with darkness?" (2 Cor 6:14). One of the dangers in the present age is to insulate ourselves by spending most of our free time with our physical families rather than our fellow church family. God's word indicates that our interactions with other believers in the local church body motivate us to reach our full potential in Christ (Pro 27:17).

Attention to the lost. Christ's mission on earth involved improving mental, physical, spiritual, and social well-being (Luk 2:51-52). Additionally, Jesus spent His short life on earth with a daily purpose—to seek and save the lost. Is that my ministry as well? The Great Commission is our great example: "Go therefore and make disciples of all nations" (Mat 28:19-10). As I go about my daily life, do I choose to interact with the people around me–in the grocery store, the cubicle next door at work, the restaurant, and the doctor's office? Do I shine my light by giving strangers a glimpse into my heart and showing them love and kindness? Do I act in such a way that people want to talk to me and learn more about me? Do I continue to grow spiritually so I am more prepared to lead others to Christ?

Knowledge of the Bible. We must "grow in the grace and knowledge of our Lord and Savior Jesus Christ" (2 Pet 3:18). If you want to increase your knowledge of God and become a better Bible student, take a deep dive into the word of God. As the brethren in Thessalonica did, we should "examine the scriptures daily" (Act 17:11). I highly recommend the NIV Chronological Bible, which reads like a novel. You will become more captivated with all you learn every year you spend in God's word. After you have mastered that daily reading ritual, add a podcast, a devotional book, or an online sermon. Listen to hymns on the way to work. Find a spiritual mentor and have weekly discussions about the Bible. Do you see the point? It is all about incremental steps and Biblical inundation that lead to long-term growth. Paul reminds us, "present yourself to God as one approved, a worker who does not need to be ashamed and who correctly handles the word of truth" (2 Tim 2:15).

I often reflect on my daily habits to see if I am preparing myself to become a better servant in the Kingdom each year. Am I setting a pattern in my life to be more like Jesus? What are my top priorities when I consider my life as a Christian, a wife, a mother, a friend, and a neighbor? Do I seek to increase in wisdom, stature, and good standing with God and man? Remember, we should strive to excel still more (1 The 4:10).

CONCLUSION

The key to intentional living is to "figure out what will please Christ, and then do it" (Eph 5:10). When put into practice daily, living intentionally changes your life. Consider Jesus as our model. In just three short years, He mentored His disciples to become leaders of His movement. That meant being intentional about the people and places He used to mold and shape His disciples. Without question, Jesus was strategic in this effort.

The well-known human rights activist Nelson Mandela said, "After climbing a great hill, one finds that there are many more hills to climb. I have taken a moment here to rest, to steal a view of the glorious vista that surrounds me, to look back on the distance I have come. But I can only rest for a moment, for with freedom comes responsibilities, and I dare not linger, for my long walk has not yet ended."[4]

How will we be remembered after we are gone? May we emulate the poor widow from the parable in Mark 12, and it will be said of us that we did all we could (12:43-44). May the Lord help us to make the most of our talents and to shine our light in the world.

4 Nelson Mandela. *Long Walk to Freedom*. (Boston: Back Bay Books, 1994). 625.

THOUGHT QUESTIONS FOR "INTENTIONALITY IN CHRISTIAN LIVING"

1. What are some specific things in life you are currently intentional about?

2. What unique talents and abilities do you have? How can you cultivate those gifts in service to God?

3. Identify certain daily habits that you can change or eliminate to engender spiritual growth.

4. Why is it so hard to change your habits or to "find the time" for increasing your faith?

5. How can you be more intentional about developing your unique talents and seeking improvement every year?

6. Can you articulate what you want your spiritual legacy to be? In other words, how will your family and friends remember you, especially as it relates to your spirituality?

GRIEF

Minerva Holk, EdD

Pure and undefiled religion before God and the Father is this: to visit orphans and widows in their trouble, and to keep oneself unspotted from the world.

James 1:27

Grief is unavoidable in our earthly lives. Fortunately, most of us have lives which blend events that bring joy as well as sorrow. I have experienced grief and have learned from those experiences. Grief is rarely comfortable and yet I have been fortunate to also see the blessings that come with it. In the chapter that follows, I will share some of the experiences that I have had which others believe give me insight into the process of grief. Grief is not a competition and I do not discount the grief others experience. I have often reminded my students that we are the product of our lived experiences, which colors our reactions to the events in our lives. Grief is painful but can also bring blessings. I know that our heavenly Father cares when we are grieving and will not give us more than we can handle together with Him.

The history of my life and my connection to Florida College begins when I was raised in Ohio, the second of four children. My mother was a Christian and my father had been raised in a Pentecostal family. Neither of my parents were faithful to their religious beliefs at the time they met and married. Mother was restored after having my older brother, and determined to bring her children up knowing our Father and the truth of His words. My family consisted of my parents and their four children. We were very close in age, "stair-stepped," having been born within a three-year, seven-month window. In many ways, my brother was a stand alone and I was the oldest child who tried to please everyone.

I attended the neighborhood elementary school and as always was a good student. I was perhaps a bit more sociable than the teachers desired. I never remember a time when my mother was not confident that her children would graduate from college, and I believed her. I remember her constant prayers for our souls and wisdom to bring us up as God would desire. My mother was a great believer in doing the best you can do, pray diligently, then "forget it" and let God handle it.

My initial plan was to become an elementary school teacher. I had always loved school and looked forward to the start every fall. The fact that my birthday fell during the first month we were back in school just added to my joy of the fall season. After my freshman year in high school, I was accepted to attend a cooperative high school downtown. After our sophomore year, all students got a job through a cooperative relationship between the school and local businesses. I majored in medical arts because I was planning to attend college, and the curriculum was more aligned to the college prep curriculum in other city high schools. My first job was at a local hospital, and I worked 40 hours a week all summer. When fall semester started, the students were divided into two sections and throughout the school year, section one would work two weeks while section two went to regular high school classes. Every two weeks we would alternate. We did this year-round for our junior and senior years of high school. I was in the medical arts program because the curriculum was most similar to the college prep curriculum at other public high schools in Dayton. I was not planning to become a nurse. I had the benefit of working with some stellar nurses for two years and considered going into nursing. My mother encouraged me to go into nursing because I would always be able to get a job and I might not be able to get a job teaching. I have pondered that many times as my career in nursing has involved teaching and working in academia most of my career. I hate calling it a career because it was never my priority. One of the reasons I went into nursing was to have the freedom of working when I wanted or needed. My future family was my priority.

During my senior year two events happened which changed the plans I thought I would be pursuing after graduation. First, the Florida College chorus performed in Dayton, and we kept two of the girls overnight. They were two of the nicest girls I had ever met. Second, in May, there was a shooting during an anti-Vietnam war expansion protest at Kent State University; four students were killed and nine were injured. There was unrest on many college campuses during the late '60s and early '70s. My mother had been pushing me to attend Florida College and I did apply but did not really plan to go. After the Kent State shooting, my father decided his first daughter to leave home was not going to a school with tear gas, armed militia, and riots—effectively eliminating all public college in Ohio. He got on board with my mother to send me to a small, private, safe school in Florida. I remember trying to convince my mother to let me stay home and attend the local college, but she was determined for me to go. She said if I did not like it after one year, I would not have to go back. She had two years of college and I think she knew I would be happy once I was there. I loved it and returned the following year bringing my sister with me. It was hard to leave after two years. I wanted to continue with my friends, many of whom were planning to attend Western Kentucky University (WKU), but the Bachelor of Science in nursing that I was pursuing was not available at WKU. The most important thing I accomplished at Florida College was strengthening my faith in our Lord and Savior and His Father—what a blessing! At Murray State University (MSU), I attended the only sound congregation in town and was welcomed by my new bonus family. I graduated in December 1974. I started working as a graduate nurse in a high-risk labor and delivery unit. I took the RN licensure exam in January and passed, although the results were not known until March 1975. After

20 months working in the labor and delivery unit, I was invited to teach for a year as clinical faculty at MSU. My mother advised me to accept the position to find out if I would like teaching nursing before spending all the money to go to graduate school. I learned so much in that year, the most important thing at that time was the decision not to specialize in nursing education during graduate school. At the end of the academic year, I had saved enough money to go with Ferrell Jenkins and a tour group to Europe. What an amazing time and so many wonderful people! I still make some of the recipes from the older widows who became friends on the tour.

August of 1976, I began my graduate education at Indiana University in Indianapolis. The congregation I attended was welcoming and as I was single, several were interested in getting me married. They thought I should meet "Buster". I was confident that the last thing I needed at the time was a Buster in my life; I also had a boyfriend although he lived in a different state. Several months later, my boyfriend and I broke up. At a potluck, my dear friend, Ruth (adoptive substitute mother), learned about the breakup and encouraged me to send a letter to Buster who was in the US Navy and stationed in Guam. I wrote him a letter, mainly to appease everyone who thought our getting acquainted was a good idea. The day after I sent the letter, Ruth's daughter caught me after Bible class and said, "I heard you sent Buster a letter." I told her I had to which she replied, "I wish they would leave that boy alone." In my head, I wished I had talked to her before I mailed the letter. To make a long story short, he wrote me back; it was the sweetest one-page letter I have ever received. We were married less than 18 months later and were blest to have just shy of 37 years together before his unexpected death. His given name was George, not Buster, which I appreciated.

I adapted to being a Navy wife and enjoyed many parts of it. My husband was a Navy pilot and flew jets on and off carriers in the middle of the ocean when he was on sea duty. We lived most of our married life in Washington state, with two tours in other states. We were fortunate to be able to visit our families in Ohio and Indiana at least once each year. I only worked two days a week during our early years of marriage. When he was at sea, I worked more. I became a stay-at-home mom after our first son was born. Our second son was born 3 ½ years later. My husband completed his time in the Navy in 1995 when he retired and went back to school to prepare for his second career. In preparation for his retirement, I took a nurse refresher course to requalify for my RN license in Washington. After I had an active license, I started working part-time in the nursing program at our local community college. I had not worked outside the home for 11+ years after the boys were born and it was extremely part-time teaching nursing which allowed me to continue teaching Bible classes, attending ladies' Bible classes, serving others, and helping in my sons' classrooms at school. I was off for their school holidays and breaks. I got longer breaks than they did which meant I was still able to be very involved in their care and activities. After two years, a full-time position became available at the college, and I was hired. I made a promise to myself that this could not displace the two most important aspects of my life: continuing to be faithful and active with our local congregation and caring for my family.

Our boys went to the Florida College Ohio Camp for three years when they were in their teens. We wanted them to associate and meet people outside of our family who were Midwesterners as they had lived almost their whole lives in the Pacific Northwest. Our oldest son earned his associate degree from Florida College in 2003.

It is so interesting to talk with people and learn their stories. We also learn that everyone has troubles and have experienced grief, and it is often difficult to see. I do not mind sharing events in my life with people who are interested but sometimes it is difficult for them to hear, and I also do not want them to feel I have been overburdened. I believe that we will not be burdened with more than we can handle but it is also important to look for God's hand in supporting us through our trials. I am a realist and try to present a positive perspective even with difficulties. Sharing some of the challenges/grief experiences from my life is meant to provide perspective on my experience with grieving. My mother was not the originator of the comment that people are as happy as they make up their minds to be, but it was heard frequently. My words are not meant to diminish the difficulties many people experience with clinical depression or imply that they can cure themselves without help. I will share a few specific examples from my life including an autoimmune disease, our son breaking his back at 16 which resulted in paraplegia, and the death of my husband.

My autoimmune symptoms began in 2002 and I was referred to my first rheumatologist. I had four appointments and did not go back for the fifth one that had been approved because she basically dismissed my symptoms as age related. Several months later I went to another rheumatologist because I was worse, the three potential diagnoses that were being considered were scleroderma, lupus, or Sjogren's. I remember looking them up and the prognosis for two of the three was a life expectancy of five to 10 years. I was so sad because I felt like I still had so much to do, and my family still needed me. It took a while to make peace with this information, but I realized that God would see to it that my sons would be taken care of if I died. He would send someone, and it would all work out. I was at peace although still trying to get healthier. Most people were unaware of my illness as I forced myself to keep going and a challenge associated with autoimmune diseases is they are often invisible or at least hidden which is not always a good thing. When I realized my doctor was not attentive to my condition, I finally went to a rheumatologist in Seattle. He looked like Mr. Rogers and when I left his office that day, it was the first time I had hope that I could get better. I remember calling my mother on the way home from the office and telling her it was the first time I had left any of the rheumatologists' offices where I was not feeling laden with waiting for the other shoe to drop. Within 36 hours, the changes he made in my medications brought a significant improvement. For the next 15 years, I was stable and able to use my hands and the swelling in my lower extremities was gone. I am so grateful that I did not have negative effects to the medications and the right combination to help me get better.

Our sons had both enjoyed going to ski school during junior high and high school on Saturdays during the winter. Our younger son went to ski school on Saturday morning, January 31, 2004. I still remember the last time I looked at my lean, tall, athletic 16-year-old as he headed to the garage for his dad to drop him off at school for the bus. We received a phone call at 10:30 from Stevens Pass that our son had been airlifted to Harborview Medical Center in Seattle. I think they told us he could not move his legs, but we expected he would still be okay. I packed a change of clothes for him to wear home from the hospital after his discharge. When we arrived at the hospital, our son was not in the ER as he was having a test done elsewhere. I saw his x-ray on the counter in his room and saw that he had a fracture subluxation of the twelfth thoracic and first lumbar vertebrae. We were at Harborview for four nights. One of the blessings of being there was each evening they would deliver email messages that had been received for our son and his parents. We got so many messages each evening from Christians all over the United States and even some foreign countries. Each one was encouraging and reminding us of the Great Physician and sharing verses of encouragement. It was a very difficult time. On the fifth day, we were transferred to Seattle Children's Hospital in-patient rehabilitation unit. Our son's days were filled with occupational therapy, physical therapy, appointments with nutritionists, psychologists, nurses, and physicians. Our total time in the hospital was 35 days. I was on leave from work from the time of the accident until the following September. Our son had a parent with him continuously while in the hospital. I stayed five nights a week and my husband stayed the other two, one on the weekend and one during the week. In the early days after the injury, I was struck by how our whole world had changed and yet to look at the world, nothing was different. It was such a rough time, and we did what we needed to do. My husband continued to meet his work responsibilities and visiting our son each day which involved driving more than an additional 100 miles per day. Our oldest son was in college when this happened, and we did not have him come home until his spring break. He said people from church would ask him how his parents were doing; he said I think they are doing what they must do. He knew we accepted that we could not change the situation and were doing what was necessary and trying to give his brother the best life possible. When we got home, I think we had appointments almost every day for a while plus I had to do twice daily physical therapy exercises and the other treatments for our son including turning him during the night. He was still in his TLSO which is like a turtle shell to keep his back immobilized as he continued to recover from surgery. I had been doing the treatments while he was still in the hospital but there was no one else to help when we got home. Our son was on prescription pain medications for six months following his injury. The medications were strictly monitored and administered. We did not know as much about addictive properties in 2004 as we do now and ultimately deal with the life changes and coping led to new challenges for our son and his parents. That is not the purpose of this sharing, but it is another form of grief. I can talk about it but will not be writing about it in a book.

God's plan for marriage is perfect and I was so blest to share my life with my husband. Together we shared much happiness, but the troubles were halved. Having been a military spouse, I had always had a fair amount of independence, but I always knew he was there for me and vice versa. In 2016, Buddy Payne took us to dinner in Washington and during the conversation, it came up that Florida College was considering starting a nursing program. Buddy asked if I would be interested in helping. My husband and I talked it over and decided we were willing to do this. We had been supporters of the College our whole married life and from the beginning he continued paying the $100.00 a year Century Club donation I committed to before we married. Later we became charter members of the Society. I had just finished my doctorate in June 2016 and needed to stay at my current school until the end of the 2019-2020 academic year to repay my nursing loans. Our plan was to move to Florida for three to four years and then decide whether to move back to Washington. Unfortunately, my husband died unexpectedly in April 2017. I was devastated,

I had never felt such a loss. It took a few weeks to realize that part of my problem was that he was not there any longer to share my burden. My husband was a CPA in his second career, and he had taken care of all our financial matters for more than 20 years. During his active-duty Navy years, I would take care of the finances while he was out at sea for long deployments, but I had not needed to do that for years. Everything was electronic, bank accounts, credit cards, paying bills. We had been to California to see our son who was getting married the following June and had driven home the past weekend. My husband had gone into our bedroom to put something away and then I heard an unusual noise. I went to check; he was sitting on the floor and said, "I think I must have fainted." I asked him what his pulse was and as he went to count it, he slumped over to the floor. I thought that was strange, but figured he was just resting, and I would help him get up when he was ready. Then I noticed his fingers were not checking the pulse on his wrist and his eyes were blank. I went out to call 911 on the land line. I turned on the front light and unlocked the door as I went back to the bedroom where I started chest compressions. I cracked his ribs on the first compression. The 911 dispatcher stayed on the phone with me until the paramedics arrived. After they started working on my husband, I called our preacher (also an elder) and his wife. They lived near us and arrived within a few minutes. I also called a work friend. They worked on my husband for about 45 minutes before transporting him to the hospital. They were not able to get an airway in and he also aspirated which I knew meant we were in trouble.

In the ER, they continued to resuscitate him. One lung collapsed and a chest tube was inserted. The other lung collapsed upon arrival to the ICU realizing another chest tube. His oxygenation was not good even though he was on a ventilator. The doctors wanted to give him a week to see if he would improve. On the following Monday evening, we took him off the ventilator anticipating that he would only take one or two breaths before he died. He did not die that night. The next afternoon we were transferred to palliative care (arranged by one of my graduate nurses) where he did not die until 7:37 Friday morning. I started this by saying I am a realist and think positive or try to take note of all the blessings God provides each day. These are my positives for my husband's death: 1) the last person he saw was me, the person he loved most in this world; 2) he did not know that he was going to his reward or that I was going to be sad and alone; 3) the event happened when we were home and not in the middle of nowhere travelling like we had been on the weekend before the collapse; and 4) we were at the hospital where I had educated so many nurses who lovingly cared for us during this time and we had our church family and long-term friends who were a constant source of support. I am so grateful that my husband was a Christian who daily walked with Christ. I decided early in my grief that I would not dishonor what we had shared by being sad and miserable continually. I also decided it was selfish to wish him back from paradise. Being able to see positives is helpful but it does not mean the grieving person is happy all the time. Even seven years later, I am still overcome at times with grief for my husband and grateful for the life we shared.

Grief is a part of life and is associated with loss. Each of us will deal with grief in our own way, and how one navigates grief will be dependent upon her experiences, faith, support systems, and relationship with the source of the grief. One definition of grief is "deep mental anguish, as from bereavement."[1] One definition of bereavement is "to leave desolate or alone, especially by death."[2] Bereavement involves suffering the loss of a loved one.

There are phases of grief. The first type is anticipatory grief. I first became familiar with anticipatory grief when I was a graduate nursing student working in a high-risk labor and delivery unit. Examples include parents who experience miscarriage or stillbirth, a premature birth, or a child born with deformities resulting in the loss of the idealized child. The parents may feel guilty, particularly if they feel they did something that caused the loss. David suffered anticipatory grief before the death of his first son with Bathsheba (2 Sam 12:15-23). It is important to provide opportunities for people who are grieving to share their thoughts about the grief they are experiencing.

Men and women experience grief differently, but finding ways to comfort both is important. Julie Cook is an author who writes and does YouTube videos about grief. She

---

1 The American Heritage College Dictionary. s.v. "Grief."

2 Ibid.

says, "Grief is like a snowflake. Sometimes it comes one flake at a time; other times, it comes like a blizzard. It melts away, but it always comes back. Just as each snowflake is unique, each person experiences grief in their own unique way."[3] Often, we are uncomfortable being with grieving people, perhaps afraid to say the wrong thing. The book of Romans is full of suggestions for strengthening our faith and relationships with fellow saints. It also includes a suggestion for grief: "...weep with those who weep" (Rom 12:15). Often, there is no need to talk. It may be a greater comfort to listen and pray with them. God provided several examples for us to learn about grief and value understanding it. He also does not intend that we stay in our grief. I find it comforting that there is a resurrection, and we will some day rejoin with the departed saints. This assurance does not remove the grief, as is seen throughout the Bible. Author Rachel-Marie Martin writes, "Sometimes you have to let go of the picture of what you thought life would be like and learn to find joy in the story you are actually living."[4] It is hard to imagine in the initial phase of grief that joy will ever return, but we are assured it will. "Weeping may endure for a night, but joy comes in the morning" (Psa 30:5).

"Grief work" must follow the painful response to a loss, which is the process of resolving grief. "Grief is like an earthquake. The first one hits you, and the world falls apart. Even after you put the world together again, there are aftershocks, and you never really know when those will come."[5] The Old Testament provides some practices used to support the grieving process. There are several examples of grief actions in the Bible. Several times, God's people tore their clothing as a sign of their grief (Gen 37:29). Times of grief included the initial week of grieving. Another example is when Jacob died when we are told that, "Joseph fell on his father's face and wept over him.... The Egyptians mourned for him (Jacob) 70 days" (Gen 50:1-3, 10). Following the death of Moses, "the children of Israel wept for Moses in the plains of Moab thirty days. So, the days of weeping and mourning for Moses ended" (Deu 34:7-8). The children of Israel also mourned Aaron for thirty days (Num 20:29). Ruth encouraged her daughters-in-law to return to their families for comfort following the death of their husbands (Rut 1:9). Other actions included wearing sackcloth

---

3 Julia Cook, Grief is Life a Snowflake: A Picture Book About the Death of a Loved One. (Chattanooga: National Center for Youth Issues, 2011).

4 Rachel-Marie Martin. The Brave Art of Motherhood: Fight Fear, Gain Confidence, and Find Yourself Again. (New York: Waterbrook, 2018).

5 Author unknown

and putting ashes on the body (Exo 33:4) and the absence of wearing adornments or ornaments when mourning (Exo 33:4).

Adults experience intense mourning and grieving (usually lasting around six months to a year) only when there is an intimate, affectionate bond with the deceased, as with close friends and relatives. Some have suggested that the length and intensity of mourning are proportionate to the closeness of the relationship prior to death. The Cocoanut Grove Fire was the second deadliest fire in the United States and resulted in the deaths of 492 people and 166 injuries. It also changed the way we understand grief and redefined grief and mental health. Erich Lindemann, a psychiatrist who specialized in caring for the grieving, described the symptoms of "normal grief" following the Cocoanut Grove Fire in 1944. The picture shown by persons in acute grief is remarkably uniform. Common to all is the following syndrome:

> "Sensations of somatic distress occurring in waves lasting from 20 minutes to an hour at a time, a feeling of tightness in the throat, choking with shortness of breath, need for sighing, and an empty feeling in the abdomen, lack of muscular power, and an intense subjective distress described as tension or mental pain…."[6]

Grief can be accompanied by a sense of unreality and a feeling of increased emotional distance from other people. The grieving person accuses himself of negligence and exaggerates minor omissions in regard to their lost one.

The duration of a grief reaction seems to depend upon the success with which a person does the grief work, namely, emancipation from the bondage to the deceased, readjustment to the environment in which the deceased is missing, and the formation of new relationships. An obstacle to this work is the fact that people may try to avoid the intense distress connected with the grief experience and avoid the expression of emotion necessary for it. It is beneficial in that it frees the mind from constant preoccupation with that which is gone. This will allow more energy to deal with the life that remains.

Morbid grief reactions or pathological grief reactions represent distortions of normal grief. These conditions must be transformed into "normal reactions," after which we can find resolution. There are two categories of pathological grief reactions. The first is delay or postponement of the reaction, which happens if the bereavement occurs during a time

---

6 Erich Lindemann. SYMPTOMATOLOGY AND MANAGEMENT OF ACUTE GRIEF. American Journal of Psychiatry, 101, no. 2 (September 1944): 141–48.

when the person has important tasks or when there is a necessity for maintaining the morale of others. He may show little or no reaction for weeks or even much longer. The second category includes distorted reactions, the first being overactivity without a sense of loss. Instead, a sense of well-being and zest for life prevails. Another example would be the acquisition of symptoms belonging to the last illness of the deceased or the development of a psychosomatic illness. There may also be an alteration in relationships with friends or relatives, avoiding former social activities, and progressive social isolation.

At first, the full reaction of grief may be delayed, or there may be a numbness or blunting in which the bereaved person acts as if nothing had happened for a few hours, days, or weeks. After that, attacks of yearning and distress occur. The grieving person may think the deceased is present, and there is a tendency to think of him as if he were still alive and to idealize his memory. The intensity of these features begins to decline after one to six weeks and is minimal by six months, although for several years, occasional brief periods of yearning and depression may be precipitated by reminders of the loss. Several researchers who have studied mourning extensively have strongly emphasized that full expression of emotional reactions in a grieving person is necessary for the optimal resolution of the mourning reaction. If mourning is impeded and not allowed to run its course, pathological grief can result. Consider how you relate to others who are grieving.

How can we support those who are grieving? Be available to them and be willing to listen or to sit quietly. "Better to go to the house of mourning than to go to the house of feasting, for that is the end of all men; and the living will take it to heart" (Ecc 7:2-4). Especially in the case of grieving widows and widowers, accept that they are no longer the person they were before the death. This is likely more pronounced in persons who have been married for a long time. If we are one as the Lord describes the marriage relationship, then if we lose half of who we are, there will be differences as we rediscover who we are in our widowed state. One simple thing to do is to talk about the person who died and use his or her name. Almost two months after my husband died, a dear friend from our church family took me out for lunch. During our lunch, she shared with me that the deacons had planted a tree by the church building in my husband's memory, and it was probably the first time they had a meeting when all the deacons were present, as often someone was unable to make it to their meeting. One of my husband's deacon duties was to make sure everyone who had a role during Bible class and worship was present and that the communion was ready. My friend shared that there was some confusion the first Sunday after he passed because they were so used to George taking care of all those details, and no deacon had taken over. Hearing these accounts brought tears to my eyes, and fortunately, she was comfortable enough to allow them. I told her what was most valuable to me from her sharing was to know that I was not alone in missing my husband. Each spring one or more members from the congregation sends me a picture of the growing tree and its blooms. I know with newborn or infant deaths, it is very common to not use the baby's name, and there is an expectation that the grief period should only last a few weeks. I was surprised at how people could easily forget someone who had lived 60-plus years. At the three-month mark, after my husband died, I received a note from Cherry Hall and a thin book (a quick hour-long read). A friend had given her four books to send to me, one every three months. Each book described typical feelings related to the grief response at three, six, nine, and twelve months. The books were consistent with what I was experiencing. I looked forward to each book's arrival and another note from Cherry. I do not know who gave them to her as the friend asked to remain anonymous, but it meant so much to me, especially because receiving the book meant she remembered my loss. The summer after my husband died, I read fourteen books--a combination of spiritual and secular. I did not realize at the time that reading provided an escape from the pain and consciousness of my intense grief. I learned later that reading can help adjust to the loss. I received several books related to grief during this time. I appreciated the thoughtfulness and found them helpful. Drawing closer to our Father through prayer and spending time in His word provides comfort. "The LORD is near to those who have a broken heart,..." (Psa 34:19). God cares for us and will provide shelter in His wings (Psa 61: 1-4). We have been given such a gift in the Bible. There is nothing new under the sun (Ecc 1:9), and God has provided everything we need to navigate our lives.

I have great appreciation for God's care for the widows and His expectations that His people also care for them. God considered this important enough to be included in His law and to impose negative consequences for those who did not follow His instruction. The following scriptures demonstrate God's expectations. The people are not to afflict the widows (Exo 22:22-24). Widows are to receive justice, charity, care, including food and clothing (Deu 10:18, 14:28-29, 16:14, 24:17-19, 26:12, 27:19). Widows were not to be sent away empty or mistreated (Job 22:9, 24:3). We should defend widows (Psa 68:5, 146:9). God's people are to assist widows when they need someone to plead for them and prevent them from becoming prey (Isa 1:17, 10:1-2). God commanded His people to amend their ways as they were guilty of "oppressing the stranger, the fatherless, and the widow" (Jer 7:6; Zec 7:10). Later in Jeremiah, the prophet declares God's command to do no violence toward widows (22:3). Ezekiel condemns Jerusalem for mistreating the fatherless and widows (22:7). The Lord will take judgment against those who exploit wage earners, widows, and orphans (Mal 3:5).

Several passages in the New Testament also address the care of widows. In the early days of the Church, the Hellenists brought a complaint against the Hebrews because their widows were neglected in the daily distribution (Act 6:1-6). The apostles instructed the brethren to seek out seven men of good reputation to be appointed to oversee the business of providing for the widows. The church had instructions about caring for widows, including distinctions between young widows and older widows as well as their respective family's responsibility (1 Tim 5:3-16). We find the final instruction in James 1:27: "Pure and undefiled religion before God and the Father is this: to visit orphans and widows in their trouble, and to keep oneself unspotted from the world." From my experience as a widow and the many widows I have come to know in the past seven years, I know this is still a needed direction.

I have a framed quote from Jeremiah 29:11, "I know the plan…." As soon as I saw it in a store, I started to cry. Each time I see it, I am grateful for the reminder that God has a plan for me, especially when the world around me seems out of control or overwhelming. The Lord knows our needs, and His ongoing care brings peace. Looking back on trials allows us to see God's hand in our lives. The life I have lived is not the life I imagined when I was a child. Even with the heartaches, it has been so much better, and looking forward to heaven after this life is so much sweeter when God will wipe away every tear from our eyes (Rev 7:17). Widows are to trust in God (Jer 49:11).

THOUGHT QUESTIONS FOR "GRIEF"

1. Make a list the people you know who are grieving or those who may be grieving. Reflect upon your actions to support them as they adjust to life without their loved one.

2. What are some actions that you can do to support others in their grief?

3. What are some actions you can take to enhance your abilities to understand grief and support those who are grieving?

4. Select a person from the Bible and study his or her life and grief response more deeply. What factors do you think contributed to the intensity of the person's grief and their ability to do the grief work and adjust to the new life without the lost loved one?

5. What comments are helpful to one who is grieving?

6. What comments are not helpful? If you have not experienced this, who do you know that you could talk to and learn more about their unpleasant or hurtful experience?

THE AMAZING GIFT OF ADOPTION

Jennifer Kearney

For you did not receive a spirit of slavery to fall back into
fear. Instead, you received the Spirit of adoption,
by whom we cry out, "Abba, Father!"
Romans 8:15

I first came to Florida College in the Fall of 1995, intending to stay for a year to have the "FC Experience." I ended up graduating with my AA and coming back to work in the library (twice!), eventually being appointed library director.

But to really tell my story, I need to go back to the mid-1960's when my father was the second of four boys, growing up in Dublin, Ireland. In those days, immigration was very common. A lot of young Irish people moved to other countries for better opportunities. My dad was no different. When he was only twenty, he and a friend, Tom Fox, flew to Toronto, Canada with $60 between them.

He was all alone in a country where he knew no one (besides Tom). But Dad did not let that stop him. He found work at an engineering company, McKinnon Mitchell, where he met my mother. She had gotten a summer job there. She was quiet and shy. My dad . . . was not. Some of the guys dared him to ask her on a date. He got down on one knee in the middle of the office to ask her out. They had their first date on New Year's Eve and were married the following October. They lived in the Greater Toronto area for the next four years before moving back to Ireland so Dad could go into business with his younger brother.

My parents could not have children, so they chose to adopt. That decision was fraught with difficulties. Mom was Protestant. All the adoption agencies in Ireland were run by the Catholic church. Mom was not required to convert, but she did have to take catechism lessons and agree to raise any children they had in the Catholic church. I was born in September of 1975. My parents brought me home six weeks later.

Around the same time that Dad moved to Toronto, his oldest brother, Steve, moved to South Africa where he met Wayne Sullivan, who taught him the gospel. Uncle Steve and his wife, my Aunt Cora, were baptized there. By 1975, they had moved back to Ireland, and my uncle began preaching full-time in Dublin.

He kept talking to my parents about the gospel, but they showed little interest at first. Uncle Steve persisted, and by the time I was five, they had started studying the Bible and were baptized. From that point on, serving the Lord became a major focus for both my parents.

So many things had to align for me to end up knowing the gospel. First, my Uncle Steve had to move to South Africa. Then Wayne Sullivan had to teach him the gospel so that he could obey it. My dad had to move to Canada to meet and marry my mom. Next, Dad and Mom had to move from Canada to Dublin at the same time my aunt and uncle were moving back there from South Africa. My parents also had to jump over the hurdles of the adoption process. My birth mother had to give me up for adoption, and finally, my parents had to be baptized. This level of complex, international coordination would be seemingly impossible to orchestrate, but our Father in heaven is not even slightly challenged by making sure His children can find their way to Him.

I started my education at a local Catholic school. I have a very distinct memory of the teachers walking us to the church next door on Ash Wednesday so that the priest could bless us. I kept wiping the ashes off my forehead, and he kept putting them back on. I was five when my parents made the decision to obey the gospel. After that, my parents moved me to a nearby Protestant school. It was a tiny two-room schoolhouse. There were only two other kids in my class. I think the largest class in the school had only seven or eight students.

I was 12, almost 13, when I made the decision to obey the gospel. We were camping with family friends at the beach. I had a nightmare about the judgment day and that was the final push I needed to ask to be baptized the next morning. We woke everyone up, and my dad baptized me in the frigid Irish Sea before breakfast.

For my secondary education, I moved to a much larger school. I think high school can be a very difficult experience for many people, and it definitely was for me. There was a lot of peer pressure to conform to unhealthy and ungodly activities. I dug my heels in, but it made those years pretty miserable. I escaped into reading a lot, to the detriment of my schoolwork. Mom would pick me up every other Thursday and we'd stop at the large public library near my school. I would max out my library card, as well as hers and my brother's, to get enough books to keep me going until the next "library day". I was a voracious reader and had wide-ranging interests. I would read Agatha Christie mysteries one day, epic fantasy the next, and Robert Ludlum spy novels the day after that. I am still an avid reader. I finish between 50 and 100 books annually.

As I was growing up, my family was part of the small congregation where my uncle preached. The group was close-knit. We often went camping or met up for picnics on bank holidays. A few times a year, everyone would come to our house for a get-together. We lived in a more rural area and had a large field behind our house. Dad would get the tractor out and pull us kids around the field in an open trailer. As we got older, we put up a volleyball net, and that was the activity of choice when people came over.

Back then, the congregation often had American preachers come for meetings, or visitors worshipped with us while on vacation in Ireland. My parents would always invite the visiting preachers for dinner. I had heard of FC from them but never had a desire to move halfway across the world to go to college. Instead, after I got my Leaving Certificate, I enrolled in a technical college and majored in Biology with the intent of being a lab tech. I loved the academic work but was less enthralled with the social side. Back in those days, a lot of Irish social life revolved around the pub. Things have changed now, and avoiding alcohol is more of an acceptable choice, but back then, if you didn't drink, you were left with few options for a social life.

When I was 20, I remember talking to my parents and telling them that I regretted not having gone to Florida College when I had the opportunity. My dad said it was not too late and a few weeks later I was in the whirlwind of applying to Florida College, buying plane tickets, and preparing to leave home and move to another country. My family understood the Lord was more than capable of watching over us no matter what continent we currently occupied.

Florida College changed my life. For the first time, I was surrounded by others of a similar age who shared my faith. I could say yes to invitations without questioning if it would be in an unsuitable location, or if booze would be involved. I took classes that broadened my horizons. I made lifelong friendships. This is by no means an unusual or unique experience to me. Many FC alumni could say the same thing. Having an extended Christian family is one of the great blessings of being associated with Florida College. It is unusual for me to travel to other places and not find some connection to friends that I have made in my time as a student and as an employee of the college. Although it was not a unique experience, it was a transformative time in my life.

After that first year, I told my parents I wanted to come back and finish my Associate of Arts degree. They were happy to oblige. After graduating with my AA, I told them some of my friends were going to the University of South Florida and sharing an apartment, and I wanted to do that too. They supported me in that also.

Buddy Payne at that time was the Academic Dean and in that role was the advisor for all international students. During one conversation with him, he suggested that I might be interested in librarianship and recommended I speak with one of the librarians. I did that and had a conversation with Wanda Dickey, who would later become a mentor and friend. I told my parents that eventually I wanted to get a master's degree in library science. With their blessing, from that point on, obtaining my MLIS became my focus.

I enrolled at USF as a psychology major. Because library science didn't require any specific undergrad major, I could study whatever interested me. What a gift that was! I had decided to major in psychology because I loved Thaxter Dickey's classes at FC, and because a friend was also planning to be a psych major and we would be able to take a lot of classes together. Some friends and I moved into a couple of apartments near USF, and my time there was filled with card games, X-Files watch parties, devos, and birthday parties alongside of my classes and study sessions, of course.

While I was researching graduate programs, I had a conversation with Joe Rose, who was the FC library director at the time. He gave me advice on choosing a program, and I ended up moving to Lewisville, Texas, and entering the Library Science program at the University of North Texas. I graduated in August 2001. Around that time, Buddy Payne called me about a job opening at the Florida College library. I initially said no, but after a couple of months struggling to find a suitable position in the Dallas-Fort Worth metroplex in a post-9/11 economy, I called him back and asked if FC was still an option. I interviewed with then-director Jim Hodges in early 2002 and began working at the library later that year. I stayed until 2005 when my work visa expired.

From Temple Terrace, I moved to Toronto where my mom's family was from. I loved living there. Toronto was an amazingly vibrant and multicultural city. And it had seasons! I found a great basement apartment in Bloor West Village and worshipped with the West End church of Christ, which is a wonderfully diverse group of Christians. John and Michelle Maddocks, who are still working with the church there, really took me under their wings and into their family. I lived there until 2009 when Wanda called to say that Brooke Ward was expecting her first child and asked if I was interested in returning to the FC library? I was, and circumstances worked out that I was first able to get a work visa and then a green card. I have been back at Florida College since 2009 and was named library director after Wanda's retirement in 2021. I continue today to serve in that role.

Working at Florida College has been a blessing. My absolute favorite time of year is the start of school. The energy on campus is electric. Students are so excited to be back on campus or here for the first time. Once everyone gets settled in, we start the run of classes coming in for library instruction. Getting to help students solve problems is the part I enjoy the most. My goal is for every student to leave with resources they can use for upcoming assignments, but also for them to be better equipped to find answers to whatever challenges them in the future.

The library underwent a major renovation a couple of years ago. We went back to the drawing board to learn how best to meet the needs of our 21st century users. We now provide greater technological access to information, host the Bowman Media Center, serve as a popular social hub, and have beautiful and comfortable quiet spaces for individual and group study. All of this and The Coffey House, too! The updates increased our usage and foot traffic significantly. It is a whole new world in the Chatlos library these days, and I am excited to see what comes next!

If you had to place your children for adoption, what would you wish for them as they grew? What kind of adoptive parents would you hope for? You would probably wish for two people to love your children as you would, for them to be part of a loving family, to have a happy home, to have opportunities that you would not be able to provide. No matter how beautiful the life we would wish for our children, it cannot compare with what God has in store for those who accept His gracious welcome into His household.

ADOPTION DEFINED

Adoption is defined by the Cambridge English Dictionary as "the act of taking another person's child legally into your family to raise as your own child."[1] Random House further explains it as "the act or process of establishing a legal relationship between a child and a parent other than the child's biological parent, thereby entrusting the designated adult with responsibility for raising the child."[2]

The word "adoption" does not occur in the Old Testament, and it was not a common practice among the Israelites.[3] The process does occur in other cultures, as in the case of

---

1 Cambridge English Dictionary, s.v. "Adoption (noun)," accessed July 27, 2024, https://dictionary.cambridge.org/us/dictionary/english/adoption

2 Random House Unabridged Dictionary, s.v. "Adoption (noun)," accessed July 27, 2024, https://www.dictionary.com/browse/adoption

3 Ronald Youngblood, ed. Nelson's New Illustrated Bible Dictionary "Adoption" (Nashville: Nelson, 1995, 23.

Moses being adopted by Pharaoh's daughter, which is explained in Exodus 2:10 as "and he became her son" (CSB). It is also likely that a Pharaoh in the days of Solomon also adopted a son named Genubath and raised him as part of the ruling family (1 Kin 11:20).

Though the practice was not common, the Old Testament does provide a few beautiful snapshots of adoption among His people. The relationships between Eli and Samuel (1 Sam 1-3), David and Mephibosheth (2 Sam 9), and Mordecai and Esther (Est 2:7) illustrate familial bonding formed under special circumstances. From the beginning God describes His people as specially His, as He draws them from out other nations and calls Himself their Father (Gen 12:1-2; Exo 4:22-23; Deu 7:6-9). God describes Israel as a foundling, lovingly rescued and raised as His own (Eze 16). Throughout the Bible, God's commandments that orphans be treated with compassion highlight for us His tender grace and abiding love for the vulnerable and lonely (Deu 10:18; Psa 10:14, 17-18; James 1:27).

Adoption in Christian theology, according to Nelson's New Illustrated Bible Dictionary, is "the act of God's grace by which sinful people are brought into His redeemed family. In the New Testament, the Greek word translated adoption literally means 'placing as a son.'"[4] During the first century, Romans practiced adoption, and their customs strongly influenced Jewish family life. A Roman adopted child was endowed with the same status and privileges as a natural descendant.[5] According to Ronald Youngblood, "In the eyes of the law, the adopted one became a new creature; he was regarded as being born again into the new family—an illustration of what happens to the believer at conversion."[6] Paul was known to incorporate modern day practices that people understood into his teaching. The word "adoption" appears only five times in the New Testament, and Paul is the only writer of the scriptures who mentions it.

BLESSINGS IN SPIRITUAL ADOPTION

In Galatians 4:4-5, Paul tells us that at just the right time, God sent His Son to redeem those under the law so that they could be adopted as sons. In Ephesians 1:5, the apostle tells his readers that God planned for us to be adopted as His sons for Himself through Jesus, and it pleased Him to do so.

---

4 Youngblood, "Adoption," 23.

5 Youngblood, "Adoption," 23.

6 Youngblood, "Adoption," 23.

Romans 8:14-15 explains that "all those led by God's Spirit are God's sons. For you did not receive a spirit of slavery to fall back into fear. Instead, you received the Spirit of adoption, by whom we cry out, 'Abba, Father!'" (CSB).[7] Paul uses the phrase "the Spirit of adoption" as an analogy for God's covenant people. When we take on Christ's name, we become more than His children. Romans 8:17 tells us we become God's children and therefore His heirs.

Romans 8:18-23 speaks of the transformation from groans to glory. It describes what God is doing for His people, for us as Christians. Paul remarks that the present groanings cannot compare with the glory that will be revealed to us, that even creation eagerly waits, anticipating the revelation of who the sons of God will be, as we await our adoption and redemption. And whether we are male or female, we will be treated as the firstfruits/sons, granted all the blessings and privileges entailed with the promise.

Romans 9:1-4, the fifth passage in which Paul mentions adoption, explains how full of sorrow Paul was that his fellow Jews were rejecting their place in God's family, for God meant for adoption to belong to all the Israelites along with "the glory, the covenants, the giving of the law, the temple service, and the promises" (Rom 9:4, CSB). God was not exclusive though. From the promises to Abraham, we see that He meant from the beginning to extend His family to all nations.

The scriptures teach that God wants us to be His children, that He planned for this from the beginning, that it pleases Him to adopt us, and that we are blessed with an inheritance like no other. In his first epistle, John beautifully expresses God's love for us and His desire for us to be part of His family: "See what great love the Father has given to us that we should be called God's children; and we are!" (3:1, CSB)

This verse always reminds me of one of my favorite hymns, "How Deep the Father's Love", which talks about the immense love God has for us to have given His only son to die on the cross to redeem us from our sins.

How deep the Father's love for us,
How vast beyond all measure,
That He should give His only Son
To make a wretch His treasure.
How great the pain of searing loss:

---

7 Scripture quotations marked CSB have been taken from the Christian Standard Bible, copyright 2017 by Holman Bible Publishers.

The Father turns His face away,
As wounds which mar the Chosen One
Bring many sons to glory.[8]

The hymn writer's scriptural reference to the bringing of many sons (and daughters) to glory (Heb 2:10 CSB) is a beautiful image. Let us praise God for His marvelous plan that not only allows us to call Him Father but gives us such a big family in which to enjoy His love.

Adopting a child means that child is forever a part of your family. Legally, you are that boy or girl's parent. My birth certificate lists Ben and Joyce Kearney as my parents. I am their child as surely as if we shared the same blood. It is not temporary or reversible. It is not a covenant to be entered into lightly or thoughtlessly. For most adoptive parents of faith, it is preceded by much longing and prayer, and it is ratified in pure joy.

Paul the apostle tells us that once we are adopted into God's family, nothing can keep us from His love, not death, life, angels, rulers, present or future things, powers, height, depth, or anything created—nothing can separate us from God's love that we have through Jesus (Rom 8:38-39). The Psalmist further explains how special our relationship is: "As a father has compassion on his children, so the Lord shows compassion to those who fear him" (Psa 103:13, CSB).

In the imperfect, sinful world we inhabit, adoption most often comes about through troubles. Potential parents often suffer infertility, and children are not able to be cared for, unwanted, orphaned, abandoned, neglected, or abused. In the best of circumstances, a biological mother gut-wrenchingly gives up her child in hopes of a better life for her offspring. These difficult circumstances can mirror the state we were in before we were rescued to serve the Lord.

ADOPTED BY GOD OUR FATHER

As adopted children, we have the blessing of a relationship with God our Father. This is a unique feature of Christianity. In Galatians 3, Paul writes that we are sons of God under this new covenant: "So then, the law was our guardian until Christ came, in order that we might be justified by faith. But now that faith has come, we are no longer under a guardian, for in Christ Jesus you are all sons of God, through faith" (Gal 3:24-26, CSB). Like

---

8 Stuart Townend. "How Deep the Father's Love." Thank You Music (admin. By EMI Christian Music Publishing) in Brentwood, TN, 1995.

children who go from desperate circumstances to a good home, for Christians, adoption is an amazing gift. We are placed into God's family, given a spiritual inheritance, and granted the hope of a perfect home in heaven.

FULFILLMENT

My mother is often uncomfortable when people talk as though she has done a noble thing by adopting. To her, at the time, it was not an altruistic action – she wanted a baby, and this was the way she and my dad could grow their family. There absolutely is an element of altruism to adoption, but it also involves desire on the part of the adoptive parents to make this child family.

This brings us full circle. God planned for us to be with Him (Eph 1:11). He truly wants us to be with Him. Peter reminds us: "The Lord does not delay His promise, as some understand delay, but is patient toward you, not wanting any to perish but all to come to repentance" (2 Pet 3:9, CSB). And for all those He adopts, He showers us with His blessings and guidance.

SENSE OF BELONGING

As children of God, we become members of His family. 1 Timothy 5:1-2 exhorts us to relate to one another as family, with respect for elders and care for younger members, reflecting the unity and care inherent in God's household. Recently I was talking with a friend who observed that even when our earthly families let us down or are not what they should be, because we are of the family of God, we have godly fathers and mothers, sisters and brothers all around us. David the psalmist expresses a similar thought when he writes, "Even if my father and mother abandon me, the Lord cares for me" (Psa 27:10, CSB), and again, "God sets the lonely in families" (Psa 68:6, NIV).

Jesus expands the concept of family when He turns from His earthly family and points to His disciples: "Here are my mother and brothers. For whoever does the will of my Father in heaven is my brother and sister and mother" (Mat 12:46-50). Knowing He is about to leave His disciples and go to the cross, Jesus reassures them that their status as His beloved family will not end but instead become even greater: "I will not leave you as orphans; I am coming to you...Because I live, you will live too. On that day you will know that I am in my Father, you are in me, and I am in you…And the one who loves me will be loved by my Father. I will also love him and will reveal myself to him" (Joh 14:18-21, CSB).

When the church truly is a family, we will fill those roles for those around us. Jesus says in Mark 10:29-31 that those who leave family for His sake will gain them one hundred times more—houses, brothers and sisters, mothers and children with persecutions—but in the end they will receive eternal life. Our Savior and elder brother, the same loving Teacher who welcomed little children and urged His disciples to do the same, has a heart infinitely open, ever enfolding newcomers into His spiritual family. We belong!

COMMUNICATION

We are given the privilege of communicating with God through prayer. In the Old Testament, God spoke to His people through prophets and priests. We, under the law of Christ, have the opportunity to bring our cares directly to our Father who is eager to hear them. Philippians tells us that instead of worrying, we should bring our concerns to God: "Do not be anxious about anything, but in everything by prayer and supplication with thanksgiving let your requests be made known to God" (4:6 CSB).

DISCIPLINE

As children, we are disciplined by our parents. It is not pleasant for anyone involved, but it is important. How else do children learn how they should act, and what they should or should not do? Just as our parents disciplined us, so God also disciplines His children. Hebrews 12:6 tells us that "the Lord disciplines the one He loves and punishes every son He receives" (CSB). He does this for our benefit.

IMITATION

In addition to learning from discipline, children learn by imitating those around them, particularly their parents. People are often taken aback to learn that I am adopted. They will tell me that I look just like my mother. We do not actually look much alike. What we do share is a similarity in personality and temperament. That resemblance in character encourages people to see a physical resemblance in us that does not really exist.

Further, Paul tells us to "be imitators of God as dearly loved children" (Eph 5:1, CSB). He is our perfect example. Paul reminds the Corinthian brethren to imitate him as he imitated Christ (1 Cor 4:16; 11:1). The apostle also told the Thessalonian brethren that they, in turn, served as an example for all who knew them: "And you yourselves became imitators of us and of the Lord when, in spite of severe persecution, you welcomed the message with joy from the Holy Spirit. As a result, you became an example to all the believers in Macedonia and Achaia" (1 The 1:6-7, CSB). As we strive to be more like Christ, we are an example to all those around us as lights to the world (Mat 5:16), shining like stars in the darkness (Phi 2:14-15).

GIVEN A SPIRITUAL INHERITANCE

I was fortunate to be adopted into a family that had a deep faith in God. My desire to follow Christ was passed on from my parents. My interest in spiritual things came from watching and seeing that He was the center of their life.

Physical adoption is a blessing for both the adoptee and the adoptive family. Adoption into the family of God is an even greater blessing for those of us who choose to follow Jesus. Generally, inheritances pass from parents to children. When we accept Christ in baptism, we are promised an inheritance that can never fade and that is reserved in heaven for us (I Pet 1:4). Our ultimate reward is not from earthly things. The Hebrew writer tells us, "For we do not have an enduring city here, instead we seek the one to come" (Heb 13:14, CSB). Our inheritance is eternal (Col 3:23-24). The hope of heaven is meant to strengthen, encourage, and fill us with wondrous joy. It is not wishful thinking! Rather, as soon as we are adopted into Christ's family, we can be certain that heaven is our ultimate destination (Joh 3:17). In fact, we do not even need to wait for our blessings. Ephesians 1:3 is phrased in the past tense: "Blessed is the God and Father of our Lord Jesus Christ, who has blessed us with every spiritual blessing in the heavens in Christ" (CSB).

THOUGHT QUESTIONS FOR "THE AMAZING GIFT OF ADOPTION"

1. What blessing of spiritual adoption resonates most strongly with you? Why?

2. We touched on a few aspects of adoption into the family of God. What are some other aspects of physical adoption that might have a spiritual equivalent?

3. What are some examples of adoption in the Bible? What similarities or differences do you see between them and our adoption as children of God?

4. What are the practical implications for knowing that you are a joint-heir with Christ?

5. How might you do your work today differently if you were doing it for the praise of God's glory?

6. How does hope in our eternal destiny shape the way we live our everyday lives?

FEARFULLY AND WONDERFULLY MADE

Jessica Miles, PhD

For it was you who created my inward parts;
you knit me together in my mother's womb.
I will praise you because
I have been remarkably and wondrously made.
Your works are wondrous,
and I know this very well.
Psalm 139:13-14

Every one of us is "broken" in some way or another – physically, mentally, emotionally... and all of us spiritually until we choose to put on Christ. And then, we are still broken but broken with the promise of grace and forgiveness and the hope of eternal life in heaven with those who have gone on before us. However, God does not see the "broken" in us but instead sees our potential. After all, He knows what was, what is, and what is to come. We are fearfully and wonderfully made, no matter what we may think of ourselves or others' opinions of us. I am no different than any other but unique in every way. He knit me together, just as He did you, giving us promises of heaven one day. Born the second of three girls to two first-generation Christians, I consider my life to be nothing but blessed. Perfect? None of our lives are. But it has been more than I could ever want or need. Hopefully, this brief story of who I am and where I come from will inspire you to see how God's unseen hand has been at work.

My story starts long before I was born. It does not begin with a long line of Christians whose faith grew stronger as the generations passed. Instead, my parents were two first-generation Christians striving to do what they believed the Lord desired of them. My daddy, Robert J. Dysart, Jr, entered the Air Force, following in his father's footsteps. Little did he know that his decision to serve his country would eternally change more than just his physical life on earth.

The Air Force stationed him in Torrejón, Spain. While in the forces, he met a fellow airman named Barry Ford, who happened to be a Christian. Barry planted and watered, and God gave the increase. God's hand was at work far before I was even thought of. I'm not sure how many conversion stories Barry had while in the Air Force, but I am eternally grateful that my dad was one.

As most men do, Dad kept his eyes open for opportunities to date, even while abroad. He landed a date with the friend of a fellow airman's girlfriend, excited to go on a date with a pretty Spanish woman. The lovely Spanish woman backed out the day before the date, but Wayne had another friend. Panic set in for my dad because he realized he would be going on a blind date with a woman from another country whose language he did not know. Dread set in, but he was committed. It was only one night, and he could make it through it.

As the story goes, he met the most beautiful woman he had ever laid eyes on, Maria Martin Sanchez. When she walked in, his jaw hit the floor, and he figured there was no way this woman didn't have a husband or boyfriend. His life changed forever as they overcame language barriers and the odds set against them. About a year and a half later, they would be married. At some point during this time, my dad decided he was not going to stay in the military, a decision he discussed with his brother in Christ, Barry; having concern for the soul and eternity of this young Christian and his bride, Barry pointed my dad toward a small Christian college named Florida College. While he had never heard of the school nor the city it was in, he was bound and determined to grow in his faith, ultimately setting this young couple's compass in that direction. That is how the Dysarts landed in Temple Terrace, Florida, within the Florida College community and amongst more brothers and sisters they ever knew existed. Time and chance happen to us all, but I firmly believe God's hand was in this beginning.

Mom and Dad quickly settled in, joining themselves to the saints at Fletcher Avenue church of Christ, befriending other young couples who were in a similar phase of their lives. Lil and Bruce Ansley "adopted" my mother, as they said it just wasn't proper for a young girl like this not to have a mother in her life (my mom's mom passed when she was just a toddler). Nana and Papa, as we would later go on to call them, had an immense impact on our lives and the faith of my parents. As they grew in their faith, Brother H.E. Phillips baptized my mom into Christ in 1979 while she was pregnant with my older sister, Sara. A few short years later, on July 2, 1983, I was born into this world, a blonde-haired, brown-eyed girl born to a family full of black-haired family members (my sister would go on to tease me and tell me I was adopted). When my younger sister Amanda came along in 1988, her hair would be light as well (though not as light as mine), and we would band together in the knowledge that we were, indeed, the biological children of Rob and Maria Dysart.

Those brown eyes would help to instill in me more passion and fire than anyone ever knew, as those brown eyes were no normal brown eyes. At about three months of age, my parents noticed something was not quite right with my vision, so they brought it to the attention of my pediatrician. After many doctors' visits and tests later, they discovered that my retinas never fully developed, diagnosed as idiopathic foveal hypoplasia, and I lacked some rods and cones. In short, it was a birth "defect." Inevitably, this would impact my entire life, but no one knew how much since the condition was exceedingly rare. None of my ophthalmologist's other patients had this condition.

I was too young to know faith or fear, but there was no doubt my parents experienced both, along with a whole slew of additional emotions, during the early phases of the diagnosis. My parents did all they possibly could for me to take the appropriate steps, giving me the care and support I needed along the way. One thing I do know, I was never treated any differently than either of my sisters. My parents loved us all equally and strove to raise us in the nurture and admonition of the Lord. Life, as I knew it, was wonderful. We went on adventures together to Lettuce Lake Park (often bike rides with the Cunningham family), Lowery Park Zoo, the Hillsborough County Library, and much more. Although the Dysart family lived paycheck to paycheck, this was never evident to my sisters or me. My parents emphasized the Lord, our family, and love. We had each other, and we loved each other. Sundays and Wednesday evenings found us at the Fletcher Avenue church building, hopefully getting orange Tic-Tacs from the "tic-tac lady," sister Elsie Taylor, or some chewing gum from the "gum man," brother Verbal Flatt.

My older sister Sara attended Florida College Academy until it came time for me to go to school, and that was no longer within the budget. That was just the same for me, as I knew no different. So, off my sister and I went to Temple Terrace Elementary, the home of the Dolphins ("...to you we will ere be true, the home of the white and blue!"). Enter once more, those brown eyes. It was here that I first remember knowing that my eyes were different than others. I could not see the board, and I hated that, but there was an "easy" fix. My teachers allowed me to move to the floor, but this made me feel different from my friends, and I didn't like it. My "vision teacher" would come to the school and pull me out of class to work with me, which also made me feel different. I didn't like it.

There were trying times through elementary and middle school. I received much mocking. I'd be called "wiggle eyes" (my condition came along with nystagmus, an oscillation of the eyes that thankfully slowed with time). "Can you please stop doing that with your eyes? You're giving me a headache," or others would mock me by repeating my response, "I can't help it, I was born this way." You name it, and I probably heard it. "Sticks and stones can break my bones, but words can never hurt me." That adage took me a while to embrace, but I eventually did. I don't recall my condition defining me but rather refining me. My mom recounts how she would walk by my room and find me playing, almost always to hear me singing and happy, playing alone or with my sisters. I loved playing outside with my sisters and friends, climbing trees, swinging, catching crickets, digging holes, and finding a bull's horns buried in the yard (which was just a pipe branching off in two directions). I lived a pretty standard "kid life." I was blessed and content with my lot in life. God had been good to the Dysart family!

As I mentioned earlier, I knew nothing other than love and support, not only from my parents alone but also from my Christian family and friends. These were friends I would have for life. Anna Cunningham, Lydia Dickey, and I were thick as thieves. When you're a child, you don't think much beyond the day you're living in. Life is what it is — until your dad receives an excellent job opportunity in Atlanta, a world away from everything I knew. I know now that my parents prayed a lot, no doubt shed some tears, and made a tough decision to leave all we knew for a better life. In June 1992, I bade my friends farewell at the skating rink during the best early birthday party I could ever imagine — except for the leaving part.

We moved to Snellville, Georgia, enrolled in some of the best schools in the state, and quickly found our place. Our house was two stories, had four bedrooms and two and a half bathrooms, and we each had our own bedroom. This move wasn't so bad after all. I didn't take much notice of it right away, but somehow, there was not a church of Christ on every corner. My parents decided we would worship with the saints at the Lawrenceville church of Christ, got to work, and settled in. We quickly bought winter coats once the daily temps dropped below 60 degrees, but only after the leaves turned brilliant colors, which didn't happen in Tampa, FL! We even had a blizzard our first year in Georgia — the Blizzard of '93.

As I grew older, the nystagmus slowed down, making the issue less physically evident to others. I played soccer and ran track and field—the 400m, 800m, long jump, high jump, shot put, and hurdles. That probably doesn't seem like a feat to most, but it sure did surprise my doctor. He didn't think my depth perception would allow such activities. He was sure I would never drive either.

Despite what he thought, I wanted to try to get my learner's license. I'll never forget that day. I was very nervous. The line was long, and the anticipation and anxiety mounted as I waited to see the viewer and see what I could or couldn't see. Although, as I waited, I noted that I heard the same two strings of numbers over and over again, and again, and again. Surely they changed the string of numbers in the viewer, right? My turn came, and I got on my tip-toes (have I mentioned I am five foot nothing). It was a no-go. I couldn't even pretend to see those numbers. "No, ma'am, I can't see those." Then 20/40. I could see that these were one of the strings of numbers! I "saw" those numbers and got my learner's permit. I would always be in the car with my dad. Long story short, I didn't get enough practice before that expired, and I had to renew it. We went to the Kroger DMV kiosk, and there was no one in line, but there was NO WAY I could see those numbers. My dreams of driving came to a screeching halt. I was deflated.

Despite the setback, these eyes of mine, with the help of my parents, sisters, and best friends, instilled in me a strong will. As far as I was concerned, nothing was going to stop me (except things like driving laws and the like), except maybe myself. I determined I was going to have a career in healthcare. In what capacity, I wasn't sure, but it would happen.

Despite moving myself to the floor to see the board, high school was easy, at least the schoolwork part. The social part of it was a little tougher. I didn't have a hard time making friends, as I had friends in many different circles and grades, but this was the first time since elementary school that I found myself at the same school as my older sister, Sara. This would be great, except for that part where I quickly found myself in my older sister's shadow – not by her choosing, but by chance. She had already been at South Gwinnett High School for three years. She excelled in every aspect of her life – soccer, social life, good looks – you name it, she had it (and still does!). I felt I'd always be in those shadows. I let this newfound shadow life define me – I let a negative self-image settle in to no one's fault but my own. It took residence there, deep within me. I had determined that I would never step out from the shadows where Sara excelled, so I dug into something I knew no one could take away from me – my smarts, grades, and GPA. That's where I dug in. I was the nerdy sister, and that was okay with me.

In my senior year of high school, I applied to the University of Georgia (UGA) and anxiously awaited the news as to whether or not I would be a Georgia Bulldog come Fall 2001. I was ecstatic when I got that "big packet" in the mail because everyone knew the small one would be a rejection letter. I was so excited to be a bulldog and to, once more, join my sister for one more year of school, college at that. I was set and ready to go until FC North Carolina Camp in the summer following my senior year. I remember the feeling of FC camp, being surrounded by nothing but Christians as far as the eye could see. To be among "my people" after being "in the world" all year. I considered FC following camp and mulled it around in my head. Ultimately, I had determined my major would be Athletic Training (AT) at UGA – combining my love for medicine and healthcare with my passion for the athletic environment and population. When my (sister's) car drove east on Highway 78 that fall, I took my spot in Brumby Hall with my potluck roommate. I did think of how things would be different at FC, but through life, I learned to bloom where I was planted, so that is what I did. I strove to live in the present and future and not in the past.

It was a good fit for me. I loved the big college traditions and the palpable feel of the first home football game of the year. Having my big sister on campus with me was irreplaceable – we grew closer then than we had ever been before. She was my rock. My choice of major was just right for me, and I met people who would leave a mark on my life forever. I even was able to get a second degree in Spanish. Spanish always came naturally to me (as if it were in my blood). There were two in particular I can think of who changed my life forever and for entirely different reasons. Jesse Prahl, a student one year ahead of me in the AT program, took a particular interest in my vision problem, as her mom was an Occupational Therapist (OT) who worked in the Center for Low Vision in Atlanta. That connection ultimately afforded me the ability to drive! I had to use bioptic lenses, mind you, but I had learned, at that point in life, to embrace my "defect" and allow it to help me instead of hinder me. I didn't care what I looked like; I was behind the wheel and no longer had to count on someone else to take me from point A to point B. I never thought I'd be driving; this was a true Godsend.

The other to whom I owe most of who I am professionally in my early years and who I have become today is Dr. Michael Ferrara, the Program Director of the Athletic Training Program at UGA. I was so excited the day Dr. Ferrara was set to come and speak about Athletic Training in my Introduction to Exercise Science class. At some point during his lecture, I determined to go up, shake his hand, and introduce myself at the end of the lecture. I learned that if you want something badly enough, you've got to work hard to get it, and I was going to be sure that when it came time for the AT faculty to select the students for my year's cohort, he would remember me. He was kind and always wore a welcoming grin with a trademark mustache. He instantly became my biggest cheerleader. When it was time to select the 2005 cohort, I was accepted! Thus began my journey into understanding how the body functioned and malfunctioned, what it did to fix itself, and how I, as a healthcare practitioner, could support healing along the way.

It was also the beginning of me realizing that my dad had some competition as my biggest cheerleader. I learned that Dr. Mike Ferrara saw far more in me than I had ever seen. He saw potential, and he was going to be the one to help me realize it, to help me see that the AT world was my oyster, and all I had to do was unlock it. He arranged an opportunity for me to translate for the Spanish delegates in the role delineation study for Athletic Training in Chicago – all expenses paid and the opportunity of a lifetime none of my peers had. He introduced me to others in the AT profession, stateside and abroad, who would be my resources for years. But, most of all, he brought life into perspective for me. One of the first times I found myself in his office crying over something that seemed like a mountain, but was certainly a molehill because I don't remember what it was now, he looked me straight in the eyes and said, "Jessica, is it going to matter when you're 60?" Through sniffles, I responded, "No." Well, then, it wasn't a big deal. That reality changed my perspective, even if I probably didn't fully embrace it until after I graduated from undergrad.

Before I graduated, Dr. Ferrara and I sat down and mapped out my 20-year plan. Master's degree at a well-known Research 1 (R1) Institution, paid for by a Graduate Assistantship because, as Dr. Ferrara said, "If you play your cards right, you should never have to pay for college" (he was right…as always). I was then to get my doctorate at the University of Georgia (I wanted to stay there for my Masters, but he wouldn't let me, saying I needed to go out, meet new people, learn new things, and then return). Once I graduated, I was to get a job at an R1 Institution, serving as a faculty member for a couple of years, rolling into the Coordinator of Clinical Education role, and finally landing the role as the Program Director within those 20 years. At the end of 20 years, the plan involved me becoming the president of the World Federation of Athletic Training and Therapy.

I haven't mentioned my faith much thus far, but my faith was strong throughout my time as an undergraduate student. Being so close to home and with many chauffeurs to carry me there, I often returned home on the weekends. Still, when in Athens, I worshiped with the saints at the Oglethorpe Avenue church of Christ in Athens, Georgia, a group who loved on their college students and supported them as best they could, though we were few throughout my entire undergrad career. Going to a big state school afforded me so much, but it did not grant me what many of my friends who went to FC had—friendships built on faith and Christ that would last a lifetime. I didn't miss this because I didn't know anything different, but sometimes it takes hindsight to see the things that weren't seen before at an unforeseen time in the future.

My husband, the love of my life, Patrick, always says he thinks God has a sense of humor. When I made that 20-year plan with Dr. Ferrara all those many years ago, I am convinced God smiled down on me from heaven and chuckled. Even more than Dr. Ferrara, God was, is, and always will be right. Within months of graduating, my plan derailed when I didn't get into my first choice of graduate school, the University of North Carolina Chapel Hill. I was heartbroken. I did not know what I was going to do. I of course applied elsewhere. I wasn't going to let this stop me. I applied to the University of Connecticut in Storrs,

CT. My dad went there with me for the interview so we could explore the area after the two-day interview. What started with lost luggage and a foot of snow, along with a great interview in the middle, ended with my dad handing me an ice scraper before we went exploring, saying, "Here, you should get used to this." A 90-minute drive to the nearest church family who only met once on Sunday showed me the true meaning of "Money can't buy you happiness." It was the greatest assistantship there probably was out there – full tuition, book waiver, partial medical, partial dental, partial vision, and a world-renowned heat expert, in exchange for working as an AT for a private school in the area. Who could ask for anything more? My faith was the trump card, as it had always been in my life, but the rubber of faith met the road of life with this one. The thought of being about 1,000 miles from my earthly family and more than ninety minutes from my church family told me that no matter how good this package was by man's standards, it didn't measure up spiritually. So, I turned them down this time and headed back to the drawing board, which was the career center website.

Purdue was another great option. I took a trip up for an interview and another visit to one of the local congregations. I also met some AT acquaintances I had met along the way, and I had the promise of something great. I was hopeful. However, in the end, I received an offer, but I still needed to find a better fit. Three big, R1 institutions – part of my 20-year plan – and three strikes. It sure did leave me feeling left out in the cold. Nonetheless, I was determined to stay the course, so I continued to watch the job boards on the National Athletic Trainers' Association website.

Samford University, a small Baptist school, was looking for four graduate assistants, and although I had never heard of it, it was close in Birmingham, AL. It sounded promising, and I thought, "Let's give it a shot." Away went my application materials, on which I mistakenly put Stanford instead of Samford, and they still returned an offer for an interview. Right away, I knew this was where I was meant to be. Mr. Wayne Kendrick, the head AT, was an upstanding Christian who embodied a servant's heart. Michelle Johnson was a young AT eager to teach and welcome us in, and Brandon and Matt were pretty decent, too. I was offered a graduate assistantship position at Samford University – far from R1, but right where I belonged.

When I told my cousin I would go to school in Birmingham, he told me, "You do know the birds fly upside down there, right?" I said not to worry since I'd be coming back after two years. I was wrong again! I lived in Homewood, AL, and worshiped with the Vestavia church of Christ, where I met a young man named Patrick Miles, who was about to graduate from UAB and had a job lined up. We made small talk each service and eventually started "hanging out." I recall telling my sister he was very attractive and fun to hang out with, but I couldn't see us dating. Fast forward eighteen years, and we will have been married for more than fourteen years. I was wrong again, but I'm more than okay with that misjudgment.

My two years in Alabama grew into four years in Alabama when the grant that was supposed to fund me for my doctoral studies fell through at the end of June. I was to start my position in the first week of July. My plan was slowly falling apart, but I came to find out that I couldn't have planned it better. I was able to line up a couple of different jobs, ultimately landing at UAB Sports Medicine, working in the orthopedic clinic during the day, and with Homewood High School athletics in the afternoons. I always said I would never work high school, but I was wrong again! That setting was my favorite, yet I only worked in that setting because my plans had fallen through. At the end of two years working with UAB and HHS, Patrick and I got married, returned from our honeymoon on a Monday, and loaded up and headed to Athens, Georgia, for our new life together that Friday. We were acting with immense faith for such a young married couple. We would be living on my grad assistant salary until Patrick found a job while finishing his master's degree in Education. Within a month of moving, God blessed him with an awesome opportunity.

We grew together as a married couple and in our faith. He finished his master's degree, and just before my third year in my doc program, I found out I was pregnant with our oldest, Ansley. Well, that wasn't part of our plan, but it must have been in His plan, and we couldn't have been happier. I loved being pregnant and was progressing in my degree – even being pregnant, I should have been able to finish up my degree in three years. With a post-partum bleed that went completely bad, a condition that "could go either way," a waiting room filled with the members of the Oglethorpe church at midnight, there to support my Patrick with prayer and hugs (along with our families), prayers offered on our behalf from all across the country and the world (there is SOME good in social media), and that strong will to live to see another day, I made it through what only a small percentage of the population with that condition makes it through. I have known the power of prayer in my life, but it wasn't until then that I truly knew the power of prayer. He brought me through something that, by medical standards, I should not have made it through. He gave me a new lease on life. He allowed us to be a family. This instilled in me a greater faith than ever I had before. He had plans for me that I didn't know. Finishing in three years was out of the question. I didn't have the energy, so we adapted.

It became evident that the salaries of a graduate assistant and paraprofessional would stretch it for a newborn and thousands of dollars of medical bills, so we began hunting for "grown-up" jobs. Eventually, a position opened at the University of North Georgia (UNG) in Dahlonega, Georgia, but this would mean leaving a church family we had grown to love, and a group we knew would be there for us. Ultimately, I accepted the position as Program Director for the Athletic Training Program at UNG, and Patrick would work with the history department at Lumpkin County High School.

In my first meeting with the Dean of the College of Education, he told me I had three years to turn this program around, and if I didn't, it was gone. Well, that was news to me. The Dean hired me to be a change agent for a longstanding program filled with alums as preceptors and adjunct faculty. I was in for a trip I never anticipated. As a rule, I had always been a level-headed, likable person. In this job, I learned that change agents are not well-liked people. It is baptism by fire. I was dealing with an "agitated hornet's nest," as one of my colleagues called it, which was not me at all. I remembered Dr. Ferrara's words, "Jess, you're just going to have to get some thicker skin." My skin was not thick. My sleep was not good. My nerves were on end. My prayer life got better. My relationship with my husband became stronger, and I was determined to turn that program around. Our second beautiful girl, Piper, was born in April 2015, and life was humming along. Long story short, I ended up working with UNG for eight years, my final two years serving as both the Program Director and the Department Chair – weathering COVID and coming out on the better end of it. I developed stronger grit and determination. Love and support from my physical and spiritual family, as well as a couple of very close allies at work, pushed me through.

In my eighth year at UNG, one of the members at Mountain View church of Christ asked me, on a Wednesday night, if I knew anything about Kinesiology – as I was currently serving as the Chair for the Kinesiology Department, I told her, "I do know a little bit." She told me that FC was looking to start a Kinesiology program, which I thought was a solid move. I told her I would be happy to help, to which she responded, "But you can't leave us." "Oh, don't worry. We aren't going anywhere." Famous last words. Where we were was happy and comfortable. We loved our church family – they were second to none. We were growing in our careers (Patrick was now at UNG, too, at the Gainesville campus), and I was two years shy of being vested. We were within 2.5 hours of all our extended family members – grandparents, aunts, and cousins. By human reasoning, we were right where we needed to be and would be foolish to go elsewhere. We tried to shut the door on the opportunity. I asked hard questions. I tried to put a hard stop to the process. After I shut the door, a window appeared out of nowhere and opened. I would shut it only to have another appear. You get to a point where you feel like you are closing the door in the face of God – and that's how Patrick and I felt. Maybe, just maybe, we were supposed to be at FC. The political climate in higher ed at a state school was closing in – how much longer could we hold to our faith and do our jobs well? Were we blinded by the physical? You're reading a book about FC female faculty. You know where we landed.

I thought we had made hard decisions as a married couple — until now. None of our other moves took us more than a couple of hours from our families. None of our other moves put into jeopardy the promise of a stable retirement. None of our other moves took us to a place where we actually "knew" no one (though there were still so many in Tampa from my childhood….30 years prior). Sometimes, you don't see God's hand until years pass. Other times, you see God's hand as it intricately moves in real-time. We tried to sell our house the year before to no avail. We put our house on the market after accepting the position at FC and had 17 offers by the end of the next day – all over the asking price. A member of the church was selling their home in Temple Terrace, about a mile from FC, by the same real estate agent, Rich Gant, who was helping us with our search. They graciously gave us a number to satisfy them, and we signed the papers before it hit the market. Things were in motion before we even knew there was anything to be moved.

Little did I know, we needed FC just as much as FC needed us. Do you know how hard it is to talk about the body and how it works without bringing God into the conversation? Do you know on what level you can connect with students who strive toward the same faith you do? Do you know what it's like to work with colleagues who are your brothers and sisters in Christ? I had some amazing students at Samford, UGA, and UNG…some who were looking for a spiritual compass, and I filled that role for them – students who caught my reference to scripture in the classroom without directly referencing scripture. If they opened a spiritual door, I walked through it with them. Leaving them was so hard. My students at FC still need a spiritual compass but in a different way. I had some amazing colleagues at UNG with whom I built strong friendships; leaving them was heartbreaking, but building relationships with colleagues striving toward heaven with me is like nothing else.

Our very first cohort of Kinesiology students graduated this past spring (2024), and I couldn't be more righteously proud of that group of students. They are the reason we are at Florida College. We have had them in our home, laughed with them, cried with them, guided them, and celebrated their victories with them. Most importantly, we have grown in our faith together – my guidance with this group is different than any other guidance I have given in my professional life. When they come to me in my office frazzled or in tears, as I once came to my mentor, Dr. Ferrara, I offer them his advice with a twist – giving him credit for the original. I tell them what Dr. Ferrara told me, but then I ask them, "But will it matter when it comes to your citizenship in heaven?" If the answer is "no," then it isn't a big deal. I assure them that we will make it through it together. If the answer is "yes," then it's of utmost importance, and we will make it through together with prayer and a reliance on God."

At FC, we are on a journey together, the most important journey of our lives. We are all broken, looking to the Lord to put us back together. We are striving every day to be more like Christ, to realize that we are fearfully and wonderfully made. FC helps me know that I spent far too much of my life allowing what others thought of or didn't think of me, whether factual or fabricated in my mind, to define who I was instead of defining myself through the lens of a Christian woman. I desire to help some Christian young women (and young men, of course!) along their way to realize just how beautiful they are, as defined by His word and not their words.

I wouldn't be uniquely me if I were anyone other than who and how God made me. Nor would you be uniquely you. We are fearfully and wonderfully made.

KNIT TOGETHER

Having been a student of the way the body functions, malfunctions, and heals itself for about twenty-five years now, I am constantly in awe of the attention and intricate detail God took into consideration when He created humans. My students probably tire of me saying, "Can you believe God thought of THAT? Can you believe God did THAT for us?" However, the exclamations of awe are nothing short of amazing and are indeed warranted. The more I learn about the body, the more I am amazed at the complexities of it. As the topic verse says, God knit us together in our mother's womb. If you have ever knitted or watched someone knit, you know that it is no easy task. Yes, God created our bodies to operate "without thinking" when we have practiced a task repeatedly, but the act requires so much attention to detail. Every knit and purl must be completed with the utmost care – one missed stitch can cause a world of worry if unnoticed and potentially result in the project's abandonment. God gives each of us such attention to detail. At the beginning of conception, an embryo is approximately 1/100 of an inch long and full of the genetic map, resulting in the baby's delivery to her parents. In the beginning, God created man from the dust of the earth in a day, whereas today, women carry their babies nine months! Regardless of the time, the attention to detail was there. His plan was perfect when He created Adam and continues to be so now, thousands of years later.

When internal or external forces challenge those intricate systems, then what? I suppose it doesn't surprise you to learn that God has put into place so many compensatory mechanisms in our bodies to assure that they function just how they are supposed to, even in conditions outside the ordinary – I am sure you can think about times in your life where some of these compensatory mechanisms took place. Let's think about something each of us has probably experienced at some point – the "simple" act of stretching. Have you ever thought about what keeps us from overstretching and tearing the seemingly fragile fibers of the over 600 muscles in our body? Let's explore that mechanism a little bit. God created our bodies to sense things, both from within and without. We typically think of our five senses of sight, hearing, smell, taste, and touch, but we also have many receptors that aid in the proper functioning of our bodies. With everything from photoreceptors to proprioceptors and mechanoreceptors, our bodies are constantly sensing the environment and automatically responding to it – isn't that incredible?! Muscle spindles keep our muscles from overstretching and resultant injury when we stretch, whether as a warm-up or as a means to catch a flying ball or keep our little one from running into harm's way. If we are in a controlled environment and hold a stretch with some resistance, Golgi tendon organs (GTOs) overcome the muscle spindle mechanism and allow for greater stretch. And this is just one of the many simultaneous processes our bodies are carrying out every moment of every day.

Everything God put into our bodies serves a purpose – I'm sure the appendix and the palmaris longus served an important role long ago! I love that the Bible repeatedly points to God's handiwork in His creation of man and compares the physical body to the spiritual body. 1 Corinthians 12:12-27 has so much to say about the bodies – physical and spiritual. Have you ever stubbed your pinky toe? You don't realize just how important that little toe is until you hurt it – whether we think about it or not, it plays an essential part of normal gait function in our daily lives. Those pesky nose hairs? They trap pollutants, keep them from entering the body, and serve as a defense mechanism. Capillaries are the smallest part of the cardiovascular system. Here, oxygenated blood that originated in the lungs exchanges with deoxygenated blood that is then returned to the heart and lungs to pick up more oxygen. I could go on and on about the small but mighty parts of the body. Likewise, Paul affirms the same importance of each member of the body in 1 Corinthians 12 – the eye cannot do the job of the ear, nor can the foot do the job of the hand. "But in fact, God has placed the parts in the body, every one of them, just as he wanted them to be" (1 Cor 12:18 NIV) – another nod to God's great wisdom in creating us. He knew just what he was doing long before we were even created.

Further, God affirms that it isn't just the big, strong muscles or the mighty bones that garner attention and appreciation. Following the notion that one part of the body cannot claim another part unnecessary, Paul says, "On the contrary, those parts of the body that seem to be weaker are indispensable" (1 Cor 12:22 *NIV*). The other day, my 11-year-old asked me, "Momma, is the brain or the heart a more important part of the body?" That one made me stop and think – our bodies cannot function without one or the other. The heart is necessary to feed the brain oxygen, glucose, and other life means. Still, the brain gives the heart the appropriate signals and input to beat in the intricate manner it does, firing at just the right millisecond to maintain the proper functioning of the brain and the rest of the body. Breathing. Sitting. Sleeping. Digesting. Running. Talking. Thinking. So many bodily functions and constant activities we take for granted run on autopilot for the most part. The heart and the brain are integral in every aspect of our physical lives. Neither is a large organ, but both are, in Paul's words, "indispensable." While my aim in this section is not of the spiritual body of Christ, it is impossible to ignore the similarities and the intentionality God had in comparing the physical to the spiritual. Hold onto this thought for a bit later – while some are smaller than others, every part of the physical body plays a crucial part in the body's functioning, just as every one of us plays an indispensable part in the body of

Christ. He made you and me to serve an important purpose in His body, just as He made each member of our bodies integral to our daily lives.

And to think, we haven't even touched the tip of the iceberg of the greatness of God's creation of man. Volumes have been written on how the body functions, malfunctions, compensates, and more. Researchers will write many more as they make "new" discoveries about the body – new to man but long known and intentionally created by God. I can't help but recall 1 Corinthians 1:25, "For the foolishness of God is wiser than human wisdom, and the weakness of God is stronger than human strength." While researchers try to learn the "how" and "why" of the body, God knows it all, and His unseen hand is in it all. And if God entrusted us with such a truly awesome body in which we can dwell while on this earth He made for us, should we also not take care of what He so thoughtfully created for each of us?

GIRDED WITH STRENGTH

As aforementioned, the scripture has so much to say about how our bodies function and how we should take care of them. God gave us an amazing vessel in which our soul dwells – "Do you not know that your bodies are temples of the Holy Spirit, who is in you, whom you have received from God? You are not your own, you were bought at a price. Therefore honor God with your bodies" (1 Cor 6:19-20) – and we are to take care of what God has given us. Specifically, in this passage, Paul is referring to fleeing sexual immorality. However, I would venture to say that the spirit of the words includes the overall care of our bodies and how we honor Him if we don't put ourselves in the best possible shape to do so.

Currently (2024), "self-care" is a buzzword you hear in many different venues, from social to academic to medical and beyond. However unpopular opinion, self-care has the sentiment that it is more about "self" and less about others, and it is not something I care much to embrace. Yes, I recognize that this can be a tricky sentiment, as how can we give our best to others if we aren't at our best? In Philippians 2:3-5, Paul brings to light this important notion, that we are to put others first, humbling ourselves as we seek to serve one another. We also see that we are not our own, but His – furthermore, "...so in Christ we, though many, form one body, and each member belongs to the others" (Rom 12:5). Have you ever had joint pain before? Having been in Athletic Training and sports medicine for 20+ years, I've had my fair share of patients with knee pain, only to find that the origin of the pain was the ankle, hip, or maybe an ailment on the opposite limb. We cannot disassociate one part of our body from the other and expect it to function in the manner

God created it to. Just as a weak link in one part of our body affects the other links in that chain (we call this the kinetic chain), our weakness or strength in the body of Christ affects the entire body. This is true both physically and spiritually! We must be at our best to serve Christ and His body's other members. Thus, we must take care of the vessels God gave us as we move through this journey on earth.

Perhaps you are thinking of another writing of Paul's in 1 Timothy 4:8 (*NKJV*), "For bodily exercise profits a little, but godliness is profitable for all things, having promise of the life that now is and of that which is to come." The sentiment here is not that we should ignore bodily exercise but rather that it is good for us in a limited sense. Yet we know that our body is passing away and the soul is forever. Therefore, our greater focus is on spiritual things. That said, we know that exercise is important per God's word. Over hundreds of years of research, man has also discovered that physical activity (PA) is important for many aspects of our lives – both physical and mental.

Once again, many well-researched books explain the impacts of PA on health and overall quality of life, so I will highlight some "discoveries" backed by research that I find essential – discoveries that God put into motion when He created Adam from the dust of the earth. To experience substantial health benefits, the American College of Sports Medicine (ACSM) recommends adults take part in 150-300 minutes of moderate-intensity or 75-150 minutes of vigorous-intensity PA per week in addition to muscle strengthening activity 2-3 days per week.[1] However, when you dive into the benefits, you find that the effort pales in comparison to the positive results that come with the implementation of the guidelines! To name a mere few of the benefits associated with regular PA, research has found participation in regular moderate to vigorous intensity PA has an inverse relationship with all causes of mortality, stroke, many different types of cancer, cardiovascular disease, hypertension, and so much more. Taking care of the temples God gave us by incorporating PA into our lives is imperative for us to have the greatest impact possible as we tarry on this earth. It bears repeating that there is no doubt that God knew the exact impact moving our bodies would have on our physical lives. It takes man "proving" this with endless research to demonstrate what God has shown us to be true in the Bible.

Furthermore, science has "proven" time and again that PA has a meaningful impact on mental health and cognition. PA results in the release of powerful endorphins that naturally counteract stress and anxiety. PA also increases blood flow to the brain, delivering

1 Liguori, Gary. *American College of Sports Medicine,* (LWW, 2022).

increased oxygen and glucose to allow the brain to function better – the impact of PA repeatedly displays a positive effect on cognitive ability across the lifespan and among various populations. I realize that I've gone far too "nerdy" for such a setting, but I am constantly amazed by God's handiwork. I am blessed to be in an area of education where I see God's greatness daily. I cannot see into the mind of God, but I can witness the design of God, as can each one of us.

Think about PA in your own life – do you turn to exercise when the going gets tough? Have you felt the positive impact of endorphin release following PA? This was no accident. God put an intricate system within us that no scientist can duplicate. He knew what our bodies and minds would need to function at their best. Do you find yourself hitting a mental block at home, in the classroom, at work, or anywhere in between? Do you find that going for a brisk walk or taking part in a session of exercise helps to "clear the cobwebs" from your brain? There is science behind that. Ultimately, God is behind the science.

While man continues to make new "discoveries" every day about the body's response to PA, I am certain that God, when he knit us together, took into consideration every positive effect PA has on the body and the mind. If not prompted to think beyond the physical, then it is likely that most of us consider the "profits a little" comment in 1 Timothy 4 of the physical nature. Still, I hope we can also consider the mental nature of the "profit," seeing that God put it into motion. And are we surprised by this? God put us on this earth to work, glorify him, bring others to him, and be active in good works. Christianity is not passive but active. If we want to accomplish all the things God set out for us to do while on this earth, we must partake in a life of being busy and doing (Mar 6:15; Mat 6:33; Jas 1:22; Mat 5:41; 16:24; 1 Joh 3:18; Col 3:18). We can see the words of action embedded within the scriptures. Go. Do. Seek. Take up. Act. How can we expect our bodies to fulfill the commands of God if we don't take care of them? How can we expect our minds to be sharp if we don't train them, as well? We must be in the right mind and body to best serve God. We must take special care of our bodies, minds, and, most importantly, souls.

Bodily exercise is only possible with the appropriate fuel to ensure our bodies can sustain the hard work God gives us. We can take part in PA all day long, and with the proper fuel, we will excel in that PA. God provides every source of fuel we need to power us through any activity, physical or mental. Along with water, three main macronutrients fuel the processes within our body – lipids (fats), carbohydrates, and protein – and when God created the earth, He made every one of those readily available to us. There is nothing our bodies need that we cannot find in the nature God created for us. Furthermore, 27 micronutrients, vitamins, and minerals are necessary for the processes carried out within our bodies daily – we can also find all of these abundantly in nature. Different tasks within our bodies require different energy systems to function correctly – God made us that way. And He would not create us without what is necessary for us to survive and thrive. In 2 Peter 1:3, Peter tells us that God has given to us all things that pertain to life and godliness, and while we do not know exactly to what this refers, we can certainly see that He has equipped us with bodies to do His will and the means with which to fuel those bodies.

VALUED FAR ABOVE RUBIES

We have focused on God's grand design as He created us – with detail and intentionality. We have also spent some time looking at the importance of PA and the impact it has on not just our physical and mental health, but also on our ability to serve God. From our studies, it is evident that there is nothing that He didn't take into consideration when He created man. He longs for us to put the bodies He gave to us to good use — to work hard to do His will and to bring others along with us. How can we not be filled with joy and love when we think of all He has given freely to us to be successful while we are on this earth? Add in the single most extraordinary gift of sending Jesus to die the cruelest of deaths on the cross for our sins that we may be with Him and the saints who have gone on before us in heaven someday. How can we not see just how much He has given to us? How do we sometimes fail to see our worth in what He made in us?

Having worked with patients and students for over twenty years in healthcare and classroom settings, it saddens me to see the daily suffering that so many go through – much of the struggle stemming from a lack of self-worth. Please understand me — all glory is to God, and everything we have here on this earth and in the great beyond is to His credit — we are nothing without Him. However, we slight God when we don't see the worth in ourselves. Going back to the beginning of this lesson, HE created YOU. HE created ME. His handiwork is in you and me; we must give Him the credit. Society has painted the portrait of the "perfect" person, man or woman: the right physique, the perfect hair, the car, the house. Society paints and pushes their idea of perfection so we will want more. I'd venture to say that the devil often pushes us to believe that we fall short of many of the world's ideals. We begin to measure ourselves against man's standards and not against God's standards. This is especially true in females, from the very young to the advanced.

In my many years of working with college-aged young women, I am often saddened by what I hear, either in conversations with them or overheard in passing, often in public places. My mind frequently wanders to Proverbs 31:10-31 and the words of the virtuous woman or wife, depending on the version you are reading. While I know this was originally written as an acrostic and not necessarily pointing to just one woman but to the acquisition of wisdom, the words are meaningful and convicting in a deep and meaningful way.

I often think of Proverbs 31:10b, "For her worth is far above rubies" and that verse pierces me deep, as it should you. This virtuous woman is valued far above rubies. As I understand it, rubies were highly regarded in ancient times and seen as a symbol of health, wealth, and beauty. And God uses this symbolism to describe the worth of a virtuous woman. Do we give ourselves the same value assigned to the virtuous woman in Proverbs 31? You have read my narrative, and you know I have fallen short – as we all regularly fall short in different ways. When we don't value ourselves the way God values each of us, we don't give Him the glory and the credit due Him. He formed Adam from the dust of the earth. He knit each of us in our mother's womb. He equipped our bodies with all we need to live on this earth and make it to heaven. Do we sell Him short by measuring ourselves up to the standards of man rather than God?

And what about our daily walk – do we see our worth as we tread this earth daily? When we look in the mirror, do we see our every flaw, or do we see the great and beautiful person God created us to be from the inside out? In our relationships with our boyfriend or spouse, do we seek out someone who values us far above rubies, or do we allow ourselves to be devalued because we think less of ourselves than God created us to be? Every time we feed ourselves lies like, "I'm not good enough," or "I'm not pretty enough," or "I'll never measure up," or "I'm not skinny enough," or anything of that nature, it's a slap in the face of God. In a way, we are telling Him that He didn't measure up when He created us, yet we know that God makes no mistakes. And as long as we don't see the value God gave to us, neither will anyone else.

Do you notice that nowhere in Proverbs 31:10-31 (*NKJV*) does the author, inspired by God, mention in a positive light the physical attributes on which we so often harshly judge ourselves? Scripture does not say that her physical appearance is beautiful or that her body is one to be desired by man. Rather, we see that it is her actions that contribute to her being a virtuous woman: "She does him good and not evil" (v 12a) – she is kind, loving, and supportive; "and willingly she works with her hands" (v 13b) – she is busy and hardworking, seeming to not do so grudgingly; "she considers a field and she buys it; from her profits, she plants a vineyard" (v 16) – she is smart and prudent; "she girds herself with strength, and strengthens her arms" (v 17) – her hard work brings forth strength; "she extends her hand to the poor, Yes, she reaches her hands out to the needy" (v 20) – she is a servant to not only her household, but she is also philanthropic; "strength and honor are her clothing" (v 25); "she opens her mouth with wisdom, and on her tongue is the law of kindness" (v 26) – she does not litter her speech with gossip but with wisdom and goodness; and finally "Charm is deceitful and beauty is passing, But a woman who fears the Lord, she shall be praised" (v 30). The last verse mentioned is where many measure their worth when it mentions charm, beauty, and physical attributes. But this is not how God measures our worth. To whose standards do we align, those of man or of God? We all know that it is better to be worthy in God's eyes than in man's.

With which attributes do we value ourselves? We have to dig deep to answer this question truthfully. Do we believe that our true beauty comes from within, desiring that others value us according to our inner beauty? Or do we try to dress the part each day by putting on the latest fashion, exposing the best curves of our bodies, arranging our hair "just so," and putting on just the right makeup to expose our outer beauty? First Peter 3:3-4 (*NKJV*) highlights where the focus should be, "Do not let your adornment be merely outward – arranging the hair, wearing gold, or putting on fine apparel – rather let it be the hidden person of the heart, with the incorruptible beauty of a gentle and quiet spirit, which is very precious in the sight of God." I find it fascinating that the women in Bible times likely struggled with the same things we struggle with today…2000 years later! If it's in the good book, then God knew it was something we would need to hear. Our true beauty is incorruptible – we do not put it on and take it off daily, like our clothes and makeup. Rather, we should strive to put on love, as it never fails and is greater than faith and love (1 Cor 13).

Ultimately, God longs for us to see the same value in ourselves as He sees in us. He wants us not to define our worth by the physical, but by that which we plant deep within us. Paul speaks clearly of love being the greatest of all things in 1 Corinthians 13. When we put on love in all that we say and do, we put on God, for God is love (1 Joh 4:16). We can all probably think of someone we know who exudes love in all they say and do. When you think of that person, do you see their face or the love shining through? God longs for us to see the incorruptible beauty within ourselves, not the failing external beauty. We need to surround ourselves with people who can see our true inner beauty and look for the best in us. I have been blessed by many who saw my true worth, even when I did not – God has been good to me.

First and foremost, I pray that God blesses each of us with an appreciation for His marvelous handiwork in us and the beautiful person he made us, truly shining forth from the inside. And I urge you to find those who value you for who God created you to be and who you are on the inside, not for who they want you to be or solely for your physical attributes. Consider your relationships with friends and significant others – do they love you for who you are and value you far above rubies, or do they diminish your worth? Define yourself in all things good and expect others to see and respect that in you. Give God the glory and the credit He deserves by recognizing that each one of us is, indeed, fearfully and wonderfully made, and He made no mistakes on us.

TYING IT ALL TOGETHER

We are all unique, and not one of us is the same. We all have a different story and have encountered different opportunities in our lives that have defined who we are. Our stories began long before we were born. God created each one of us uniquely for our place in history. He allowed me to be born without all of my retinas, which some may see as a mistake. I see it as "time and chance" (Ecc 9:11). What could have easily held me back propelled me forward with the help of loved ones around me. What my body lacked in visual acuity, it compensated for in other ways, like exceptional balance and agility. Our bodies are fascinating, knit together by God. Research has shown us so much awesomeness of God's creation, but man still doesn't know all the greatness within each of us. As such, we should take special care of the awesome bodies God created for us – one way we can do so is with PA. Finally, we need to recognize our value in God's eyes and surround ourselves with those who see our worth, not those who will diminish it. Our stories are all written as we live each day under the sun. Ultimately, what binds us all together is a common love for our great and awesome God by whom we were fearfully and wonderfully made.

THOUGHT QUESTIONS FOR "FEARFULLY AND WONDERFULLY MADE"

1. Read 1 Corinthians 12:12-27. Think about both the physical and the spiritual body. Consider a small but mighty part of your physical body – you can think of your own experiences or look to the internet to discover something new. Think of how God intentionally placed that in our bodies with a specific purpose. Now, think of your role in the body of Christ and how you uniquely play that role. Finally, think of someone whose role is "seemingly weak, but indispensable."

2. Have you ever heard the phrase "cold hands, warm heart" before? This phrase points to our body's natural response to being cold, pulling blood supply from the extremities to the core where our vital organs are; while the hands may be cold, the heart and other organs are warm. As you go about your day, think of the many processes that take place to keep you functioning normally - you will be amazed when you slow down and pay attention!

3. Read 1 Corinthians 6:19-20 and think about your physical body and how you use it to honor God. What changes can you make in your daily life to best equip your body to honor God?

4. Take a look at the recommendations for physical activity made by the American College of Sports Medicine - do you reach those markers that help you to best serve our God? How can you increase physical activity in your life to create a healthier version of yourself?

5. Read Proverbs 31:10-31 that describes the virtuous woman. Notice her worth and that it is far above rubies. Now, consider your relationships with your significant other, friends, family, and others. Do those whom you hold dear treat you in a manner that shows they value you far above rubies? Do you value yourself, that which God carefully formed, far above rubies? Do you value you other virtuous women with such worth?

THE PLANS OF GOD

Abigail Orf

Many are the plans in the mind of a man,
but it is the purpose of the Lord that will stand.
Proverbs 19:21

If you had asked me at twenty years old where I would be at thirty, the answer would be living in Oregon, working as a nurse, and, Lord willing, married with at least one child. However, at thirty, only one of those was true. My life was almost entirely the opposite — I lived in Florida, worked as a nursing student recruiter for Florida College, and had been married for less than a month. Life is funny that way. The more we plan, the less things go according to plan. We spend our lives planning the next chapter and every move, yet we have little control. I have repeatedly seen this displayed in my life.

In 1991, I was born in Oregon. Despite moving away at six years old, it always felt like home. I had powerful relational ties with people there. I visited Oregon many times throughout my childhood and always planned to settle there when I graduated high school. We moved several times due to my dad's occupation: from Oregon to Colorado, then Indiana, followed by Texas, all in two years. Shortly after we landed in Texas, my dad was unemployed due to the company closing. For years, he hopped between jobs to provide for my mom and his four daughters, but we remained in Texas from my second-grade year through high school graduation. As we got older, my mom also held various jobs, eventually returning to nursing school and becoming a registered nurse when I was a junior in high school.

My parents came from very different homes, which shaped them into the people I knew. My dad's father passed away while my dad was a senior in high school, so after graduating and working a few different jobs to support his mom and sister, he joined the Marine Corps for four years. His lack of a college degree created some difficulty in his future job searches, but he was willing to accept work in many different areas to care for us.

My mom did not grow up attending church but was introduced to it by a friend in high school. She went to Florida College for a year and then moved to Montana, where she worked at Glacier National Park. She met my dad at a church in Kalispell, where he lived after his Marine Corps service. They were married less than a year later and had me the following year.

I had a happy childhood. I loved school and was involved in everything, from sports to student council to band. Growing up in a small town and attending a small school (K-12 were all together on one campus) was a huge blessing because it allowed me to explore many activities instead of choosing just one or two in which to participate. I was always busy with something, especially planning my ideal future. I first planned to teach elementary school. Then I wanted to attend Texas A&M to become a veterinarian and open a vet clinic with one of my best friends. Soon, that plan changed to becoming a pediatrician, and I finally landed on being a nurse. I always did well in school, and after graduating as valedictorian of my small high school class, I had many different colleges I could have chosen to attend.

Instead of remaining in Texas to attend school, I followed my childhood plan and set out on my own Oregon Trail. I attended nursing school in Oregon, one of the few plans that worked out as I intended! I did not date much throughout my high school and college years, but I prayed for the Lord to bring my future husband into my life sooner rather than later. In 2013, I thought I had found him. He had graduated from FC, completed an internship in Texas, and was starting his first full-time preaching work at the local church I was attending. I thought it so convenient that God placed my dream guy in the pulpit before me. He was a strong Christian, funny, handsome, good at interacting with everyone (even the kids!), taller than I am, his teeth were straight, and his head was the perfect size! Though it sounds silly now, I have often reflected on my dating days, shaking my head at the insignificant characteristics I included in my plan for an ideal husband. I knew this must be the man the Lord intended me to marry, and I made it clear to anyone who would listen that I loved him. I did whatever I could to try to impress him, from playing Ultimate Frisbee, studying extra hard for the Bible Jeopardy games he would host, and even being super brave at a haunted house we attended with a group of friends. Alas, my plan did not seem to be his plan, and I watched as he dated other girls and eventually married and moved away.

I was confused about why God would have placed someone who seemed perfect into my life but not allowed it to work, so I thought about God's plan for me. Maybe I was supposed to be single forever and serve Him and others in a different capacity than I could if I were married and had children. I wanted to want what God wanted for me; I wanted my plan to be His plan, but that is easier said than done. Even though I was not sure exactly what God had planned for me, I knew I wanted to be married, so I continued to search for a husband. I dated a few different people, but none of them stuck. When I was twenty-seven, I had been dating someone for around eight months but decided to end the relationship. Unfortunately, this man did not take that well. He broke into my home in the middle of the night and attacked me. By God's grace, my landlord heard the commotion and called the police. While the whole ordeal is a long story for another time, I include it not only to highlight how that experience certainly was not in my plan but also because if there is anyone out there who has gone through a similar domestic violence incident and is afraid to talk about it, I want to be a resource. I was not living a high-risk lifestyle, yet this still happened to me. If you have experienced something similar, it is not shameful or sinful, and you should feel comfortable talking about it and find support from your Christian brethren.

The incident above was not the end of the difficulty. Throughout the next few months, we went through court appearances as the justice system tried to determine the repercussions of his actions. Though my life had been negatively impacted in a significant way, and most people would not have faulted me for being angry, I found I was strangely at peace with the whole ordeal. I did not blame God for allowing it to happen, but I was confused again about how this could fit into His plan for my life. How was I going to tell people about this experience? How would I talk to others I dated about this in the future? How was it going to affect me in future relationships? There were many questions that, at the time, seemed unanswerable.

Though I had planned from a young age to live in Oregon for the rest of my life, this event caused me to rethink that decision, and then God started opening doors. At FC Oregon Camp in the summer of 2019, I learned from some campers about a woman from their congregation in Washington planning to move down to Florida to help start the nursing program at FC. This news sparked an immediate interest in me, and after getting her contact information, I reached out to her. She told me she had received my information from Buddy Payne and had planned to contact me. We continued to communicate through email over the next few months, and then, in September, I attended the Volunteer Leadership Summit event at FC. I met Dr. John Weaver, who was Academic Dean at the time and had an impromptu interview, after which he asked me if I would like to be on the committee working on getting the nursing program started and eventually plan to teach in the program. I happily agreed and began making plans to move to Florida. Initially, I planned to move down early and get a nursing job while I waited for the program to start, so I started looking into different hospitals and how to get my Florida nursing license. Then, another door opened. FC was planning to hire a nursing recruiter in the year leading up to the program's start, and I was asked to interview for the position. So, over Zoom, amid Covid, I shared coffee with the FC Admissions team in my favorite interview I have had to date. I met the girl who would become my roommate through her sister, who had been a camp friend at Oregon Camp. Everything fell into place. I often joke that even though I did not go to FC as a student, I still got my FC experience. I got to be at FC, find a fantastic roommate, create lasting friendships, attend events, and even be on a society (Go Pelicans!).

Everything looked perfect for this next chapter in my life, and I was excited and looking forward to this move to Florida. I admit some excitement was over the prospect of finding a new pool of eligible bachelors. Yet, again, the Lord seemed to have different plans. I planned everything to move in August 2020, but a few months before I moved, I received a text from a friend that was not necessarily unexpected. Still, when the texting continued over the next couple of days and turned into a phone call, I thought something might be happening. My dream guy from seven years before, who had married and moved away, found his life was also not going according to his plan. His wife had been unfaithful, and they had divorced. He was reaching out to see if I might be interested in talking and getting to know each other as potentially more than friends. I was so surprised after his phone call that I could not even really offer him a response. It was not my plan to marry someone who had been married before, yet the many reasons I had loved him from the moment I met him were still there. I prayed about it and decided to trust that the Lord would guide our paths — if His plan were for us to be together, it would happen. Since it was during Covid and he was living in Missouri, our communication was primarily virtual, with a couple of trips scattered over the next several months. After my move to Florida, we continued to date, and he was soon looking for jobs in Florida, hoping to move there. Again, life did not line up exactly like we thought it would, but an opportunity came up for him to interview at Florida College Academy (FCA), and he got the job as a middle school Bible teacher. We were engaged in May 2021 and began planning for a November wedding.

During this time, my parents were going through some struggles and ended up getting a divorce. Even though I was an adult then, it profoundly impacted me, especially as I planned my wedding. Things that should have been easy decisions became difficult, and I struggled to navigate through all the potential discomforts that would arise. The day did not look like I had planned (not only because of the family situation but also because it was not a June wedding like the song in Seven Brides for Seven Brothers), but it was beautiful, nonetheless. We had so many family members and friends who contributed to making it a memorable day, and I will forever be grateful.

After we had been married for about a year, we decided we were ready to grow our little family. I have wanted to be a mom for as long as I can remember, so I was ecstatic when I found out I was pregnant. I planned this intricate scavenger hunt to tell Brian I was pregnant. We shared our joy with both our families on Thanksgiving Day, and the following day, I miscarried. This was not my plan. I was devastated. How could something I was so excited about be gone in just a moment, something I had looked forward to for what seemed like forever? I did not know how my heart could take something like this happening again, so when I found out I was pregnant again a few months later, I was cautiously happy.

The whole process of pregnancy, birth, recovery, and parenting reminded me again of the futility of planning. Around twenty weeks into this pregnancy, the doctor let us know there was a chance our baby would have spina bifida, that the hole in his heart that all babies have was more significant than it should be and would potentially need surgical correction after birth. There was also an increased risk of stillbirth. We had to go in for more detailed ultrasounds and scans throughout the pregnancy and ended up scheduling an induction shortly before the baby's due date. Thankfully, he was born healthy after a relatively uncomplicated labor and delivery. He does still have a small hole in his heart, but it is one doctors think will resolve on its own over time without any need for surgery. Despite all the physical changes and challenges that come with the territory and the concern of the unknown, I loved being pregnant. It is incredible to feel and see how the Lord designed our bodies to bring forth the miracle of life. I was constantly in awe of the maternal blessing of being able to carry and give birth to a baby. It is something I will never take for granted. I am thankful that my plan and the Lord's plan coincided once again. As I write this, looking at my beautiful, sleeping boy, I recall the One who made all things and the One who holds my future, his future, and the future of everyone in His hands.

Another thing I did not plan for was facing a natural disaster in the form of Hurricane Milton and dealing with the aftermath. We do not live in a flood or evacuation zone, so though we prepared for the prospect of no power for several days following the storm, we did not prepare for the flooding we experienced throughout our entire home. The loss of property and the need to tear out everything that had come in contact with flood water was a significant financial and emotional burden. However, the Lord provided, and He showed up in His people. We had brothers and sisters in Christ all over the country helping us in various ways: prayers, demolition, cleaning of our home, storage of items we were able to save, multiple places to stay, childcare, dog care, food, supplies, clothes, financial support, and so much more. Before we could even ask for assistance, many stepped in and provided. God provided so much more abundantly than we could ask or think. He displayed His power by working through His people. Although it was not our plan to learn how to remodel a home or complete mold remediation, among other things, God used this opportunity to display His incredible plan for the church and teach us to humbly receive the blessings poured out from others.

Though life has not gone "according to plan" in many ways, I am thankful for all the ways I have seen God's hand present in my life. I am grateful that He has a plan for me and that it is bigger and better than anything I could ever accomplish on my own. I pray I will continue to seek His plans above my own and trust that wherever He leads and whatever He leads me through, He will be right beside me.

> "Many are the plans in the mind of a man, but it is the purpose of the Lord that will stand" (Pro 19:21).
>
> "The plans of the heart belong to man, but the answer of the tongue is from the Lord. All the ways of a man are pure in his own eyes, but the Lord weighs the spirit... The heart of a man plans his way, but the Lord establishes his steps" (Pro 16:1, 9).

Almost from the time we can talk, we are encouraged to start planning. "What do you want to be when you grow up?" is a frequently asked question beginning in early childhood and continuing into adolescence and adulthood. We plan what we want to be involved with in school, where we want to attend college, what career path we should pursue, who we are going to date and marry, how many children we will have, what retirement is going to look like, and the list goes on. Moving through life successfully without planning anything is impossible, even if you are planning subconsciously. Considering the verses above, understanding God has a far more excellent knowledge of us and the way we interact with the world, and realizing it is the purpose of the Lord that will stand despite all we might strive for, how do we plan in an effective and God-honoring way? How can we know God's plans for our lives and live in a way that will align with them?

The Bible includes many examples of planning with various outcomes, and the overall lesson of these examples is that planning is reasonable and necessary but must include a proper focus. Proverbs 6:6-8 provides us with the example of the ant and urges us to consider her ways of planning and laying up for the future and, through that, be wise. In contrast, the parable of the rich fool provided in Luke 12 warns against planning motivated by greed, storing possessions for self, but not being rich toward God. Though at first glance, the remainder of Luke 12 may seem to suggest futility in planning, on deeper reflection, we can see how it highlights the difference between worrying and planning and the importance of looking to God as the ultimate supplier of all we need.

Paul planned many actions during his ministry, but God often sent him in other ways (Act 16:6-7; Rom 1:9-13; 15:20-25, 29; 2 Cor 1:15-23; 1 The 2:17-18). Even though Paul's reasons for wanting to go where he planned were good, there were factors at play he could not see, and God created new opportunities that would otherwise have been unavailable through the change of plans. As we read through scripture, we can see how some of Paul's plans did not work out in the time he originally intended but ultimately would come to pass. Sometimes, the answer to our prayers and plans is not "no," but instead, "not yet." God knows there are situations we must experience to help prepare us for something later in life.

Despite our inability to see the future and how our lives will play out, we can implement strategies to succeed in our planning. First and foremost, you should employ the tool of prayer. Ask Him to guide you in making decisions that align with His will for your life. Implore Him to place people in your life who will help you accomplish His good plans. Beseech Him to open your eyes to the opportunities He has set before you. David said, "Make me to know Your ways, O Lord; teach me Your paths. Lead me in Your truth and teach me..." (Psa 25:4-5a). Elsewhere, he says, "For You are my rock and my fortress; and for Your name's sake You lead me and guide me... Into Your hand I commit my spirit..." (Psa 31:3, 5a). David's constant attention to prayer is a lesson for each of us. "Let me hear in the morning of Your steadfast love, for in You I trust. Make me know the way I should go, for to You I lift up my soul" (Psa 143:8).

Another strategy we see used with effectiveness in the Bible is seeking advice. There is a reason Paul instructs older Christians to teach younger Christians: they have life experiences they can use to inform their advice. Looking to others to assist us is essential when we struggle to make decisions. It is important to have others who can give advice, but we must carefully consider the kinds of people with whom we surround ourselves (1 Cor 15:33). Are they people like the young men who counseled Rehoboam poorly in his management of Israel, or will they be like the elders offering us wise counsel even when it may be difficult to hear (1 Kin 12:1-20)? Solomon is known as the wisest man in the world. Even he taught that "Without counsel plans fail, but with many advisers they succeed" (Pro 15:22, 11:14, 20:18). It may not always be easy to hear the advice offered us from well-meaning sources, but we are strengthened to know, "Better is open rebuke than hidden love. Faithful are the wounds of a friend; profuse are the kisses of an enemy" (Pro 27:5-6; 25:11-12). We are encouraged as older Christians to instruct those who are younger and, as younger Christians, to learn what we can from those with more experience than us (Deu 32:7; Tit 2:1-8).

Whatever you choose to do after praying and seeking advice from others, commit those plans to the Lord and work heartily for Him (Pro 16:3; Col 3:17, 23-24). We often struggle with wondering whether we are making the right decision, but frequently, there is no one right choice. Yet, the one way to make sure we are making the right choice is when we choose to glorify God, regardless of which place we move or what job we accept. The Bible holds many reminders that we will find success through our commitment to Him. "Trust in the Lord with all your heart, and do not lean on your own understanding. In all your ways acknowledge Him, and He will make straight your paths," (Pro 3:5-6) and "The steps of a man are established by the Lord, when he delights in His way; though he fall, he shall not be cast headlong, for the Lord upholds his hand" (Psa 37:23-24).

Despite our feeling that life is moving fast and everything seems immediate, I encourage you to take your time. Take the time to plan before rushing into action. Create opportunities to pray, seek advice, and make an informed decision. The Bible provides many examples of rushed and rash decisions that contrast with those that are more thought out and prayed over. Each example reminds us of the wisdom in seeking God's guidance and waiting for Him to lead (Pro 24:27; Luk 14:28-32). "The plans of the diligent lead surely to abundance, but everyone who is hasty comes only to poverty" (Pro 21:5).

Seek the Lord and His will first. God knows what we need and will provide (Mat 6:25-34; Luk 12:22-34). His thoughts and ways are higher than ours, and though we can never fully grasp the implications of all we plan for or the results of failed plans, He sees and knows (Isa 55:8-9). When we place Him above everything else, the other pieces will fall into place. Having the right priorities does not mean we will live without trial or difficulty, but we have assurance that the Lord will be there through those hard times and guide us in His right way. "I know, O Lord, that the way of man is not in himself, that it is not in man who walks to direct his steps. Correct me, O Lord, but in justice..." (Jer 10:23-24a; Pro 20:24, 21:2; Isa 30:20-21). Consider this passage in James 4:13-15 that reminds us to live our lives according to God's will and not our own:

> "Come now, you who say, 'Today or tomorrow we will go into such and such a town and spend a year there and trade and make a profit' -- yet you do not know what tomorrow will bring. What is your life? For you are a mist that appears for a little time and then vanishes. Instead you ought to say, 'If the Lord wills, we will live and do this or that.'"

Be flexible and keep the end goal in mind. Even when we practice all the steps outlined above, there will be times when our plans are unsuccessful or do not meet our intended timeline. That is okay. That is life. The important thing is how we handle what we may consider setbacks, but the Lord intends to provide opportunities for growth. When Paul encountered trials on his journey (shipwrecks, imprisonment, etc.), he did not let it stop him but continued to press on to the goal. His example encourages us to handle life gracefully when it gives us the unexpected. Reminding ourselves that this world is not our home can help to remove some of the pressure we place on ourselves to get everything right here on earth.

> "Not that I am speaking of being in need, for I have learned in whatever situation I am to be content. I know how to be brought low, and I know how to abound. In any and every circumstance, I have learned the secret of facing plenty and hunger, abundance and need. I can do all things through Him who strengthens me" (Phi 4:11-13).

> "Not that I have already obtained this or am already perfect, but I press on to make it my own... But one thing I do: forgetting what lies behind and straining forward to what lies ahead, I press on toward the goal for the prize of the upward call of God in Christ Jesus" (Phi 3:12-14).

Knowing that the Lord has a plan and a purpose for each of our lives is one thing. Discovering what that plan and purpose is presents a struggle for many. Because everyone does not have a personalized instruction manual for serving and honoring God, we must look to His Word to help determine the Lord's plans for the faithful.

Part of that plan is a future and a hope. In Jeremiah, the Lord promised His people that He would bring them back to Jerusalem following their seventy years in Babylonian exile. This time in exile was not necessarily a time of suffering for the people: God instructed them to have families, build homes, and seek the welfare of the cities they were living in, but it was also not God's final plan for them. Just as Babylonian captivity was a stop on the way to the fulfillment of God's promised deliverance, our life here on this earth is just a stop on the way to the fulfillment of God's promised heavenly rest to those who are faithful. We can know, with confidence, that we have a future and hope in Jesus and that if we seek Him, we will find Him (Mat 7:7-8; Rev 3:20).

> "For I know the plans I have for you, declares the Lord, plans for welfare and not for evil, to give you a future and a hope. Then you will call upon me and come and pray to me, and I will hear you. You will seek me and find me, when you seek me with all your heart. I will be found by you..." (Jer 29:11-14a).

When we love God, He promises us everything will work together for our good. This promise does not necessarily refer to good in the sense we tend to think about it on this earth, but ultimately to the good we will experience through eternal life with Him. Certainly, a life lived following Christ will be good in many ways, but we need to maintain a proper perspective when considering this verse and this promise. "And we know that for those who love God all things work together for good, for those who are called according to His purpose" (Rom 8:18-28).

We spend most of our lives planning ways to improve, comparing ourselves to others, and wondering if we will ever be good enough. Paul reminded the Philippians that God would complete the good work He had begun in them (Phi 1:6). This encouragement can be ours also. God has promised that He will never leave or forsake us. This assurance enables us to "grow through what we go through," knowing a faithful walk with Him will lead us to a state of perfection and completeness we could never achieve alone (Heb 13:5-6). "Where is there an instance of God's beginning any work and leaving it incomplete? Show me for once a world abandoned and thrown aside half formed; show me a universe cast off from the Great Potter's wheel, with the design in outline, the clay half hardened, and the form unshapely from incompleteness."

Another part of God's plan is learning to rely on His people. Maintaining our joy and faith can sometimes be challenging when we encounter various trials and tragedies in this life. God is with us in all things, and we can rely entirely on Him to supply all our needs. However, He can do that in various ways, including through His people. We are stronger together than we will ever be alone, and when we fall, God has designed His church so that we will be supported and lifted by others. We are encouraged to do good to everyone, especially those of the household of faith (Gal 6:9-10). We need to support others in our strong times, but we must also be willing to lean on our brethren during our times of need.

> "Two are better than one, because they have a good reward for their toil. For if they fall, one will lift up his fellow. But woe to him who is alone when he falls and has not another to lift him up! Again, if two lie together, they keep warm, but how can one keep warm alone? And though a man might prevail against one who is alone, two will withstand him--a threefold cord is not quickly broken" (Ecc 4:9-12).

Reflecting on my life to this point, I can see the many plans I have laid for myself and how some have come to fruition while others ended opposite of my original intentions. However, I can also see how the Lord's hand has been working to establish His purpose and how my life can glorify Him. My prayer for anyone reading this is that you will find fulfillment by opening yourself up to align your plans with the will of the Lord and that your success will lead you continually closer to Him.

THOUGHT QUESTIONS FOR "THE PLANS OF GOD"

1. How can we use biblical examples to inform our planning?

2. Have you made any plans in your life without consulting God first? How have these plans turned out?

3. Have you ever made plans that didn't work out initially but later did? How has this helped you develop a greater trust in God's plans and timing?

4. How have you been able to cope with the uncertainty of life when you place your plans in the Lord's hands?

5. When things don't go according to your plans, what actions can you take to move forward?

EMOTIONAL STABILITY

Melissa Paquette

And He shall be the stability of your times, a wealth of
salvation, wisdom, and knowledge;
The fear of the Lord is his treasure.
Isaiah 33:6

My mother is from Massachusetts, and my father is from Indiana. They met during the last couple of years of the Vietnam War, just as Dad was shipping overseas from Boston when his draft number came up. At this time, the world and my parents' lives were in great turmoil, and once they found one another, they held on tightly. My parents had opposite natures. Dad, with his "John Lennon" eyeglasses, was friendly and gregarious, and Mom, with her long, dark, "Cher hair," was quiet and shy. Dad asked her if he could write to her while he was away serving in the Navy, and she gave him her address. People who knew my dad would say, "He could talk a hungry dog off a meat wagon," and I can imagine the letters he wrote to Mom were interesting and detailed about his life in the Midwest and his new surroundings in Southeast Asia. Mom wrote back and invited him to come visit her family home 30 miles north of Boston when he made it back.

When Dad returned to Boston, he went straight to Mom's door. Mom's family of seven children loved my dad and enjoyed hearing his stories. He even tried to teach my grandmother to drive. After Dad was discharged from service, he packed Mom up in his van and took her to his hometown. Their commitment to one another and our family would endure until death.

Once settled in Indiana, they made plans because I would be arriving in the spring. Three months before I was born to my young hippie parents, my father became gravely ill and was hospitalized for several days. Mom didn't drive and walked to the hospital every day to see Dad. He was diagnosed with type 1 diabetes mellitus. The physician who delivered the news painted a grim picture of life as a diabetic. Mom believes Dad felt he would never be able to control what happened to him, so there was no reason to try to get better. The resources we have today were not accessible to them then, and he would spend the rest of his life suffering from low blood sugar reactions. Their happy home would now become one of constant chaos and instability.

They bought a small, mint green house in the northwest corner of Indiana and welcomed my brother, 3 years after me. The home had a nice yard, and we could run around outside playing tag, climbing trees, and riding our bikes in the neighborhood every day until the streetlight came on. My parents tried to figure out the puzzle of diabetes. Dad was always in great shape: he worked out, bicycled, and hiked. Dad would take me on bike rides by padding the crossbar with a towel. We would ride all around the neighborhood. I loved his strong arms around me as the wind blew across my face. Dad would take his insulin, but he didn't know what to eat to keep his blood sugar from dropping. Suddenly, Dad would get pale, clammy, quiet, and glassy-eyed. These hypoglycemic reactions happened at home and work. Our daily lives were unpredictable and sometimes frightening.

My parents became involved with the Nazarene Church, and our family attended these services. Mom was always willing to study the Bible with anyone who asked. We had a large children's Bible in our house. One day, I began reading it and didn't want to put it down. I read it cover to cover twice. I was amazed at the power of God and His plan for mankind. This was the first time I remember feeling like I had something solid I could hold onto in my life. I could pray my worries and troubles to God, and He always listened. He had a plan for me. He always had time for me and wanted me to call on Him. Despite external turmoil, I had found a place of emotional stability and security. I didn't quite understand the impact God would have on my life, but it was the beginning of an awareness that I should respect the power of God and seek Him out.

Our family moved to Massachusetts when I was ten to explore new opportunities. Mom enrolled in nursing school, and Dad became a custodian in the local school district. They enjoyed their work, but Dad's illness was getting worse. He had laser surgery for his eyes, toe amputations, and dialysis for kidney failure. He would ride his bike to work because his eyesight was failing. Whenever I felt ill, I would think, my dad must feel like this all the time.

Despite living in an inner city, Mom and Dad tried to shelter me. Mom had grown up in this city, and knowing the dangers, she watched out for me. They bought a comfortable home in a closely settled neighborhood. We joked that you could put your hand out the window and be in someone else's house. The house had a tiny yard, and it was not a good street to play outside. Instead, my brother and I would come home from school and play Super Mario Bros. on our Nintendo every day, where it was safe.

I respected my parents and didn't want to get into trouble. This was not the case for my brother. He was rebellious, and Dad's worsening illness only made the situation worse. Public school was intimidating; however, I made friends as I settled in and did well in school. In high school, I rode a city bus downtown, with other students riding to school and adults riding to work. Instead of taking the city bus home, I would walk the mile from school. The walk home was across a large bridge above a river that was boarded up on one side in the winter to block the biting wind, but the boards didn't come all the way down to the ground, so my ankles would freeze. I did this through all New England weather including rain, sleet, and snow.

I got my first "real" job at a local fast-food restaurant at sixteen. I had babysat the neighbor's children for many years, but now I was in the workforce. The restaurant was also only a mile away, and I could walk to work and back home in the daytime. I loved meeting new people and interacting with customers and coworkers, especially Eric, who was friendly and hardworking. The first day Eric and I spoke to each other was on Eric's 19th birthday. About a year later, Eric and I began a relationship. Eric sometimes talked with me about my home situation, especially when life was difficult. I struggled to talk about these things, but Eric was compassionate. Eric helped me more than anyone when he shared his faith with me. My home life felt unstable, but his home life was wonderful. He invited me to church with him, and something clicked when he said he was simply a Christian and wouldn't let me pin a denomination on him. Eric's faith in God was like a breath of fresh air to me because I believed too. My parents encouraged my growing faith and my connection with Eric. My family had become distracted and busy with the world and had stopped attending church. Unfortunately, we needed the Lord more than ever before. Eric brought me to the Heavenly Father just as I was about to lose my earthly father.

I fell in love with Eric. His family studied the Bible with me and lovingly welcomed me into their home. Eric's mom was an excellent role model for me. The Christians in Tyngsboro were also kind and encouraging and some of the most wonderful people I have ever met. I had many questions, and they patiently helped me to see what I needed to do. It was difficult for me to understand the need for baptism. In 1993, as I was about to graduate high school and after pondering the Scriptures, I responded to the Gospel call and was baptized for the forgiveness of my sins one Wednesday night. At the end of that summer, Eric and I became engaged, and we told both our parents, who were genuinely happy for us.

We decided to drive an hour to Portsmouth, N.H. every Sunday for worship. Eric's brother, Kurt, was preaching, and we wanted to encourage him and this small church. This experience was positive for me because I learned about encouraging and being encouraged. Kurt was well prepared after graduating from Florida College. Kurt prepared excellent lessons and classes which helped me grow in my knowledge, faith, and service. Most Sundays between services, we would head to Kurt's apartment, order pizza, and watch football. I also got the opportunity to write my college writing papers on Kurt's home computer, which was much better than using Eric's typewriter. It was difficult when we left this church after almost 2 years when Eric joined the Navy.

In September of 1993, I started college at the local university as an undeclared health major. That first semester was difficult for me, and I struggled to find my footing, probably because I wasn't exactly sure what I wanted to do for a career. Dad was also getting more seriously ill. Although he still had a job, he was out on sick leave more than he was able to work. Because he was such a beloved and well-known worker within the school department, many coworkers donated their own sick time to him. I cried when I saw the staggering list of names of those who showed this great kindness to Dad.

In January of 1994, Dad's mother passed away unexpectedly from a brain aneurysm. We traveled to Indiana for a few days to attend my grandmother's funeral. This was challenging, with Dad requiring dialysis treatments. Soon after we returned to Massachusetts, my dad was having more difficulties and felt as though he needed additional dialysis treatment, but he was unable to make this arrangement. That night, our family of four was home together, and we had a wonderful, harmonious chat before bed. Not one of us thought that it would be the last time.

I awoke to my mother's cries for help and attempts to perform CPR on Dad, who was lying unconscious next to their bed. My brother and I were essentially helpless except for calling 911. I was frightened and wanted to help Mom to somehow help Dad. We began praying diligently. At the hospital, Dad received the care he needed to survive a cardiac arrest, but he would never be the same. His brain had been without oxygen for too long and had irreparable damage. That semester, I did not go back to the university; instead, we worked on long-term plans to care for Dad at home. There were numerous complications and procedures to sustain Dad's life. It's difficult to look back on my father's suffering and my mother's anguish over him. Ultimately, he survived five more months before passing away. He was only 41 years old.

Eric was amazing with the amount of care and understanding he had for me during that time. He was a rock for me, driving me to the hospital to see Dad, sitting for hours at his bedside, and praying with us. After Dad passed, Mom asked Eric's father, Skip, to speak at Dad's memorial service, even though they had never met. He did a fine job; my family appreciated it, although we were all numb. There were many Christians at the service. Despite our devastation, their presence touched my family in incredible ways. This outpouring of support proved vital to maintaining my faith, even though my prayers were not answered as I had hoped. I still felt security in my faith in God and a constancy in His ability to provide comfort and strength. Through my sorrow, I tried to find ways to comfort my mother and brother.

Around this time, Mom suggested I apply to the nursing program in the hospital where she worked. The Licensed Practical Nurse (LPN) program was only eleven months of training followed by a national licensure exam. I had not registered for classes at the university, and I wasn't even sure I wanted to be a nurse. At this time, I was working full-time as a pharmacy technician at a chain drug store, but I agreed to take the entrance exam and apply. Full-time LPN school was five full days a week for eleven full months. The nursing school was based in a state hospital and provided long-term care to patients with advanced needs. The amount of work and the level of care were not for the faint of heart. I remember the first patient I cared for began yelling when I introduced myself and explained I was there to prepare her for the day. I ran from the room and was about to leave the nursing program, but a kind, older nursing student saw my distress and assisted me in providing care to this patient. Today, as a nursing professor, I attempt to consider the perspective of my nursing students and the stresses they might be feeling. Despite my initial concerns, I discovered within the second week that nursing was something I could do well.

My love for nursing grew over time. I was young, and it took me a little time to make the connections between the information I learned through studying and the application and art of nursing. Blending the necessary nursing skills and knowledge with the critical, caring component can be challenging. These skills develop over time with reflection and a willingness to refine one's practice to gain the trust of the patient. I continue to do this all the time, even now, decades later.

Eric and I were planning to marry after I graduated nursing school in 1995. He had been working for his family's paving company. However, when he enlisted in the Navy and went off to boot camp and air traffic control training school, we had to postpone our wedding until he could take time off at Christmas. We had a snowy, white wedding on a Friday evening in New England with many loved ones in attendance. I was 20 years old, and Eric was 23. Then, we headed to Virginia to live in Newport News for five years.

We found a small congregation in the area and had some wonderful times living and working in that area. The Harpersville Church of Christ had many young married couples, and we had the opportunity to host and be hosted by many encouraging Christians. Eric was away on a six-month Mediterranean deployment on the aircraft carrier the first year there. As a nurse in a long-term care facility, I had to work some holidays, including Christmas. Although I was unable to go back to Massachusetts to be with my family for the holiday, one

Christian family invited me to sleep at their home and be with them Christmas morning, complete with presents for me, too. We met so many thoughtful and encouraging people in Virginia.

His loneliness was evident when Eric called for the first time on the six-month deployment. He asked if I thought I could visit him at some point during the trip. We looked at the itinerary and decided on the week his ship was docked in Livorno, Italy, at the midway point of the deployment. Eric requested the time off from the ship, and I made travel arrangements to meet him in Florence. I was 21 years old, flying out of Washington D.C. alone to Paris and then to Italy, and I was a little nervous. However, I knew Eric needed me to support him emotionally. I could finally give back to him after all he had given me.

My flight overseas was delayed five hours, and because this was prior to cell phones, Eric had to wait and worry about me. A friend called Eric's parents, and they sent an email to Eric's chief on the ship to tell him about the delay. He never got the message. Instead, Eric talked his way onto one of the first helicopters off the ship and then jumped on a train to Florence. After several anxious hours in the hotel lobby, he called his parents to hear about the flight delay. When I finally arrived, it was a wonderful reunion. We had a blessed visit, and I believe it was such an important moment in our marriage. I'm glad Eric voiced his emotional need and that I trusted the Lord would protect me.

In my last two years in Virginia, I worked for an endocrinologist and a diabetes specialist. This was a great opportunity to teach patients newly diagnosed as diabetic how to manage the disease. I showed them how to give themselves their first insulin injections and check their blood glucose levels. We discussed ways to prevent the terrible complications my father had to face. This was rewarding work. In helping patients with diabetes gain control over their lives, I felt I was honoring my father.

After five years, Eric left the Navy, and we moved back to Massachusetts. We would have two sons, Connor and Sean, and live there for the next 20 years. We worshipped with the group of Christians in Tyngsboro once more. During that time, we dealt with many challenges, including the heartbreak of miscarriage, an ongoing cardiac problem, and financial struggles. Together, by the grace of God, we have made it through those difficult times. During Connor's senior year of high school, Connor visited Florida College and decided to attend beginning in the Fall of 2021. It was bittersweet for us to see him leave and be so far away, but we were happy for him to be going to a great school.

Over the years, I had returned to college, and I was now a registered nurse working in the recovery room in a local community hospital. As a nurse, I have seen much pain and suffering, but I have developed resilience through difficult times because of my faith. I was volunteering with the medical sweep team about a block away from the finish line during the Boston Marathon bombing, and I witnessed the terror of that horrible attack. During the pandemic, I worked as a nurse at the bedside in the post-anesthesia care unit (PACU) and the intensive care unit (ICU), providing care to many patients with COVID-19. The Lord blessed me with a family who loved and supported me throughout these difficult times.

In 2021, I completed a master's degree in nursing education, and I began working part-time as adjunct faculty in a nursing program at a local community college. Months later, a nursing program started at FC, the same year my son Connor decided to attend. As a family, we decided to leave our home and the dear people in Massachusetts and move to Florida. The Lord has blessed us with the opportunity to stay together as a family for a little while longer. Eric and I have worked and supported one another for many years, and we were ready to continue this journey together in a new place. We understand we will face challenges and uncertainty, but we place our trust in Christ.

The students at FC are amazing. They are kind, caring, and eager to serve. I am genuinely excited to share my love for Christ and my passion for nursing with them. I continue working part-time for a local hospital in the PACU to keep up to date with direct patient care practices, and I truly love caring for people.

Teaching nursing at FC has been rewarding and satisfying. I may care for someone like my father at the bedside, but in teaching these FC nursing students, they will care for many people like him for years. I know the difficult times have helped to shape the person I am today. The Lord has richly blessed me and my family in many ways, even as we navigate challenges. I believe the plan of our Heavenly Father was for our family to come to FC, and I pray we will continue to look to Him for strength and guidance, both mentally and physically.

GOD'S ENDURING LOVE

In writing the narrative of my early life, I quickly identified the great desire and constant search for peace and emotional stability. While growing up in my family, I was often anticipating some chaotic event, many times related to my father's illness or my brother's rebelliousness. My home life was emotionally upsetting, and I did not encounter a sense of constancy until I began reading a children's Bible and saw the power of God to help people through challenging times. The Lord has provided a safe refuge for people to turn to from the earliest times up to today. In Ephesians 5:2, we have an example of the Lord's love, "and walk in love, just as Christ also loved you, and gave Himself up for us, an offering and a sacrifice to God as a fragrant aroma." It has always been the same enduring love and sacrifice that people can rely on.

FAITH IN CHALLENGING TIMES

In Genesis 37-46, we can read about Joseph and the struggles he endured with his family. He had the love of his father, Jacob, and God's blessing of prophetic dreams. However, his home life was not happy because of the jealousy of his brothers. He was mistreated and sold into slavery, but he was able to endure those hardships and remain faithful to the Lord. It was likely difficult for Joseph to consider the suffering his father, Jacob, endured those many years he was presumed dead. Yet, Joseph allowed God's plan to unfold how it was always supposed to and trusted His will would be done. In Genesis 45:8, Joseph, after telling his brothers he is alive, says, "Now therefore, it was not you who sent me here, but God; and He has made me father to Pharoah and lord over all the land of Egypt." Seeing a reason or plan during difficult times that seem unfair, painful, and prolonged can be challenging. We must hold on tightly to our faith in our savior, Jesus, who planned all along to save us even from the time of Joseph when his enduring faith maintained a remnant that God preserved to rescue us even today.

HOPE IN CHRIST

Most of us seek safety and security daily, but this is an unpredictable world in which we live, and we lack control over many things. The enduring peace we are searching for can only be found in Christ. Christians understand this when we recognize the burden of sin; the only way we can lift that burden is through repentance and baptism. "And Peter said to them, 'Repent, and let each of you be baptized in the name of Jesus Christ for the forgiveness of your sins; and you shall receive the gift of the Holy Spirit'" (Acts 2:38). Before this moment, we are all wandering, seeking some reassurance, relief, and hope.

SECURITY FROM GOD

Growing up with a loving but unhealthy father was challenging because I could not trust he would always be around or be able to care for me. As a daughter, I greatly desired love and security from my father. I did not know the emotional stability of a loving father until I understood the love of God. 1 John 3:1 states, "See how great a love the Father has bestowed upon us, that we should be called children of God; and such we are. For this reason, the world does not know us because it did not know Him." It is amazing to think about being a child of God and the love we have from Him.

There are several verses related to emotional stability in the scriptures. Isaiah 33:6 declares, "And He shall be the stability of your times, a wealth of salvation, wisdom, and knowledge; The fear of the Lord is his treasure." We need to understand there will be times of great hardship, and we may wonder what we should do or where to go for strength. The Lord is reliable, and we should search His word for wisdom and remain steadfast in our thoughts and actions as we work through challenges, seeking to do His will. God's word is powerful, and no matter how many times I read a verse, a passage, or a book, I am still amazed at the timelessness of the message. When I feel stressed or anxious, I must remember to call upon the Lord. I cannot handle the world's thoughts, worries, and concerns as my own. God has given me wonderful people to help me gain more perspective, but ultimately, I must trust Him.

In Matthew 11:28-29, we read, "Come to me, all who are weary and heavy laden, and I will give you rest. Take My yoke upon you, and learn from Me, for I am gentle and humble in heart; and you shall find rest for your souls." This verse provides such great comfort. We all face difficult times and need a place of refuge that we can always count on. Losing someone we love and who has been with us our whole lives can shake us to our core. This is especially true if we have fervently prayed for God to restore that loved one's health. Despite this, I feel so grateful to God for His grace in sending me Eric and for Eric sharing his faith in our Heavenly Father with me just as I was losing my earthly father. It is unimaginable for me to consider the course my life might have taken if I did not know the love of God at the time of my father's death.

In 2 Samuel 12, Nathan the prophet rebukes David for his sins involving Bathsheba. When David learns that the consequences of his sins will result in the loss of his child with Bathsheba, David's grief is profound, and many in his household are worried about him. He fasted, wept, and lay on the ground. After seven days, the child died. Upon hearing the news of the child's death, he accepted the Lord's decision and realized he would not be able to change the Lord's mind. He chose to comfort others, and the Lord blessed him. In Psalm 34:18, David wrote, "The Lord is near to the brokenhearted, And saves those who are crushed in spirit." I prayed and wept when my father was critically ill for those five long months. Once he passed, I had to find ways to honor him. I did this by trying to comfort my mother and brother.

THE POWER OF GOD'S WORD

In Colossians 2:5, Paul writes, "For even though I am absent in body, nevertheless I am with you in spirit, rejoicing to see your good discipline and the stability of your faith in Christ." Paul is pleased with the Colossian Church as they maintain their faith in Christ even if they don't physically have him there with them. We must develop our faith even when we are no longer around those who brought us to the Gospel or helped us grow in our knowledge of God. In my own life, when Eric went overseas and I was living in a new place, I had to model the characteristics of a Christian wife and act when my husband said he needed me to visit him. I was worried about his emotional stability, being away from me and other Christians for so long. This trip served several purposes: putting Eric's needs above my own, returning the gift of support he gave to me when my dad was ill, and helping me overcome my fears of traveling alone. The Lord blessed us with safety, emotional support, and a memorable trip.

In the first chapter of the Book of Esther, King Ahasuerus requests his wife, Queen Vashti, to come to him, but she refuses. He is outraged and punishes her by replacing her for wronging him and setting a poor example to other wives, who might model her actions with their own husbands. Later in Esther chapter 4, Queen Esther (Hadassah) is told by her uncle, Mordecai, that she needs to act by going to the king to save the lives of the Jewish people as they are about to be annihilated by Haman. Esther is afraid because the law states that anyone who goes to the king without being summoned can be put to death if he does not hold out his golden scepter to them. However, Esther trusted her uncle's words in Esther 4:13-14: "Do not imagine that you in the king's palace can escape any more than all the Jews. For if you remain silent at this time, relief and deliverance will arise for the Jews from another place, and you and your father's house will perish. And who knows whether you have not attained royalty for such a time as this?"

Esther plans a banquet, organizes, and prepares to see the king and defeat Haman's plot. When she goes to see King Ahasuerus, he accepts her, she reveals Haman's plot against the Jews, and the tables are turned on Haman. Haman hangs, Esther saves the Jews, and the king promotes Mordecai. In life, we can stay where we feel safe and comfortable and perhaps fool ourselves into thinking everything will be fine. Esther fasted in anguish about the situation Mordecai told her about, but she also knew she needed to act because of her position. We must look at our circumstances, pray for guidance and emotional support, and act when needed.

RESILIENCE THROUGH CHRIST

Resilience is important as a Christian, wife, mother, daughter, nurse, and educator. It is essential to overcome painful, difficult times and become stronger despite them. There have been several moments in my life where I have had to endure hardships, but nothing was as difficult as the loss of my dad. In the Book of Ruth, Naomi has suffered famine, the loss of her husband and two sons, and now feels the Lord is against her. However, Ruth is a support for Naomi. Ruth does not abandon Naomi and loves her so much that she will not leave Naomi alone in this terrible emotional state. I can only imagine Naomi's suffering, but she allowed Ruth to stay with her, which was a great blessing for both. We must acknowledge the people God puts in our lives to help us handle difficult times. Eric has always been that person for me, pointing me to Jesus. I try not to take this blessing for granted. I pray I will always seek strength in God and help from the many other wonderful people He has blessed me with in my life. Ruth meets Boaz while she collects grain for Naomi and her. She listened to Naomi's guidance, married Boaz, and became part of David's lineage through her child, Obed. Those challenging, painful experiences led to great blessings. Ruth 4:14-15 says, "Then the women said to Naomi, 'Blessed is the Lord who has not left you without a redeemer today, and may his name become famous in Israel. May he also be to you a restorer of life and a sustainer of your old age, for your daughter-in-law, who loves you and is better to you than seven sons, has given birth to him.'"

The early struggles in my life prepared me to realize I would not live in a perfect world; my hope was in Christ. However, I take comfort in this verse, Romans 8:28, 31: "And we know that God causes all things to work together for good to those who love God, to those who are called according to His purpose… What then shall we say to these things? If God is for us, who is against us?" If I had been able to plan out my own life, I would have removed the loss of my father, which would likely have changed the course of my life in many ways. I am not sure I could emotionally endure the challenges I have faced. Thirty years later, I am still following Christ, married to a wonderful Christian man, and we have two sons who also obeyed the Gospel call. I feel blessed to work as a nursing professor at Florida College, teaching students from a biblical perspective alongside other servants of Christ. The nurses graduating from FC will be more prepared to face the pain or suffering of others and not be disappointed and disillusioned with this world. We equip them with more than nursing skills, but also with a hope of Heaven and the emotional strength of a patient, loving, and omnipotent God.

THOUGHT QUESTIONS FOR "EMOTIONAL STABILITY"

1. When was the first time you realized God had a plan for you and that He was a source of emotional support in difficult times? Was there a verse, a story, a lesson, or something else that helped you gain this reassurance?

2. What verses provide insight into the enduring love of God and demonstrates the superiority of this love over other kinds of love?

3. Can you think of a time in your life when your faith was challenged? How did God help you overcome doubt or despair?

4. Has anyone ever asked you to do something that was important, but also challenging, stressful, or frightening? How did God help you manage your emotions so you could act?

5. How do we build resilience through Christ in ourselves and others? What scriptures provide support or examples to consider continually to maintain our focus on the power of God to save us?

CONFIDENCE

Molly Taylor

Let us draw near with a true heart in full assurance of faith, with our hearts sprinkled clean from an evil conscience and our bodies washed with pure water.
Hebrews 10:22

I am a career woman. I never asked for this. I didn't want this. What I had asked for was a husband and a family. If I could count the number of times I have been discontent with my lack of relationship, the tears I've cried over feeling lonely, and the dreams I've had that include a nice man who takes care of me and loves Jesus just to wake up and find the man of my dreams was imaginary, it would add up to—well, too many times. Singleness is not for the faint of heart. It is a lifestyle that seems thrust upon many out of necessity, not choice. People try to encourage me and say things like, "It will happen for you someday," or, "Have you tried online dating?" or, "I know someone who got married later in life, so don't lose hope." For those wondering, I have tried online dating. It was horrible. I know that these words come from a place of a sincere desire for me and other singles to find the love that they have found, but they are frequently unhelpful. People want me to have everything I have ever dreamed of, which makes me happy. However, these words don't always have the desired effect on someone who has tried so hard to put themselves out there with no results. When someone says one of these lines to me, I can't help but wince a little on the inside and silently scream, "I don't know what else I can do to get a husband and finally start my life!" That faulty thinking has clouded the amazing things God has allowed me to do as a single person.

I grew up in Colorado Springs, CO, with two loving parents and three beautiful, hilarious, musical sisters. One would never guess about our humble beginnings because my parents kept our monetary needs out of family conversations. I remember a few times when I was little that people from the congregation brought our family groceries or meals. I did not equate that with poverty because where it counted, we were happy. It never felt like we were suffering. Mom shared with me that during that year, she prayed that my feet wouldn't grow because they could not afford new shoes for me. God answered her prayers, and my feet didn't grow. I did not need new shoes until later that year when my parents could afford them. Not long after, God provided my dad with a job that allowed my parents to pay back debts, support the family, help others, and start to save for the future. My dad showed us how to work "as unto the Lord" (Eph 6:7) and prioritized time with the family. My mom showed us how to keep a house, love our husbands, and show hospitality at a moment's notice. With two godly parents at the helm, we sang together, played games, spent time with each other, and learned to love like Jesus. God indeed blessed me with a happy childhood.

My sisters are a big part of my life. Emily is the oldest of the four of us. As an elementary-aged girl, I admired Emily for her ability to make people feel included and make friends. She seemed to be hanging out with friends or talking to them on the phone. I watched closely as she greeted everyone with a smile and knew how to effortlessly start a conversation. As I get older, I still admire that about her. I admired Kaitlin for her imagination. Kaitlin and I would play together all the time. We put on original musicals, complete with choreography, and performed them for whoever was in the house (sorry to our guests), working on the house (sorry to Rusty, the college-aged fix-it guy), and for extended family (thank you uncles and aunts for still talking to us). When Kerri was old enough to join, it was a full production. I admired Kerri for her energy. She completed our family in a way that no one else could. Her ability to diffuse a situation with humor and wit was almost always perfectly timed. My sisters were my best friends because we did not have many kids our age at our home congregation.

The churches in Colorado Springs were scarce. I spent my early years at a congregation called Northeast Church of Christ. When I was about eight years old, the Northeast congregation outgrew its building, so my parents and two other families decided to start a new church on the city's north side—more specifically, in our living room. The kids in the congregation consisted of my three sisters and me, and three to four other children who would split up into our bedrooms for bible study, then join everyone in the living room for the sermon, communion, and contribution, which was gathered by passing a Styrofoam tortilla warmer the first couple of weeks. The Lord added to the congregation, and we were soon able to meet in a daycare facility for Sunday services. As I was coming of age during this time, I still had very few friendship opportunities. It was at a Florida College camp where I developed the closest relationships that I would see in my life until attending Florida College.

As a wide-eyed, positive, make-friends-with-everyone personality, FC camp was one of my best experiences. Christian kids from all over Colorado and other states were there to sing, play, worship, and learn. It is what I imagined heaven would be like. I obeyed the gospel at this camp and was baptized in the campground hot tub. That environment cultivated the type of person and Christian I wanted to be. I wanted to make everyone feel welcomed, loved, and included, which has translated to my church connections. There is always an opportunity to make someone feel welcomed, loved, and included. Each year, when camp was over, I stayed in touch by letter-writing to several of my friends and cried when I could not see them until the next year.

My first connection with Florida College was at a "Friends" concert when I was 9 years old, too young for camp. My family hosted a singer from the group who fit right in with our musical musings. I was star-struck. I had been singing my whole life, and the prospect of singing with a band was my new dream. The girl that stayed with us that summer left a note on the bed which I kept on top of my dresser in my room and read it often. Every summer I would ask my parents if the Friends were coming back and looked forward to seeing them every few years. My second connection with Florida College was the Camp Friend groups. I still fondly remember camp cheers, cabin time, and sitting next to them at our Bible studies and campfires. Having older teen Christians gave me another blueprint for who I wanted to be and how I wanted to act as a Christian. The influence those FC students had on me was positive and faith-forming. As I got closer to their ages, I could see myself as one of them and decided to attend Florida College in 2005.

Making connections at Florida College brought new challenges. Besides the one week at camp each year, being surrounded by Christians my age who were happy, driven, and positive was a new experience, and it was overwhelming in the best way. I was a member of the volleyball team, so my first semester was full of volleyball practices, games, and tournaments that would claim my time as the rest of my peers were experiencing society sports and finding their groups of friends. After winning our first National title at the end of October, I spent the next six weeks trying to find my group of people. I was in chorus, Friends, and music classes, and I sang for the jazz band, which allowed me to be around people with the same passion as I did, but the music program was still small. My roommate and suitemates were kind, and I enjoyed spending time with them.

Like many girls on campus, I eventually got my first boyfriend. Having no previous experience in dating, I assumed that it would be easy; emotions would not be complicated; communication would just magically happen; we would be best friends and eventually get married in two years. That was not the case. I was the most confused I had ever been. I did not know what to make of this relationship or how to create a life with another person. My confidence waivered. What questions do I ask? How do I know if it's right? What do I do if it doesn't work out? And the most dreaded question was, who am I if I end up alone? With every question I encountered, I am ashamed to say that I did not approach God. Prayer had fallen to the wayside, even at a school that prays together in chapel every morning, prays at mealtimes, and prays at the many devotions throughout the week, I did not make it a priority to approach God with my questions. Eventually, the questions left un-prayed were answered, and the relationship ended. In the next three years, it was not just about the relationships. I went on to win two more National volleyball championships with the team, tour with the Friends group and chorus, had a role in all the musicals, became a Camp Friend, then a Camp Friend leader, and developed a singing voice that I am happy to share with others.

Though FC is not all about finding your one true love, it was a big part of why I wanted to be there. So, imagine my surprise when I graduated with a four-year BA in Music and had to start supporting myself. Right out of FC, I worked a short-term job at the Straz Center, a performing arts facility in Tampa, as an assistant to the musical director for a new musical that was being written and staged with hopes of making it to Broadway. I helped alter musical arrangements and ensured the cast had the new pages in their folders before the next rehearsal. I got very familiar with fixing broken copy machines, and I sang for a few choreography rehearsals when the leads were taking a break or absent. I was mesmerized by the process of starting up a Broadway musical, but it was not a sustainable career path. The people I worked closely with were the only ones to acknowledge that I did not curse. They consciously tried to watch their language around me, and I was grateful. At the end of my work for the Straz, the musical director offered me an intern position in New York City at a casting firm. Reflecting on the lifestyle of most people in the musical theater world, I knew it was not for me. I kindly refused and started to look for another job. That is when Starbucks came into my life.

Starbucks brought me the next love of my life—coffee. Coffee was smooth, loyal, and kind. Coffee was there for me during my 4:30 a.m. shifts. This tall, dark, handsome drink would provide my income for six years. (Insert "I like my men how I like my coffee" jokes here). I worked in a Tampa store for two years and could still be involved in the local church and see my younger sister Kerri thrive in the volleyball program. I also assisted the FC fine arts department with the musicals each Spring. It was a good environment for me, but I did not feel completely confident in a career choice as a barista. When I felt like I had explored all there was to explore in Tampa, I moved to Nashville, TN.

My move to Nashville was easy. I got plugged into a Starbucks store just up the road from my apartment. I had a roommate who was easy to live with and a church family who cared for me immediately. As I held my full-time job with Starbucks, I got several part-time jobs to see if there was a facet of music that I wanted to make a career. In Nashville, everyone searched for where they could make it big in the music scene. I worked with and served coffee to producers, artists, musicians, writers, and studio workers. Starbucks became a networking hub for many who wanted to break into the music business. My first part-time job was at a music school, where I became a piano and voice teacher to children. In my free time, I dabbled in songwriting, recorded backup vocals on a couple of studio albums, recorded a demo for a songwriter, and took a third part-time job as a personal assistant to a musician/studio owner for a few months. None of these jobs satisfied me enough to continue pursuing one track.

Since Starbucks was the one constant job in Nashville, I determined to move up in the ranks and became a store manager in Franklin, TN. This job was fun and fast-paced, but despite the extra caffeine, it was tiring and still not my passion, so it was difficult. I learned more about myself looking back on those days than I did when I was in them. During that time, I remember feeling anxious, unsupported, and unfit for the position, and I took it personally when my employees quit. Between the hard times, I made new friends, acquired new skills, and put in the longest hours at a job I would ever work. After two years, I still felt anxious and tired. I knew I did not want to be at Starbucks forever, so I decided to step down from my managerial position and become a shift leader at another store in downtown Franklin. This was a much better position because it freed me up to spend more time with friends and gave me more time to rest.

I worked with some great people and saw several famous Nashville-ians come in and out of that store. We had many regulars I got to know and love, one of whom was Ted, the husband of a fellow barista. One day in early December, I had just completed my shift when Ted approached me. He asked about my shift and said, "I have been praying for you. I don't know your specific situation, but I think I got an answer from God for you." I was taken aback because, first, I had very little personal interaction with Ted, so the fact that he prayed for me was overwhelming. Second, I had not considered the possibility of God talking directly to someone to give them an answer for something they had prayed for. Third, I had been thinking about, and minimally praying for, what my future life would look like. I felt stuck and disregarded my talent for music while living away from my family. I was also discouraged because I was still single and felt unfulfilled. Ted continued, "The answer does not make sense to me, but maybe it will for you. Whatever you are searching for is not here in Nashville." I was floored. I got goosebumps then, and I still get them when I recount the story. I told him, "Thank you," and slowly walked away with many thoughts running through my mind. When I reached the parking lot, I called my dad, a dependable and wise voice of reason. I said, "What if instead of flying home for Christmas, I move back and apply to school for music therapy?"

Dad responded, "Ok…What is keeping you in Nashville?"

I said, "My church and my friends."

"Is that enough?"

"Not anymore."

"Ok," Dad said, "Let's move you back home."

Two weeks later, I was driving myself, my cat, and all my stuff from Nashville to Colorado Springs to pursue grad school for music therapy.

I applied to two schools and got accepted into Colorado State University's music therapy program to start in the fall of 2015. This era catapulted my musical skill and motivation to help others into overdrive. For those who are curious,

> "Music therapy is the clinical & evidence-based use of music interventions to accomplish individualized goals within a therapeutic relationship by a credentialed professional who has completed an approved music therapy program. Music therapy interventions can address a variety of healthcare & educational goals." [1]

I usually describe it as using music as the catalyst to achieve non-musical goals. For example, leading a "music and movement" group at an assisted living facility to help older adults maintain mobility and mental clarity. I could go on for a whole chapter about music therapy, but that's not why you are here. During my schooling, I worked in a memory ward for older adults with dementia, a private music therapy clinic serving clients with autism in a one-on-one setting, a middle school with a group of students who had various developmental and physical disabilities, and a day home for adults with developmental disabilities. I learned to play guitar and hand percussion and use my voice and piano skills to help others.

The final semester of coursework brought a songwriting class that collaborated with a non-profit organization called Chase the Music. This organization commissions songwriters to write music for children battling critical or terminal illnesses. Each student was paired with a child and put what we were learning in class into action. I requested to be paired with a Christian family close to the area I had known almost all my life. Their

1 Definition from https://www.musictherapy.org/about/musictherapy/

11-year-old son was battling brain cancer. The song I wrote for him was the first of four I wrote for Chase the Music over four years. This opportunity awoke a songwriting side I did not know I had. Writing for a child's legacy and telling stories important to hear gave purpose to my writing. I feel so blessed to be a part of these families' lives in some small way. I used this skill when I went on to complete my internship at Covenant Children's Hospital in Lubbock, TX. This was my favorite placement in my music therapy career. I focused on the Neonatal Intensive Care Unit (NICU) and the oncology ward but also served the main pediatric floor and the Pediatric Intensive Care Unit (PICU). I wrote legacy songs for infants with no voice, helped normalize the hospital situation for some timid children, and sparked conversations about childhood cancer with families who did not know how to deal with the diagnosis or prognosis.

When I completed my internship, I moved back to Colorado to work for a home health company. I traveled all around Colorado Springs with instruments in the trunk of my car, providing music therapy to many, ranging from children to adults with physical and developmental disabilities. My next music therapy position was at a mental hospital. I was not fully aware of what music therapy in mental health looked like, and this hospital was not familiar with music therapy but was trying to expand what it offered to patients. I started the music therapy program at this facility, built my repertoire and experience, and after a year, another full-time music therapist was hired to help me. I worked mainly in the teen and adult units, and once a week, I would lead a group with the 28-day rehab clinic. It was rewarding to see the way people responded to music. Many times, patients came to that hospital after the worst day of their lives, and through the medium of music, they were able to express emotion, feel peace, verbalize goals, and learn coping skills. In addition to growing my musical skills, I also grew in empathy. I felt more capable of talking to people who lived a completely different lifestyle with compassion and understanding. It reminded me of how Jesus could sit with and talk with people who did not follow him. I desperately wanted others to know how to do this, too.

I worked at the mental hospital for a year and a half when I received an email saying there was an open teaching position in the music department at Florida College. I immediately thought, "That would be a really fun job when I'm 50 and have more work experience under my belt." Within a week, I received a screenshot of the posted position from my friend, Shane Scott, who said, "Have you seen this? I think you'd be great at it!" I responded, "I did see it, but it's too much change right now. Thanks for thinking of me."

In the next couple of days, my oldest sister, Emily, said, "Hey, did you see that the music department at FC is hiring?" I said, "Yes, but it's too much change and I'm not looking to change my job." She said, "If I were you, I'd at least apply. You never know." The next day, I was having dinner with my parents, and my dad said, "Hey, did you see that they are hiring for the music department at FC?" I felt like the man in the flood who had just turned down the canoe and the helicopter, so I applied.

In the next three months, I accepted the job offer at FC and put in my notice at the mental hospital. I was terrified. I was thinking of all the professors I had as a student and knew that I was not the serious-minded academic that I thought FC was expecting. It was not the career path that I had expected. The uncertainty was so present in my approach to the job that I was unsure I had made the right decision. Did you see prayer in any of that? Neither did I. I had lost confidence in my ability to trust God with His will for the new course of my life, though I could see He was present. I did not know how to pray for this new job. I did not want to be a career woman. At 35, I was not expecting to start a new career. My other friends in their 30s were at least married, if not with a handful of children. This comparison was keeping my thoughts on worldly expectations rather than embracing the gift that I had been given.

I am currently working in a place that puts God first, values the souls of its employees and students, and allows me to grow in my skills and social life while surrounded by sound churches and people. What more could I want? Well, I wanted to learn to trust God more. I wanted to learn how to pray. I wanted to be content with my situation. I wanted to be confident in my decision. It took another two years before I learned how to trust in the position God has put me. I have grown immensely through friends who hold me accountable for keeping a regular prayer life, and I hope that soon, that will become second nature. My prayer for a spouse has changed. Instead of praying that it will happen, I now pray, "God, I trust you to bring him into my life if it is your will. I am shifting my focus to use the gifts you have given me, and I know that you will not let me miss the opportunity." This perspective has brought me peace in thinking about my marital status. It has helped me grow in my skills and spend more time reaching out to my students, showing hospitality, spending time with people, and serving my local congregation. If it is God's will, I have confidence that He will not let me miss it. If it is not God's will, I will have spent my time serving Him, which is the best use of time I can think of. I no longer ask for a husband or family. I am a career woman striving to serve God.

Imagine you are at a group function – a party, gathering for work or school – and someone asks, "Who are you? What do you like? What are you about?" The usual response would be, "My name is (insert name here). I love to travel. I'm a musician. I have three kids. Etc." The way you tend to describe yourself is how the world attributes value. It is what you are confident in letting people know about you. It does not cause ripples. It is expected. What if you introduced yourself like, "My name is (insert name here). I love the Word of God, and using my gifts for God is my passion." Would you feel comfortable talking that way and letting people immediately know you are a die-hard Christian? This will take practice.

As women, we are not usually a confident group of people, at least regarding our looks. Hair, wrinkles, weight, clothes, and makeup are just some of the ways society has told us that we are inferior. The "Girl boss" mentality and pay-gap disparity, which I will not cover, have permeated feministic rants all over social media. Think of confident people in your life: parents, celebrities, siblings, church leaders, historical figures, etc. What do they have in common? They know who they are, what they believe, and what they represent. The same is true for the confident figures in the Bible; they know who they are or, at the very least, who their God is – which is sufficient.

Confidence is not a prideful sentiment. It does not uplift someone's arrogance or increase their trust in their own abilities. Confidence is a steadfast reliance on God. Synonyms for confidence are certainty, assurance, and conviction. These are all biblical concepts. Hebrews 10:22 says, "Let us draw near with a true heart in full assurance of faith, with our hearts sprinkled clean from an evil conscience and our bodies washed with pure water." We have full assurance in our faith. This verse exemplifies the purity that is found in drawing near to God with a clean conscience. It brings to mind snuggling into bed with a parent after just getting out of the bath. There is safety, security, and rest. This confidence and assurance of our faith is because God is who He is (Exo 3:14). All He has promised has come to pass. That is why 1 John 1:9 is so comforting, "If we confess our sins, He is faithful and just to forgive us our sins and to cleanse us from all unrighteousness." Great is His faithfulness (Lam 3:23). God has fulfilled all His promises, assuring us that He will continue to follow through.[1]

Doubt is the opposite of confidence. Some think if they doubt, their faith is invalid. However, confidence and doubt can exist simultaneously. Doubt brings up questions that require answers. It sparks a search and a longing to know the truth about something. It is ok to doubt. Many Christians that I have talked to about this have doubted some or all of their faith at some point in their walk with Jesus. However, doubting to satisfy an ongoing sin is divisive. If someone claims to be repentant but never changes, there is more faith-building to work on beyond simply, "Do I really believe that?" That individual needs to question whether he or she is truly saved. This is not the doubt I am talking about. The doubt I am addressing brings questions such as, "Why is the Bible the only guiding book for the life of a Christian?" or "Do I believe that Jesus is the only way to get to heaven?" You can still have faith while questioning these things. The caveat comes when you decide how to find your answers.

Doubting can grow your confidence. You can observe toddlers learning how to put a square-shaped block into a square-shaped hole. Their confidence spikes when they figure out how to do it, and now they want to figure out the rhombus! Well, maybe just the circle or triangle next, but you can see the point. When you do some digging on your own, you are left with the satisfaction of figuring it out, and you will have confidence in your findings. Like any good researcher, you must rifle through sources to see which are the most reliable. Make a mistake like Rehoboam (1 Kin 12:8–9), and you will receive the answers you wanted to hear from those who already agree with you. One list of sources to consult would be parents, church leaders or mentors, Bible teachers, commentaries, concordances, and the Bible itself. Most people are happy to help answer questions and lead someone to the truth if he or she knows that someone is genuine in their search. Even in prayer, you can push against God with your doubts, and He is strong enough to take those on. He is also able to point you in the right direction through scripture and credible sources.

Some people in the Bible did not have confidence but God chose them to accomplish His will anyway. The first that comes to mind is Moses. "Who am I that I should go to Pharoah and bring the children of Israel out of Egypt?" (Exo 3:11). "What if they do not listen to me?" (4:1). "I am not eloquent, either in the past or since you have spoken to

1 See the list of scriptures at the end of this chapter to read more about confidence

your servant, but I am slow of speech and of tongue" (4:10). Many times, we may be confused between having humility and being cowardly. God knows who He made and who He chooses to accomplish His will. Just after Moses' first question, God reveals His name for the first time in the Bible, "I AM WHO I AM" (3:14). God used Moses despite his self-doubts. God gave him the words, the tools, and Aaron, his brother, to help him. Moses saw that God was faithful and could accomplish great things through him. "Moses was one hundred and twenty years old when he died, yet his eyes were not weak, nor his strength gone" (Deu 34:7 *NIV*). Moses remained faithful throughout his life and was still strong at the end. May we live for God the way Moses did.

Another Bible character who lacked confidence was Gideon. An angel of the Lord even appeared to him while he was secretly threshing wheat in a winepress (Jdg 6:11). The first words from the angel's mouth were, "The Lord is with you, O mighty man of valor" (6:12). My picture of a mighty man of valor is not someone who is hiding from the enemy in a winepress hoping they will not steal the wheat. God thinks differently than you. The angel continues, "Go in this might of yours and save Israel from the hand of Midian" (6:14, emphasis added). The continuing mention of Gideon's "might" is curious when Gideon responds, "Please, Lord, how can I save Israel? Behold, my clan is the weakest in Manasseh and I am the least in my father's house" (6:15). He admits to being the least of everyone God could choose. How could he have "might"? Gideon does not immediately believe in his might. God asks him to tear down an idolatrous altar, which he does, but at night, because he was afraid (6:27).

Most are familiar with Gideon asking for further signs from God that Israel will be saved and interpret those signs as Gideon's doubt that God will be with him. Gideon then watches as God takes 32,000 soldiers and whittles them down to 300 (7:1–8). Looking back on Gideon's attitude, Gideon could have backed out. He could have refused. Even though he had doubts, hid when he was afraid, stated his weakness, and asked for signs, he still moved forward and trusted God to accomplish His purpose through Gideon. God did not chastise Gideon for expressing these doubts. God knows Gideon so well that He tells Gideon that He has given the enemy's camp to him but says, "But if you are afraid to go down, go down to the camp with Purah, your servant. And you shall hear what they say, and afterward your hands shall be strengthened to go down against the camp" (7:10–11). Gideon does just that. God knows us and our weaknesses. God takes the weakest among his people and uses them to accomplish His purpose. If you are doubting, weak, or unsure of how God will use you, have confidence that God's will can be accomplished despite your shortcomings. He can still use you.

We can speak of Jeremiah, who thought he was too young (Jer 1:5), Isaiah, who was a "man of unclean lips" (Isa 6:5), Esther, who was called on to save her nation, or the centurion, who did not feel worthy to have Jesus step foot in his house (Luk 7:6–7). God will always find a way.

Some characters appeared to be confident, but their confidence was misplaced. We often see Peter speaking on behalf of the disciples. When Jesus says He is going away, Peter is the first to ask, "Where are you going?" and "Why can I not follow?" (Joh 13:36–37). With these questions, Peter reveals his naivety through confusion and an earthly mindset. Peter tells Jesus that he will die for Him, and Jesus immediately foretells Peter's denial (Joh 6:37–38). An action of Peter's that shows his misplaced confidence is in the Garden of Gethsemane. Judas greets and kisses Jesus, and the men with Judas grab Jesus. Peter draws his sword and cuts off the ear of Malchus, a servant (Mat 26:47–51). This action seems brave at first. Peter sees the guards arresting his Lord and is ready to fight for Him. However, a closer look at the context before this event, Peter lacks understanding of what Jesus is about to do. Peter trusted the power of the sword rather than having confidence in the power of Jesus.

Those who seem to have never-wavering confidence in God are the heroes of faith, some named in Hebrews 11. Noah builds an ark to save his family from a storm he has yet to witness. Abraham trusts that God will fulfill the promises of land, nation, and seed, none of which came about during his lifetime. David, as a small shepherd, slays the giant soldier Goliath and goes on to become a prominent king of Israel and a "man after God's own heart" (1 Sam 13:14), a nickname given to him by God Himself. People who, through faith, "conquered kingdoms, enforced justice, obtained promises, stopped the mouths of lions, quenched the power of fire, escaped the edge of the sword, were made strong out of weakness, became mighty in war, put foreign armies to flight" (Heb 11:33–34) and the list goes on. People. Humans. Like you and me. We can have confidence in God's ability to use us for good.

How do we increase our confidence? The other synonyms for this are faith and trust. How do we increase our faith? How do we increase our trust in God? Through studying the scriptures, prayer, and obedience.

"So faith comes through hearing and hearing by the word of Christ" (Rom 10:17). If we want to increase our faith, we start by hearing the word of Christ. "Be diligent to present yourself approved to God as a workman who does not need to be ashamed, accurately handling the word of truth" (2 Tim 2:15 *NASB95*). When we accurately handle the word of God, we are proving that we are willing to work for God without shame. Learning the scriptures is the first way to have confidence in your faith.[2]

Prayer can help a lot with confidence, and we should have confidence when we pray. Jesus tells his followers, "If you abide in me, and my words abide in you, ask whatever you wish, and it will be done for you" (Joh 15:7). This verse combines the necessity of knowing the scriptures and praying. If we know the scriptures and the word dwells in us, we can ask God with confidence for what we want, and He will do it. As long as the request is a part of His will, it will be done, but it is comforting to read "what you wish" and not "what you need." Sometimes, I find myself shying away from asking for things I only want and asking for things I need instead. I am limiting God by thinking He cannot handle both. The worst that can happen is the answer is no, but "you do not have because you do not ask" (Jam 4:2). Let us become better pray-ers, knowing that God hears us and will do what we ask of Him. "Rejoice always, pray without ceasing, give thanks in all circumstances; for this is the will of God in Christ Jesus for you" (1 The 5:16–18).[3]

Obedience is the true test of confidence in what we have read and prayed for. Promises given for a life of obedience fill the New Testament. We read earlier in Romans 10:17 that "faith comes through hearing and hearing by the word of Christ," but James tells us to "be doers of the word, and not hearers only, deceiving yourselves" (1:22). It takes action on our part to act on what we read and live a life worthy of the calling to which we were called (Eph 4:1). God has called us to a life of obedience, filled with freedom in Christ. We are not called just to have faith but to grow our faith. The apostles learned this lesson after they had attempted to cast out a demon. They asked why they could not cast it out and Jesus replied, "Because of your little faith. For truly, I say to you, if you have faith like a grain of mustard seed, you will say to this mountain, 'Move from here to there,' and it will move, and nothing will be impossible for you" (Mat 17:20). Even those with little faith can accomplish much in God's service. Paul gives thanks to God when he sees the faith of the Christians at Thessalonica growing (2 The 1:3). The writer of Hebrews admonishes his readers to long for more than the milk of the Word but that they should grow in their

2 See also Acts 17:10–12, Romans 15:4, 2 Timothy 3:16, and Hebrews 4:12 for more inspiration on the importance of knowing the scriptures.

3 See also Matthew 6:5–15; 26:41, Mark 11:24, Romans 8:26–27, Philippians 4:6 and James 5:16.

maturity beyond basic principles (Heb 5:12–14). Too many Christians are content with the milk of the word and not challenging themselves to grow. Let us not fall into the trap of complacency. We must constantly search the scriptures and pray to grow our faith and confidence in God.[4]

Confidence can come in the form of looking good, feeling prepared for something, mental clarity, having good people around you, trusting in the safety of a situation, and having courage; however, many of these attributes are how the world views self-confidence. It is not bad to be confident in yourself, but our confidence does not come from self. It radiates out of us because of who God is. "We have this as a sure and steadfast anchor of the soul, a hope that enters into the inner place behind the curtain" (Heb 6:19). The most comforting verse that brings confidence in the relationship we share in Christ comes from Romans 8:31–39. I encourage you to memorize these verses as a reminder that "in all these things we are more than conquerors through Him who loved us" (vs 37).

Other Scriptures of Confidence: Psalm 16:6–9; John 10:28–30; Acts 17:24–27; Romans 8:31–39; I Corinthians 2:4–5; 2 Corinthians 12:9–10; 2 Timothy 1:7; James 1:16–18.

4 See also Luke 11:28, John 14:15, Romans 2:6–8, 2 Corinthians 10:5, I Peter 1:14, 2 John 1:6.

THOUGHT QUESTIONS FOR "CONFIDENCE"

1. Identify some confidence "killers" (people talking behind your back, self-esteem issues, doubts, etc.) then find at least one scripture that counteracts that killer. What scripture helps you hold on to your confidence?

2. Who are some Bible characters whose confidence may have been misplaced in self or others? What could have prevented that way of thinking?

3. What are the hardest things to pray about? Why? (consider emotions, sins, needs, dreams, desires, pain, gratitude, forgiveness).

4. What will your spiritual walk look like when you are confident and secure in Christ?

5. How can you express confidence in God when introducing yourself to people? Is it difficult to think of who you are in Christ? Why?

KEEP THE HOME FIRES BURNING

Kathleen Trigg

Be hospitable to one another without complaining.
Like good stewards of the manifold grace of God,
serve one another with whatever gift
each of you has received.
1 Peter 4:9-10
(*NRSV*)

I was born in a small steel town into a big Catholic family when Kennedy and Nixon vied for the presidency, the Pirates were about to beat the Yankees in the World Series, and Walter Cronkite and David Brinkley read the evening news without viewers doubting their veracity. It was a wonderful time, and I thank God that He planted me where, with whom, and when He did. I have always known that my parents love each other, they love me, and God loves us all. Those certainties provided inimitable comfort and security in my youth and have continued with me through the pitfalls and pinnacles of adulthood.

I had an ideal childhood. My parents nurtured, trained, and disciplined me. They taught me to work hard first and have lots of fun after. Dad was a meat packer and Mom a full-time homemaker. Our family was traditional in that sense, but my father and mother were not your typical married couple for that era. Dad joined in the cooking, cleaning, childcare, and grocery shopping while Mom repaired the washer, painted the house, reupholstered furniture, and, when the youngest kids were in high school, served as a local politician. My sisters and brothers and I played sports, took tap dancing lessons, and cooked, cleaned, and did laundry. My parents were equal partners and a dynamic duo who presented a united front to us kids; they expected all their children to develop all the talents the Lord gave them, regardless of what gender roles dictated back then. At the same time, my father was the undisputed head of our household, and my mother was his willing accomplice.

Religion played a foundational role in my upbringing. We were old-world Roman Catholics. I received the sacrament of Baptism (sprinkling) when I was a week old and always attended Mass and holy days of obligation. Mom and Dad taught us all the prayers to recite and how to pray the rosary before we were old enough to attend school. I went on to receive the sacraments of Communion and Confession when I was seven and Confirmation when I was eleven. Our family prayed together before every meal, and I said my prayers when I woke up, began a school day, and went to bed. As a teenager, I gave serious thought to becoming a nun. I was so immersed in my faith that I had even convinced two of my boyfriends to become Catholic.

The faith we lived led us to share the blessings of our happy home. The young, middle-aged, and elderly all gathered at our house. We hosted holidays, birthdays, and other special occasions. Our doors were open to all our friends and neighbors—all the time. There were frequent volleyball matches, Pinochle games, and Monopoly marathons. Our friends brought their musical instruments, and song and laughter emanated from our back porch most summer nights. Parents joined their children at our house, and some families took daily refuge there—escaping troublesome situations at their own homes. We also tended to the elderly in the family and the neighborhood. Taking food to the sick, visiting the lonely, cutting grass, shoveling snow, and running errands were normal activities. Hospitality and service were core values we practiced religiously and enjoyably.

Our devotion to God, family, and friends only slightly surpassed our commitment to the Pittsburgh Pirates, Steelers, and Penguins. We gathered in front of the television or around the radio for games as consistently as we attended Mass. To this day we all bleed black and gold even though our teams are less successful than they were back in the '70s and '80s. The Olympics also garnered our undivided attention every four years. We watched sports and we played sports. My parents even started a booster club for girls' athletics at our high school. They raised funds to provide female athletes the same kind of support and awards that the boys' teams had. Sports kept us entertained, healthy, and out of trouble.

We were also a very crafty family. My mother taught us to sew, embroider, draw, and make candles. We made all our Christmas presents. I later learned to knit, crochet, and do counted cross-stitch. My family ran the crafts booth at the fundraising bazaars for our church. Through the years, I have also done woodworking, rubber stamping, and scrapbooking. We were taught to work with our hands to avoid wasting time. To this day, I rarely sit in front of a television without needlework of some kind so that when I am finished with the program, I have something productive to show for that time.

Our family also spent time entertaining others. Our weekly dance classes turned into performances for orphanages, county fairs, veterans' hospitals, and women's clubs. I first took the stage when I was three years old and performed throughout my younger years in high school, community, and college musical theatre productions. I learned from an early age that bringing joy to others is worthwhile and exhilarating.

Education was also paramount. Mom and Dad read to us and then taught us to read. We had library cards before we were of school age. My eight siblings and I went through eight years of an excellent Catholic grade school, excelled academically in high school, and paid our own way as first-generation students through college. I graduated with honors in 1982 from what was then Clarion State College with a Bachelor of Arts degree in Speech Communication and Theatre. I spent much of my extra-curricular time on stage or traveling on weekends to compete in public speaking and oral interpretation of literature. Our forensic team was ranked in the top ten in the nation. I enjoyed every minute of performing, competing, traveling, and speaking. Those abilities paved my way to securing a Master of Arts degree in Communication and Rhetoric from Ball State University. I received a graduate assistantship to teach speech and coach the individual events team. I drove a fifteen-passenger van all over the Midwest helping young people master the skills of speaking in public and interpreting literature. There in Muncie, Indiana, I honed my teaching and coaching skills with a fellow graduate student who was an alumnus of a tiny college that I had never heard of in Temple Terrace, Florida.

Randy Richardson and I attended every class together and traveled on weekends together with the team. The more time we spent together, the more we realized that we were not like the other graduate students who celebrated their good fortune and misfortune at bars. Even when arriving back to campus at four o'clock on Sunday mornings, after a long exhausting weekend of coaching and judging tournaments, we would see each other five hours later leaving the graduate housing complex; I was headed to Mass and he to worship. I will be eternally grateful to him for causing me to question why the Catholic Church taught doctrine contrary to the scriptures. I was convinced my faith was the only true way to worship God, but since I was not familiar with much of the Bible, I decided to read the New Testament to prove to Randy that he was mistaken. The Holy Spirit accomplished something very different that weekend.

It took me six months to count the cost. I knew what the scriptures said, but I could not believe that my family and the nuns and priests could miss what seemed so plain to me. They would not intentionally mislead me. They loved me. I knew that. If I chose to leave Catholicism and be immersed for the remission of my sins, I worried that my family, like the Catholic Church, would excommunicate me. It was almost more than I could bear, but Jesus' words from Mark 10:29-30 worked on my heart: "Truly I tell you, there is no one who has left house or brothers or sisters or mother or father or children or fields, for my sake and for the sake of the good news, who will not receive a hundredfold now in this age—houses, brothers and sisters, mothers and children, and fields with persecutions—and in the age to come eternal life" (*NRSV*).

At the end of the Spring semester of 1983, I was baptized at the Calvert Avenue Church of Christ in Muncie. That same week, I met a dear friend named Julie Koltenbah who had just returned from Florida College. Her father was an elder at the congregation and my first Bible class teacher. Already the Lord was fulfilling the promise of Mark 10 in my life with new brothers and sisters. Only the Lord knew back then that thirty years later Julie and I would be colleagues at that small Christian college that Randy had attended. I spent that summer of my spiritual birth soaking up the scriptures. I had so much catching-up to do. I was years behind my peers in Bible study! Then and there my ardor for the Word of God took hold, and the Word Himself has been holding on to me since then, bringing me through joy and grief, love and loss, success and failure, strength and weakness, pleasure and pain, and everything else woven into the tapestry of my life. When I broke the news to my family that fall, forty years ago, it broke my parents' hearts and shocked my siblings, but they did not disown me. Ever since, I have been trying to love them closer to Christ as they attempt to do the same for me in their way.

After Ball State I served as a program director in a market research firm in Cincinnati. For my first six months there, I worshipped with Royce, Hope, Luke, Todd, and Laura Chandler at the church in West Mason. The Chandlers also performed with the Mason Community players where two of my sisters performed. The Chandlers and I would take the stage together thirty years later in Broadway Comes to Camp, and Royce, Hope, Luke, Todd, and I would serve together as faculty at Florida College. Later that year in Cincy, I joined myself to the work at the Eastern Hills church of Christ where Dennis Allan and his wife Benita fed me spiritually and physically. They welcomed me often to their home that had little children, centenarian Aunt Mary, and plenty of love and laughter to share. Through their hospitality and spiritual nurturing, as well as that of the Chandlers, the Lord once again was demonstrating His promise in Mark 10 to provide brothers and sisters and houses.

One year later, I was recruited away to work on my PhD at Wayne State University in Detroit. Again, I joined Randy in teaching public speaking and coaching the forensic team. I studied Organizational Communication and Speech Education on a Rumble Fellowship. While there, I worshiped with the Downriver congregation that met in a daycare center. What we lacked in size we made up for in zeal. Paul and Sharon Ayres, who were supported by the church, welcomed me into their family of six and even added a toothbrush for me in the family holder. Bob and Doris Johnston, also known as Grandma and Grandpa to everyone in the church, would have me over on a regular basis to feed me roast beef and mashed potatoes, and they would urge me to bring my laundry. They gave me a key and had me housesit for them when they traveled. They lived in the country where it was peaceful and quiet, and at night you could see all the stars that Abraham was not able to count. It was quite a contrast to the noise, crime, and filth of Detroit. The Doug and Janice Tellinghuisen family hosted the monthly potlucks, and as my spiritual family grew, I felt more and more at home with the family the Lord was providing. In my early fifties when my family relocated to Temple Terrace, Janice was the first person to welcome me to Florida, and we reconnected after all those years.

My first year in Detroit was 1984. I could see the lights of Tiger Stadium from my dorm room. In my first month, I saw eight games from the cheap, bleacher seats in centerfield, and the Tigers went on to win the World Series. Family, faith, and fandom were still flourishing in my life.

Three years later I persuaded four women from nearby congregations to start a small Christian women's magazine called *Contents of the Weaker Vessel*. For the next fifteen years we wrote and edited articles, poetry, book reviews, and lyrics for children's Bible songs. Our mission was to encourage Christian women to deepen their own faith, provide a venue for women to hone and share their writing, and encourage other women to serve the Lord fully whether single or married, at home and/or at work. Before we published our final edition, we had women subscribing and writing from more than forty states and at least ten other countries. It was an enriching and rewarding venture. Through that work I grew even closer to sisters in Christ, ending up with family all over this country and in Europe, South America, Asia, Africa, and Australia. I also met Tom Hamilton who would 35 years later become my Provost at Florida College. He graciously and professionally type-set our publication for free from his home in Indiana—the home of my spiritual birth. The Lord was weaving an intricate tapestry through His word and His people and surrounding me with the warmth of faith and family.

When the Rumble Fellowship ran out before my studies were completed, I became a part-time, adjunct professor at Wayne State University and added Persuasion and Communication in Business to the courses I taught. I also branched out into corporate and non-profit communication consulting and was invited to be a part-time adjunct professor in the University of Michigan's Ross School of Business.

When my coursework was finished and while I began the research for my dissertation, I spent a couple of years working at a hotel in Dearborn, Michigan. At that time, I was involved in a newly formed work of the Lord in Jackson, Michigan, with L.A. Mott, Jr., and his family. Part of our evangelistic work involved hosting Bible studies for students at Wayne State University, Eastern Michigan University, and the University of Michigan. It was not unusual for me to attend five Bible studies a week while hosting two of them in my apartment. The three Mott siblings were Florida College alumni and had a heart for the Lord and the lost. Since they had all been or were currently in graduate school, our congregational studies were deep and engaging. Learning from a man who had diligently been studying the Bible for forty hours a week from the time he had graduated from college gave me the opportunity to learn how to study more productively while having someone to help me answer my most challenging questions. It was during that time that my roommate and her boyfriend were baptized into the Lord. I will forever be grateful for that time of growth and fellowship where I learned from the older generation and daily gathered with my peers to study the word and sing songs of praises. R.J. Stevens and Dane Shepard had just published *Hymns for Worship*, and we set out to sing every song in the book starting from zero. What a blessing! That was before Dane's children Nathan and Kaylan were even born. I have since had the privilege of coaching and teaching them at Florida College.

Eventually I left the hotel and became the Executive Director of the local American Cancer Society. While supervising over 1,500 volunteers, I managed to pass my written and oral comprehensive exams. All that remained of my PhD work was to finish the dissertation. The Cancer Society kept me busy days, nights, and weekends, which left little time for writing. When a position opened as the Executive Director of a county substance abuse prevention agency, I applied and was hired. It was rewarding work, but just as demanding of my time as my previous job. One blessing of that job was when my secretary began studying the scriptures with me and attending our small congregation. She chose to obey the gospel and another sister in Christ entered my life.

For three years, I supervised employees, created substance abuse prevention curriculum, presented at school board and PTA meetings, taught in classrooms, facilitated support groups for at-risk kids, and supported the needs of the Board of Directors. Then my dear friend Jerri Hamilton, who served with me as an editor of *Contents of the Weaker Vessel*, introduced me to my husband. John Trigg was a preacher at the church of Christ near Augusta, Georgia. Jerri had invited the two of us to her home in Russellville, Alabama, one October weekend in 1992.

I was 32 years old and assumed I would be single the rest of my life, since I had not found anyone who wanted to marry me that I was willing to put myself in submission to. John was 34 and had been waiting for the Lord to bring someone into his life. We found that we had a great deal in common, and when I heard him preach that Sunday, I knew he was someone who could feed me and lead me spiritually. We spent the next month writing letters and talking on the phone late into the evenings. I invited John to join my family in Pennsylvania for Thanksgiving, and that Sunday he proposed. He was not put off by my response, "Marry you? You don't even know me. I could be an axe murderer!" So, I prayed and talked to every Christian I could find that knew him and his family, and at Christmas I agreed to marry him. I flew to Atlanta, and he gave me my engagement ring on New Year's Eve at Pat and Pam Duff's home in Stone Mountain, Georgia. I would be blessed to teach public speaking to their grandson Connor more than twenty-five years later.

John and I married on May 29, 1993. We will celebrate our 32nd anniversary this spring. With John established as the preacher at Martinez, I left my work at the South-Central Michigan Substance Abuse Prevention Agency and moved to Martinez, Georgia, to become the preacher's wife. I left Michigan with ten house keys that were not my own. Along with family, the Lord had given me access to the same number of homes as there are members of my immediate physical family. The Lord has most definitely been mindful of me.

At that time, I had every intention of finishing my dissertation at a distance. For our first six months together, I was a full-time homemaker. Then I took on part-time work as an assistant in an office of psychiatrists and psychologists to supplement our income when our health insurance would not cover the medical expenses resulting from a miscarriage. The family in the Lord at Martinez embraced me and loved us through that challenging time.

Our first child was born in October of 1994. Maggie was a bright, beautiful baby, but she tried to enter the world unconventionally. Breach birth is not a complication of pregnancy according to Blue Cross and Blue Shield; therefore, they refused to cover my Caesarean-section. Oppressive medical expenses led John and me to decide that I should put my advanced education back to academic work at the University of South Carolina-Aiken. Since the church building did not have an office space to work, John would be working at home with our baby. Like my father, my husband was an actively involved dad, and our Maggie was in good hands.

At first, I taught part-time, but then another former member of the Florida College family, Dr. Guy Warner, told me about a full-time temporary position opening at Augusta State University where he was teaching. I applied and was hired. That was the beginning of my 18 years employed there. Most semesters I did my teaching on Tuesdays and Thursdays so that I could be at home more. As it turned out, I never did complete my PhD. My priorities had shifted dramatically, and I just could not find the time to fulfill my responsibilities at home and work and write a dissertation. I wish that I had finished, but I do not regret putting my husband and my children ahead of completing it.

Our son Andrew joined the family in 1998. We were overjoyed with our bright, beautiful, bounding-with-energy boy. A year later, a fire at my sister-in-law's home in Texas gave us the opportunity to have John's mom live with us while the house reconstruction took place. John's mom had type I diabetes as well as Parkinson's and advanced osteoporosis. My aunts and uncles and parents set the example that taking care of the elderly in your family is service that you provide without question, so we learned all we could about Mom Trigg's health concerns. She joined us in January of 2000, and rather than return to her beloved Texas, she lived with us until her death in December of 2012. During those years, I continued to teach at Augusta State, and John continued to preach at the church in Martinez. We also began home schooling Maggie and Andrew. When I was two months shy of my 44th birthday, the Lord answered our years of prayer and Hannah was born. She was happy, clever, and outgoing from birth. Three healthy children born after the age of 34. My doctors back in Michigan said it was unlikely that I would ever have children. They had not consulted the Lord on that matter!

It was a busy time in our lives, but the Lord saw us through it. I wore many hats: wife, mom, caregiver, professor. It was a season in my life that I felt my time was not my own, but I trusted the Lord and He provided. As Mom Trigg's health declined, we had to make some tough decisions. Her health challenges were too complex for a nursing home to handle, so John resigned after 22 years of preaching there and gave full-time attention to his mother. Our finances were restricted, but by God's grace, we managed.

My work at the university had become increasingly stressful. Our school had been merged with a nearby medical college, and restructuring was taking its toll. Also, I worried over the success of my students who were taking the communication skills I had taught them and using them to advance causes and philosophies I believed were ungodly. I prayed about what to do. I was practicing "whatever your hand finds to do, do it with your might," (Ecc 9:10, *NRSV*) but the results of my teaching often helped others more effectively oppose the Kingdom.

After my mother-in-law went to be with the Lord, I received a call from Dan Petty, the Academic Dean at Florida College. There was a position in the Communication Department, and a few Christians had recommended me. John and I assumed it was an answer to prayer, and I joined the faculty in August of 2013. For the first six years I taught and helped coach the Oratory Union and earned tenure. For a few years I also was the faculty representative to the NAIA, the athletic association for the Falcons. I currently teach and serve as the

Coordinator of the Communication and Organizational Communication degree programs. In my tenth year, I graduated with a second Bachelor of Arts degree, this one in the New Testament. After decades of hearing about FC and receiving the love and blessings from its alumni, I can now finally call myself an alumna. I serve my students, my department, and the college on campus, and—like my parents—we open our home as often as possible for lodging, food, coffee, games, or laundry. My colleagues are my dear friends and my spiritual siblings, and I tell FC parents that I treat their children as if they were my own. As a result, my spiritual family continues to grow. God is so good.

My life is still full. No. My cup runneth over. Maggie and her husband Jed brought our granddaughter Maeve into the family and are expecting a son in February. Andrew lives in Alabama with his wife, Desiree, who is carrying our third grandchild. Hannah is in her junior year at Florida College majoring in Music. John is retired from his weekday job but preaches part-time for the church of Christ in Wesley Chapel where he serves as an elder. Like I did back in Michigan, we meet in a daycare center. I teach children's and women's Bible classes, organize ladies' days, and keep sharing what I know about communication with young people who take their knowledge and skills and put them to work for good. I love my husband, I love my children and grandchildren, I love my students, I love my coworkers, I love my school, and God in His abundant graciousness continues to love us all.

During World War I, the song "Keep the Home Fires Burning" was a popular anthem that people on the home front sang to keep their spirits up. The chorus encourages:

> Keep the home fires burning,
> While your hearts are yearning.
> Though your lads are far away
> They dream of home.

There's a silver lining
Through the dark cloud shining.
Turn the dark clouds inside out
Till the boys come home.[1]

I hope we never have to live through a world war, and I cannot imagine what it was like back then without our communications technology. It must have been agonizing to be brave and carry on without regular news from loved ones at home or abroad. Thank the Lord we do not face the physical warfare that is currently raging in Ukraine and Israel, but we must remember that every day we are engaged in spiritual warfare. First Peter 5:18 tells us the devil is prowling around like a lion looking to devour us. Our enemies are not flesh and blood, but covert evil spirits (Eph 6:12). If we turn on any news broadcast or access the internet, we see the results of their work. We are surrounded by negativity, sin, evil, and darkness in this world that we are in, but not of (Joh 17:14-16).

We cannot control the chaos, but we can combat it with comfort. God gave women the privilege of transforming houses into homes, and He commands us to share our blessings with the needy (Eph 4:28), to pursue hospitality (Rom 12:13), and to do it without complaining (1 Pet 4:8-10). It is even a way married women can help their husbands prepare to be elders (1 Tim 3:2; Tit 1:8) or be taken care of as widows if they have no children to do so (1 Tim 5:10). Hospitality benefits the giver and receiver. By the grace of God, our homes can be a haven for our family, our friends, and even the "foreigners in our land."

HOSPITALITY AMONG THE GENTILES

The scriptures are filled with the practice of hospitality among the Israelites and Christians, but hospitality was also a custom in the Gentile Middle Eastern, Greek, and Roman cultures. The *Dictionary of New Testament Background* explains the five different types of hospitality practiced in the Mediterranean world.[2] Public hospitality was a form of foreign policy or diplomacy. Temple hospitality entailed organizing housing for travelers on pilgrimages. Commercial hospitality provided food and housing for a price, much like our hotels with restaurants. *Theoxenic* hospitality occurred when people provided hospitality

1 Lena Guilbert Ford. "Keep the Home Fires Burning (Till the Boys Come Home)." Ascherberg, Hopwood, and Crew Ltd. in London, 1914.

2 J. T. Fitzgerald, "Hospitality," in Dictionary of New Testament Background, eds. Craig Evans and Stanley Porter, eds. (Downers Grove, IL: InterVarsity Press, 2000), 522-525.

to gods, heroes, and other semi-divine guests. Lastly—the focus of our study—private hospitality was when people shared the food and shelter of their home or provided care for those who needed it. This private hospitality "...was widely esteemed and encouraged throughout the ancient world as a moral virtue."[3]

The Roman Empire's marvelous system of roads and sea routes made travel easier for people in the Greco-Roman period, and commercial hospitality grew as a result. While there were some acceptable places to stay, robbery was a common danger in most, and many locations became nothing more than brothels. Therefore, travelers preferred the safety and comfort of private dwellings where they were treated with friendship and honor.[4] Extending hospitality to strangers was seen as generous and protective. Such characteristics were part of the normal practice of gracious living then. An example of this can be seen in Acts 28:7 when Publius entertained Paul and his shipwrecked companions in his estate on the Island of Malta.

From the days of old to modern times, the people of the Mediterranean area have practiced hospitality. *Nelson's Illustrated Bible Dictionary* states that Bedouin people of the Middle East greet their guests with the words, "You are among your family."[5] When we share the safety and solace of our homes, we carry on an ancient and noble activity that serves humanity and, therefore, pleases God.

HEBREW HOSPITALITY

There is no one word in Hebrew to denote hospitality. Therefore, we do not find it by name in the Old Testament.[6] There are, however, many examples of God's people demonstrating it. We are probably all familiar with the stories of Abraham and Lot entertaining angels in Genesis 18 and 19, Rahab protecting the spies in Jericho (Jos 2:1-16), the Widow of Zarephath in 1 Kings 17 sharing water and her last bread with Elijah, and the Shunamite woman in 2 Kings 4 feeding Elisha and having her husband build an upper room for the prophet so that whenever he visited, he would have a place to stay. There is

---

3 Ibid., 522.

4 Ibid., 523.

5 Ronald Youngblood, ed. Nelson's New Illustrated Bible Dictionary "Hospitality" (Nashville: Nelson, 1995) 580.

6 John Koenig, "Hospitality," in The Anchor Bible Dictionary, ed. David Freedman (New York: Doubleday, 1992), 299-301.

also Rebekah in Genesis 24 giving water to Abraham's servant, watering his camels, and inviting both man and animals to her father's house where there were straw and feed and a place to spend the night.

Less well known is the hospitality of Jethro the priest of Midian recorded in Exodus 2:15-21 after Moses fled from Pharoah after killing an Egyptian. Jethro invited Moses to break bread and stay with him. Nehemiah fed 150 Jews and officials at his table along with guests from nearby nations (Neh 5:17-18). David in 2 Samuel 9 brought Mephibosheth, the crippled son of his dear friend Jonathan, to eat at his table for the rest of his life and provided for his family. Job, also, in his defense before his accusing friends, expressed how he dared not neglect caring for others in his service to God:

> If I have denied the desires of the poor
>   or let the eyes of the widow grow weary,
> if I have kept my bread to myself,
>   not sharing it with the fatherless—
> but from my youth I reared them as a father would,
>   and from my birth I guided the widow—
> if I have seen anyone perishing for lack of clothing,
>   or the needy without garments,
> and their hearts did not bless me
>   for warming them with the fleece from my sheep,
> if I have raised my hand against the fatherless,
>   knowing that I had influence in court,
> then let my arm fall from the shoulder,
>   let it be broken off at the joint.
> For I dreaded destruction from God,
>   and for fear of his splendor I could not do such things. (Job 31:16-23, *NIV*)

These children of Israel obeyed God's commands to care for others, and their obligations did not end with their own people. Leviticus 19:33-34 states, "When an alien resides with you in your land, you shall not oppress the alien. The alien who resides with you shall be to you as the citizen among you; you shall love the alien as yourself, for you were aliens in the land of Egypt: I am the LORD your God." (*NRSV*) When the nation of Judah complained that God was ignoring them even though they were fasting and lying in sackcloth and ashes, God directed Isaiah to tell His people that they were neglecting His ordinances, and their behavior was rebellion. In verse 7 of chapter 58, we see what God expected instead: "Is it not to share your bread with the hungry, and bring the homeless poor into your house; when you see the naked, to cover them, and not to hide yourself from your own kin?" (*NRSV*)

Taking care of others is a wonderful way to let our light shine. When we care for those in need, we emulate our Father in heaven. Deuteronomy 10:17-19 says, "For the LORD your God is God of gods and LORD of lords, the great God, mighty and awesome, who is not partial and takes no bribe, who executes justice for the orphan and the widow, and who loves the strangers, providing them food and clothing. You shall also love the stranger, for you were strangers in the land of Egypt." (*NRSV*)

In *The Jewish Wars*, Josephus recorded that Herod was so committed to hospitality that he had 100 bedchambers built into his palace for guests.[7] We are not expected to go to such extravagance, but it was clearly God's desire that the Israelites be hospitable by feeding, clothing, sheltering, and protecting others, and their behavior was recorded for our example. The importance of hospitality was not just conveyed in the old law. We see it continued to be observed by the children of God in the first century.

CHRISTIAN CARING

The basic form of the Greek word for hospitality is *xenia*, which is related to *xenos*, or "stranger."[8] This term originally connected hospitality to guests not previously known to the host. Another Greek word for hospitality adds the word philos. It means love. Philoxenia, therefore, is literally "love of strangers."[9] In contrast to that, xenophobia is a fear of strangers and can subject strangers to neglect or abuse such as the men of Sodom's desires toward the angels in Genesis 19 and the horrific treatment of the concubine in Judges 21.[10]

Fortunately, the New Testament provides many examples of the Lord's people providing hospitality to friends, foreigners, and even foes. In Mark 1:29-34 the mother of Peter and

---

7 Flavius Josephus, *Jewish Wars* 5.4.4. c. 75 ss 177

8 Fitzgerald, "Hospitality," 522.

9 G. B. Funderburk, "Hospitality," in The Zondervan Pictorial Encyclopedia of the Bible, Ed. Merril C. Tenney (Grand Rapids, MI: Zondervan Publishing House, 1975), 214-215.

10 Fitzgerald, "Hospitality," 523.

Andrew serves Jesus and His earliest disciples and opens her home to all the sick and possessed people of the area as Jesus healed them and cast out demons. Martha welcomed Jesus into her home (Luk 10:38), Dorcas sewed clothing for the widows (Act 9: 36-42), and the Samaritan bandaged the wounds and further provided for the needs of the injured man on the roadside (Luk 10: 29-37). The earliest believers shared all their belongings and sold their possessions and goods so that the proceeds could benefit other believers, and some even sold land to donate to those in need (Act 2:44-45; 4:32-37).

While spreading the gospel, Peter was hosted in Joppa by Simon the Tanner (Act 9:43) and in Caesarea by Cornelius (Act 10:5, 23-48). In Corinth, Paul received hospitality from Priscilla and Aquila, as well as Titius Justus (Act 18:1-3, 7). In Philippi, Lydia housed Paul and his traveling companions (Act 18:26), and after the earthquake, the jailer washed Paul and Silas' wounds and fed them (Act 16:33-34). In Rome, Paul's faithful co-workers Priscilla and Aquila hosted the church in their home (Rom 16:3-5).

MAKING HOSPITALITY OUR MISSION

We have established that hospitality was important throughout the ancient world, and the word of God provides many examples of it. Matthew 25:34-46 teaches us that hospitality is also imperative. Practicing it can be a matter of spiritual life and death. Those who feed the hungry, quench the thirst of the parched, clothe the naked, care for the sick, and visit those in prison will inherit the kingdom prepared from the foundation of the world. More importantly, practicing hospitality gives us the opportunity to be more like our Lord. Psalm 23 mentions the Shepherd preparing a table and anointing the head of the sheep causing his cup to overflow.[11] The psalm ends with the Host sharing His house forever. As modern-day members of the flock, it is now our responsibility to carry out the noble tradition of hospitality in our homes and communities.

We can begin with prayer and meditation. Whatever our circumstances, whether physically well-prepared or worried that we do not have the means to provide for others, praying about providing hospitality is a great place to start. We can remember how others have extended hospitality to us and use our creative thinking to determine how we can use what the Lord has given us to care for the needs of others.

We also need the proper attitude. This is our opportunity to participate in fulfilling God's promise to Abraham that all the families of the earth will be blessed in him (Gen 12:3).

11 Youngblood, "Hospitality," 581.

Just as Abraham rushed to serve the strangers in his midst, we as his spiritual descendants must be ready to do so. We do not do it out of guilt because we must, but out of gratitude for the many gifts God generously gives us.[12] We also must not do it to receive hospitality back.

> Then Jesus said to his host, "When you give a luncheon or dinner, do not invite your friends, your brothers or sisters, your relatives, or your rich neighbors; if you do, they may invite you back and so you will be repaid. But when you give a banquet, invite the poor, the crippled, the lame, the blind, and you will be blessed. Although they cannot repay you, you will be repaid at the resurrection of the righteous." (Luk 14:12-14, *NIV*)

We host or give of our means not expecting anything in return, because that is how God freely gives to us.

In some cases, hospitality is hard work, but we must not focus on that. It is not a burden; rather, it is a blessing. My friend Julie Gant enlightened me to the abundant benefits received by those in the scriptures who practiced hospitality. It is a wonderful study. I have more stories than I can include here of the many ways God blessed my family when we shared our home or our possessions.

We should create a welcoming atmosphere in our homes. After receiving the Nobel Prize for Peace in 1979 for her work among the poorest of the poor in Calcutta, Mother Teresa was asked what the average person could do to promote world peace. She replied, "Peace and war begin at home. If we truly want peace in the world, let us begin by loving one another in our own families. If we want to spread joy, we need for every family to have joy."[13] Our peaceful, loving homes can bring joy to the world!

In Titus 2:5, God gave women the responsibility to be keepers of the home. We need to maintain order, calm, and safety. Yes, we need to keep our houses clean and functioning, but let us distinguish between housekeeping and homemaking. The welfare of the people within the household is more important than the efficiency in running it. We must prevent chaos, but if our family members cannot relax in their own home due to rigorous maintenance of schedule or too many restrictions, our focus may be off. I remember a dear friend of mine

---

12 George Ross, "Hospitality in the New Testament," May 3, 2023, https://www.nobts.edu/geauxtherefore/articles/2021/HospitalityNT.html

13 Michael Collapy, center fellow and project consultant for Architects of Peace Project at the Makkula Center for Applied Ethics at Santa Clara University, New World Library scu.edu/mcae/architects-of-peace/Teresa/essay.html

who kept an immaculate home. She visited me once when our kids were young, and I had been on the floor playing with them in a fort made of chairs and a bed sheet. The house was in disarray with toys strewn everywhere, laundry half folded on the couch, and dishes accumulating in the sink. There was no place for her to sit down. I was mortified. It looked a mess, but we had really been enjoying ourselves. When I apologized for the state of things, she told me she regretted having made organization and cleanliness her top priority when her kids were small. She said to stop worrying about things that do not matter in the light of eternity, and she got down on the floor and played with us. We need to maintain cleanliness and order in our homes, but we must not go overboard and sacrifice joy.

I do have to admit that fun and games were not always the order of the day at our house. I am sorry to say that when the stresses of life interfered, I could lose my patience, raise my voice, and take my frustration out on the people closest to me. That kind of upheaval is what we need to guard against more than untidiness. We should cultivate an atmosphere of love and respect and comfort and joy. It will attract others. In his study of New Testament hospitality, Dr. George Ross determined that "hospitality is a catalyst for the advancement of the gospel."[14] He further shares that the early church exploded through its practice.

We must not worry about the style or size of our house or the elegance of our offering. We do not practice biblical hospitality to impress people. If we wait until everything looks the way we want, we may never welcome others to share in the blessings God has provided. In my single days when I secured my first real job, I found the perfect apartment. I lived in it for nine months before I had money to buy any real furniture. I had only a card table and a small rocking chair in the living space and a mattress on the floor in the bedroom. All my friends hung out at my place anyway. When we wanted to get together, I would always offer my place, and everyone would come and have a great time while sitting on the floor. Hospitality is not about the outward appearance of our home, but the love found within it.

As the years went on, I had more furniture and many more things with which to entertain. For a while, I got caught up in wanting everything to be just right. I would spend more time, money, and energy than needed, and rather than enjoying our guests, I was burdened with following through on my grandiose plans. It was exhausting. It is nice to have special gatherings, but we do not always have to host that way.

---

14 Ross, "Hospitality."

When my husband and I were first married, I had moved from Michigan to Georgia, and I did not know anyone. We started going to Jim and Faye Warner's house every Wednesday and Sunday evening after worshipping and studying with the saints. We lived one house down from the church building and they lived down around the corner. They had six kids. They would feed us, and then we would play Pinochle. Faye was a good cook, but she was more concerned with the quantity and quality of the food than the dining experience. It was perfect, just what we needed as newlyweds: nourishment and nurturing. Our twice-a-week eating and card-playing went on for at least ten years. (We were not completely freeloaders; when their oven died, we bought them a new one. We figured we owed them after all the food we had eaten.) In that decade, two more couples and eventually five more children joined the gatherings. The Warners' house became a second home to all of us. Their doors were always open because their hearts were.

Our congregation today is smaller than many. We gather in each other's homes once a month for a potluck, and we enjoy ourselves immensely. Occasionally, though, Robb and Michelle Mitchell tell everyone after worship to grab lunch at a fast-food spot or the Publix deli and bring a bag lunch to their house to visit with one another. We love that time together, too. There is no one right way to be hospitable. Be creative, open your home, and see what the Lord brings about.

There is no need to go to great expense. We can just share what we have. When we have the means to put on a feast, we can do it! If we do not, we can invite people over for a hot dog roast or after dinner for a movie and popcorn. We can host an afternoon tea or make breakfast for dinner, hold a Bible study, a book club, a singing, a hobby night—anything just to get used to having people in our home. We may start with friends, but we need not limit our hospitality to them. Bringing people into our homes and our lives is one way they can come to know Jesus naturally.

If our current home really cannot accommodate guests, we can take someone out to eat or pack a basket, bag, or cooler with tuna or egg salad sandwiches, a bag of chips, some grapes, and water. If we add a nearby park, we have a picnic. Hospitality does not need to be confined to the indoors.

When needed, we can make room for overnight guests. The hospitality of the Bible often involved giving people a place to spend the night when they were traveling through town. Today, the hospitality industry extends to almost all the remotest parts of the earth, but we miss out on so much when we put someone up in a hotel instead of bringing them into our homes. Our hospitality can also save money for others. It is good stewardship!

When my family arrived in Florida, we could not close the sale nor move into the house we were buying because it did not pass the electrical inspection. Half the old house needed rewiring. It would have meant financial disaster if Dan and Kathy Petty had not insisted that we stay with them rather than at the expensive Extended Stay America down the road. They housed our family for at least a month, and we will be grateful forever.

If we have a guestroom, it can be easier to host guests, but if all the bedrooms are full like ours were at one time, we do not have to decline the opportunity. Our kids were always good at trading their bedrooms for a sleep-out in the living room, which teaches children to share.

Through the years we have benefited greatly from housing extended family, friends, visiting preachers, college students on breaks from school, and parents of students needing a place to spend the night. We do not have a big house, but we always seem to have room for more. We are not the Hilton, but we like to help when we can.

We can also practice hospitality away from home. Perhaps the most common example of this is when we receive or provide food for those who are sick or new parents or grieving the loss of a loved one. We have probably all visited others in the hospital. For those who are single or away from loved ones, we can even spend the night at the hospital with them. Being an advocate who will look out for others when they are incapacitated is a great service and such a relief to those who are suffering. Another worthy way to spend our time is to write to or visit those in prison or support others who do.

There are also volunteer opportunities to minister away from home. We can care for mothers-to-be at pregnancy centers. We can serve cancer patients by driving them to their appointments. The American Cancer Society has a Road to Recovery program that matches patients with drivers. They also have programs where cosmetologists and hair stylists help patients cope with skin issues and hair loss, and cancer survivors can be matched with those who are recently diagnosed and in need of a mentor. If we are good at wielding a hammer or paint brush, Habitat for Humanity allows us to work alongside a new homeowner. If we have the time, Big Brothers and Big Sisters, Inc. is looking for people willing to meet regularly with a boy or girl who needs a caring role model.

We do not need an official organization or program to care for others. I remember one former student, Noah Diestelkamp, ran a "Ziploc mission." He would put a bottle of water, a couple granola bars, new socks, a plastic hooded rain cover, soap, and a small New Testament in big zipper bags and hand them out to homeless people he saw in Tampa when he was out riding in his big van. If we pray for opportunities, the Lord will provide creative ways. Do we know any single parents who could use a free babysitter? Are there caregivers who would benefit from an afternoon or evening away from their responsibilities? Can we substitute for them to attend worship or a Bible study? Can we drive or walk a busy neighbor's child to school? We need to keep our eyes and ears open to the people the Lord puts in our path. As we spend time in their lives, they will see the Lord in us and be attracted to Him.

We can be hospitable even when our strength and mobility are limited. If we are not able to entertain or visit others, we can always write old-fashioned notes of encouragement to those who are sick or discouraged or confined to their homes or places of retirement. Phone calls are a good substitute for visiting as well. In our notes we can remind people that we are praying for them, and in our calls we can pray together. If we have the means, we can tuck a gift card for gas or groceries in a note or Venmo cash to those in need. Today there are so many ways to practice hospitality.

As we welcome others into our homes with open hands and open hearts and serve them through action and affection,[15] the Lord blesses us with the most wonderful guests and future friends. If you are a veteran at hospitality, weary not in well-doing, sister (Gal 6:9). Could now be the time to take someone under your wing and share your expertise? Is it time to consider foster care or adoption? If you are a beginner, join us in this ancient and enriching way to love one another. Hospitality is an activity and an art form in which we all can excel. Let us shine our lights by keeping our home fires burning brightly so that others may bask in the warmth that glorifies our Father in heaven.

---

15 Logan Murphy, "The What and Why of Biblical Hospitality," September 30, 2019, openthebible.org/article/what-why-biblical-hospitality/#:~:text=The%20word%20

THOUGHT QUESTIONS FOR "KEEP THE HOME FIRES BURNING"

1. Describe a time when you or someone you know received gracious hospitality in a time of need.

2. Hospitality has many facets. What is your favorite way to show hospitality and why?

3. There is a strong connection between showing hospitality and being blessed. For these scriptural incidents of people practicing hospitality, discover the blessings they received.
   a. When Abraham and Sarah showed hospitality to three visitors in Genesis 18:1-8, what were they promised (Gen 18:9-14)?
   b. When Lot showed hospitality to the same strangers (Gen 19:1-3), how was his family blessed (Gen 19:15-22)?
   c. In Joshua 2:1-21, when Rahab sheltered the spies, what did she receive in return (Jos 6:22-25)?
   d. Ruth 2:1-17 tells of the hospitality Boaz showed to Ruth. How was he blessed (Rut 4:9-17)?
   e. Abigail fed David's mighty men (1 Sam 25:2-31). In what ways was she rewarded immediately (1 Sam 25:32-35) and in the future? (1 Sam 25:39-42).
   f. When the widow of Zarephath fed Elijah in 1 Kings 17:8-13, in what ways was she rewarded? (1 Kin 17:14-24)
   g. When the Shunammite woman fed and made a place for Elisha (2 Kin 4:8-10), how was she blessed? (2 Kin 4:14-37)
   h. Mary and Martha of Bethany were hospitable to Jesus on multiple occasions (Luk 10:38-42; Joh 12:1-3). How did Jesus respond? (Joh 11:38-44)
   i. When the Philippian jailer cared for Paul and Silas (Act 16:25-34), what blessings followed?
   j. When Dorcas/Tabitha took care of the widows (Act 9:36-42), what blessings resulted for her and others?

DEVELOPING A LIFE OF SERVICE

Brooke Ward

And the King will answer them, "Truly I tell you, whatever you did for one of the least of these brothers and sisters of mine, you did for me."
Matthew 25:40

I am Brooke Ward, the wife of Nathan Ward and the mother of Silas and Judah. I was born and raised in the village of Chippewa Lake, Ohio, but have now spent more than half my life living in Tampa, Florida and working at Florida College. If you could go back in time and ask high school Brooke if she could see herself here 25 years into the future, she would likely say this was not her plan. As I sit and reflect on my life, my mind recalls the people, events, and choices that brought me here. I currently serve Florida College and her students as a librarian and adjunct professor, teaching about human development and aging. My own life emphasizes how my decisions and factors in my life have formed me. We are molded into the people we are especially because of our relationships with others. I cherish several key relationships in my life, and many are because of my time at Florida College.

In high school, I had set my mind on becoming a doctor. I had been looking into local schools in northeast Ohio until I became a Christian. I still laugh about it, but on the day I was baptized, I came out of the water to hear, "So, are you going to Florida College?" I had no idea what Florida College was or what it had to do with being a Christian. Eventually, during a High School Days event during my senior year, I visited Florida College for the first time and decided it was where I wanted to be—at least for a semester. My academic focus did not change, and I pursued courses required for medical school.

I attended Florida College from 1997-1999 and transferred to the University of South Florida (USF) when Florida College was predominantly a two-year institution. Next, I needed to find a job. After a short stint in retail, a friend told me that Florida College was looking for someone to work in the bookstore. I worked there full-time for a few months and cut back to part-time when classes started at USF. My class schedule would not allow me to work at the bookstore as much as they needed me, and they decided to search for another full-time employee. At a luncheon that August, I found myself at a table with Dr. Colly Caldwell, the president of Florida College at the time. He asked so sincerely how I was doing, and I explained the situation. I told him I would have to start searching for another job. His response was, "Let me see what I can do."

Within the week, I had an appointment with Dr. James Hodges, director of the library, about a part-time job. Even though Dr. Hodges' first words to me were, "Oh, I was expecting a boy," I was welcomed on board. I spent around 10-15 hours per week assisting with the Phillips University library collection that Florida College had recently acquired. A good portion of the job required physical labor—lifting, moving, emptying, and repacking heavy boxes of books—but another part of the job was the blessing of spending time with

Mrs. Cecil Norman. I had known Mrs. Norman from Barberton, Ohio, where she and her husband opened their home to teens and young adults from all over Ohio, West Virginia, and elsewhere on the first Friday of each month. This gathering was immensely helpful to me during my formative years as a young Christian. Soon after, I would also get to know Mary Ann Pope, Jeannie Culp, Jan Romkey, and Wanda Dickey.

Meanwhile at USF, I changed my major to gerontology, the study of aging and older adulthood. It was a decision I never regretted. While completing that degree, I took on more responsibilities at the library when Mary Ann Pope moved to Houston, and Jan Romkey left the library because she and her husband were adopting their first child. By March 2000, I worked full-time at Florida College and took a full load of night classes at USF. I completed my bachelor's degree, only one semester behind schedule, in December 2001. When my job search did not pan out as expected, in a post-September 11 economy, I remained at the library. Around that same time, I was engaged to be married and decided against continuing a job search while planning a wedding. I had finished school, had a full-time job, no student loans, and was about to get married. I was happy to remain on that path.

In 2004, with encouragement from Wanda Dickey, the library director at that time, I started my master's degree in library and information science at USF. I took classes part-time and completed the degree in May 2007. I transitioned to the role of librarian that summer and worked full-time until the birth of our first child, Silas, in August 2009.[1] After a couple of months off, I adapted to motherhood with the intention of returning to a reduced 32-hour contract after my leave. Wanda thought that was not wise and encouraged me not to commit to so many hours. She was right. I started back to work in October 2009, working ten hours a week, and moved toward 15 hours a week as the year progressed. I could not have done that without Wanda and my co-workers' flexibility and kindness.

Now, as I look back at 25 years of history in the Florida College library, I am still not back to my full-time status in the library (at least not on paper), but I've taken on new challenges and responsibilities on the side. When the nursing program was first proposed, my husband saw that there would be a gerontology class. He encouraged me to have a conversation with Dr. John Weaver, then the Academic Dean, about whether I could eventually teach that class. It would require taking more graduate courses to meet accreditation standards, and I am not a nurse. I was sure the answer would be "no." I was pleasantly surprised to be given the opportunity to teach Gerontology on a temporary

---

1 As a side note, he was supposed to arrive in September but decided to come three and a half weeks early.

basis and to become an instructor in Lifespan Developmental Psychology--a course I was not expecting or asking to teach. So, I returned a third time to USF to complete 18 hours of graduate work in gerontology—and then some. I cannot leave things unfinished. The addition of 12 more credit hours meant completing another master's degree. So, I did. I graduated in May 2023. I could not have accomplished this without the understanding of my husband, children, and library colleagues. At Florida College, I have continually worked with people who sought my best interest and gave me opportunities not only to be employed but also to be employed with an atypical schedule, to try new things, and most importantly, to prioritize God and family above all.

I am thankful for the many faculty and staff I have worked with over the years. Leaders who took a chance on me, mentors who taught me and saw what I could be, and co-workers I have collaborated with and formed friendships with have played key roles in making me who I am. The other significant aspect of working in higher education is the students I have had the opportunity to interact with. With each summer comes the much-needed pause at the end of the academic year, followed relatively quickly by the anticipation of the return of students, making our jobs and lives meaningful each day. The imparting of knowledge and wisdom in the classroom is important, but forming relationships that go beyond the classroom is what Florida College is all about. We have enjoyed having colleagues and students in our home. I cannot imagine that relationships like these are formed in many other colleges and universities. Watching students mature, find a spouse, find meaningful careers, grow their families, and ultimately serve the Lord with a joyful heart gives you the fuel to keep working, improving, and rededicating your life to serving these students to the best of your ability.

I use the title Developing a Life of Service to tie my academic interests to my journey. Each fall I teach a course called Lifespan Developmental Psychology. In that class, we follow human development from conception to death, investigating the many factors that affect our development and the numerous areas of our lives that can be affected. Teaching this course has encouraged me to be increasingly forward and backward-thinking—to trace my own history and influential factors in my life. Beyond a doubt, the gospel and the encouragement of faithful Christians have been factors that guided me to where I am today, in a place where I can influence others for good. Many have made sacrifices for my benefit and exemplified Christ-like service so that I would grow in my faith and service. The remainder of this chapter will look to the Bible for instruction about godly service and how we can apply Biblical examples to our own lives.

Each Christian has the responsibility to sow the seed of the gospel. Each person we have contact with represents an opportunity to share Jesus or to support another disciple in his or her walk of faith. How we serve within our communities and occupations should reflect how we serve within our churches. As members of God's church, we should know our purpose as God's people and how we can serve others—those inside and outside the fold. We can begin to see our purpose in reading Romans 12:1-21 as we explore how we carry out the unique work God intends for us. Continuing with that image of the body of Christ, consider 1 Corinthians 12:12-27. Not only do we all have our individual way of contributing to the body, according to the strengths God has given us, but we also serve one another, cover one another's weaknesses, and empathize with each other. We also see in Ephesians 2:19-22 and Ephesians 4:15-16, 25 that the body of Christ is a dynamic being. We join together to grow into His holy temple and carry out our work. Serving together and serving one another requires submission and humility. Ephesians 5:21 says that we submit to one another in reverence to Christ. Let us examine ourselves to ensure that we are inclined to serve others, not out of a desire to glorify ourselves, but to glorify the Lord.

When we think about the church, we must consider the body and its members. We meet in a building at certain times for certain purposes, but being a part of one another and serving one another does not cease when we part ways and go home. Being part of the Lord's church involves having a relationship with the Lord and each other that walls or other physical divisions cannot sever, unless our thoughts and attitudes allow it. We must think about these verses in that way. This next section intends to discuss ways we can serve the body as a whole and the members individually, whether inside the meeting place or without. I will start with biblical examples and draw applications afterward.

BIBLICAL EXAMPLES OF SERVICE

Let us look at biblical examples of volunteering in the church. We will start with the gospels by looking at examples of Christian women. Serving the church, our brothers and sisters in Christ, was carried out in various ways among women in the New Testament. Luke 8 mentions Mary Magdalene, Joanna, and Susanna serving Jesus and providing for His ministry by their own means. While we may not know exactly how they carried this out, these women contributed to paving the way for Jesus's ministry. We have Martha's example in Luke 10:38-42. Martha sometimes receives criticism for her reaction to Mary's devotion to sitting at Jesus's feet while Martha was working hard to prepare food. Martha's devotion to hospitality was appropriate for the context and what was expected of her culturally. Jesus conveyed that He did not require that from her in His presence, and she was not to scold Mary for what she had chosen. We are responsible for making our own decisions and taking advantage of opportunities to learn and serve.

What about the Samaritan woman at the well in John 4? The conversation between Jesus and the Samaritan woman begins with a discussion about drawing water, and Jesus offers living water that allows those who drink it never to thirst again. Jesus then reveals to the woman that He knows of her five husbands; she confesses that she believes the Messiah is coming; Jesus tells her that He is here, and, she begins to proclaim Jesus as we read in John 4:28-29, 39-42. Her influence spread like wildfire. Because of one woman's faith and the choice to proclaim Jesus as the Christ, many more believed for themselves. How often do we radiate the light of Christ in our day-to-day walk? If Jesus is important to you, show that to others. Some of us, myself included, are not very outgoing and do not have the boldness to strike up a conversation with strangers. Think of alternatives. Be an example in your attitude, actions, and dress. Others notice those things. We can make a big impression without saying a word. Do not be afraid if someone asks why you are so happy, generous, or modestly dressed. That is a good place to start a conversation about Jesus.

Phoebe, noted in Romans 16 as a servant of the church at Cenchrea, was called a "patron" of many including Paul. The word, as used here, usually meant a woman in a supportive role or a benefactor. In the same chapter, Paul sends greetings to Mary, "who has worked hard for you" (Rom 16:6). Again, the specifics are not provided, but these women were doing work worthy of recognition by those spreading the gospel far and wide. Whatever role they were performing was instrumental in spreading the gospel. Some denominational churches are supportive of having women preaching from the pulpit. That is not what is happening here, but the supportive work of Pheobe and Mary was important and complementary to the work Paul and the disciples were doing.

Again, in Romans, we read about Priscilla and Aquilla, a couple working for the Lord in many places, often hosting the assembly of the Lord's church in their home. They "risked their necks" for Paul's life (Rom 16:3-5). They are spoken of also in 1 Corinthians 16:19 and 2 Timothy 4:19. Are we willing to give up the sanctity of our home to host our brethren? Are we ready to risk our own lives for the furtherance of the gospel? These were not the only ones mentioned as providing a place for local churches to meet. Consider also Nympha in Colossians 4:15 and Philemon 1-2. While many of us are in communities with established churches with comfortable buildings where we worship freely, imagine yourself in a country where worshipping the Lord and evangelizing is illegal or subject to great persecution. Brethren around the world meet, often secretly, in homes, hotel rooms, and other remote places so they might come together and study the Bible. Could you risk your neck to provide a place for the gospel to be preached or house a needy Christian?

Other women in the Bible were known for the encouragement they provided. In Romans 16:13, Paul mentions Rufus's mother, "who has been a mother to me as well." We also have several examples of women in the book of Acts who served to further the gospel. The women at Philippi came together to pray in Acts 16 and here we are introduced to Lydia. Lydia is baptized into the Lord and invites the apostles to stay at her house (Act 16:13-15). She serves her newly found brethren without hesitation. This is not the last time we read about Lydia. Paul and Silas visited Lydia after being released from prison (Act 16:40). Lydia provided a place of meeting for the apostles and other Christians to be restored and encouraged before continuing their journey.

Tabitha, or Dorcas, was "filled with good works and acts of charity" (Act 9:36). She died and was brought back to life to continue serving. Still, before her resurrection, we get insight into her character and reputation. The widows praised her for the garments she made, and pairing this with what we know about her "good works and acts of charity," she likely used her skills to provide garments for others. Her selfless nature was valued and honored. Her generosity was a great part of her identity—it filled her life. Let us all find room for service and fill our lives with good works.

In Philippians 4:2-3, Paul speaks about Euodia and Syntyche, who served side-by-side with him in his work of the gospel. Although we do not know what this service involved, I believe this is another example of women paving the way for the gospel to be preached.

Suppose we can use our financial means, social connections, community relationships, skills, expertise, love, generosity, encouragement, confidence, and humility to serve others. In that case, we, as members of the body of Christ, can carry out God's plan for us and His church. Find a way to serve—which may be very different from how your mother, sister, or friend can serve—and continue in it.

HOW WE CAN SERVE

There are other teachings about giving and doing so generously without expecting to be seen and praised. We have no command to tithe as the Jews did, but our giving, and the extent of it, needs to come voluntarily and from the heart. In 2 Corinthians 9:6-7, we are encouraged to give and to do so cheerfully. Jesus says to give cheerfully (Act 20:35) and He tells us to give in secret, with humility, not to be seen by others (Mat 6:1-4). When we think we have given enough to others, be ready to give more (Mat 5:40-42). What we have is not our own anyway. All things belong to God.

Our giving can be done in many ways. We can save and give directly to a Christian in need. We can use our money to buy things for others, feed others, and even use our precious gas in our cars to provide transportation to someone. Of course, congregations have weekly collections on the first day of the week, as the Corinthians did (1 Cor 16:1-3). Giving monetarily, even if equivalent to the widow's two mites (Luk 21:1-4), is still a way to contribute to the saints. While we give, think about who we are serving. Proverbs 19:17 says, "Whoever is generous to the poor lends to the Lord," and Matthew 25:35-40 says, "The King will answer them, 'Truly, I say to you, as you did it to one of the least of these my brothers, you did it to me.'" Look at the big picture. Our actions carry greater weight than the immediate consequence, whether good or bad. Christ knows our hearts and our deeds and will reward us accordingly. Colossians 3:23-24 says, "Whatever you do, work heartily, as for the Lord and not for men, knowing that from the Lord you will receive the inheritance as your reward. You are serving the Lord Christ." When we serve others, we serve the Lord. Does it change our perspective and motivation when we think about doing things for Christ and to Christ when we serve others? Think about how Christ feels when we refuse to serve. We must be aware of how we will be judged. "Judge not, and you will not be judged; condemn not, and you will not be condemned; forgive, and you will be forgiven; give, and it will be given to you. Good measure, pressed down, shaken together, running over, will be put into your lap. For with the measure you use it will be measured back to you" (Luk 6:37-38). We are wealthy in Christ. Rich beyond measure. Sometimes we let our material, economic status be the measure of our worth and wealth, but that is insignificant considering the spiritual resources we have to offer. Think about this in Luke 6:30-31: "Give to everyone who begs from you, and from one who takes away your goods do not demand them back. And as you wish that others would do to you, do so to them." This is the golden rule, right? Let me argue that this pertains to more than physical goods. Our time, knowledge, kindness, wisdom, and service are valuable too. This is also stated in Matthew 7:12: "So whatever you wish that others would do to you, do also to them, for this is the Law and the Prophets." Reciprocation of good deeds, kind gestures, thoughtfulness, and love (in my class, we call this prosocial behavior) should be taught to our children and carried out throughout our days.

Can we fall into the trap of not serving others? The writer of Hebrews says, "Do not neglect to do good and to share what you have, for such sacrifices are pleasing to God" (Heb 13:16). Are we sometimes stingy with our resources? Proverbs 3:27-28 says, "Do not withhold good from those to whom it is due, when it is in your power to do it. Do not say to your neighbor, 'Go, and come again, tomorrow I will give it'—when you have it with you." Sometimes we fool ourselves, thinking we have nothing to offer others, when we have an abundance of intangible blessings to offer. Time, labor, hugs, and prayers can carry someone through a difficult time, not to mention a meal, a warm bed, or a car ride. The Bible gives us many examples of how we can serve at different times in our lives.

Before discussing additional applications, let us look at a few passages that discuss the spirit of our service, so to speak, and the repeated calling and expectation for the people of God to carry out good works. Colossians 3:12-17 says:

> Put on then, as God's chosen ones, holy and beloved, compassionate hearts, kindness, humility, meekness, and patience, bearing with one another and, if one has a complaint against another, forgiving each other; as the Lord has forgiven you, so you also must forgive. And above all these put on love, which binds everything together in perfect harmony. And let the peace of Christ rule in your hearts, to which indeed you were called in one body. And be thankful. Let the word of Christ dwell in you richly, teaching and admonishing one another in all wisdom, singing psalms and hymns and spiritual songs, with thankfulness in your hearts to God. And whatever you do, in word or deed, do everything in the name of the Lord Jesus, giving thanks to God the Father through him.

Notice how many times Paul says to be thankful or to give thanks. It should be an honor to serve. Subsequently, we thrive in helping others. Titus says that devotion to good works is "excellent and profitable for people" (Tit 3:8). A widow who was deemed worthy of support from the congregation was expected to have "a reputation for good works: if she has brought up children, has shown hospitality, has washed the feet of saints, has cared for the afflicted, and has devoted herself to every good work" (1 Tim 5:9-10). This widow's reputation is ripe with humility, selflessness, and devotion. Surely, this is a reputation built over a lifetime.

Additional analogies of our reputation of service include the use of salt and light, such as this description in Matthew 5:13-16:

> You are the salt of the earth, but if salt has lost its taste, how shall its saltiness be restored? It is no longer good for anything except to be thrown out and trampled under people's feet. You are the light of the world. A city set on a hill cannot be hidden. Nor do people light a lamp and put it under a basket, but on a stand, and it gives light to all in the house. In the same way, let your light shine before others, so that they may see your good works and give glory to your Father who is in heaven.

I have pondered how to find the light even in seemingly dark situations. We can take disappointment, grief, loss, and life stresses and use the experiences to gain resilience and life lessons. We can, in turn, use these to guide, teach, and encourage others. Find the light. Dwell on the scriptures in troubled times as well as joyful times and let it be the focus. When we let our light shine, this does not mean flipping the switch on only when you are in a crowd or doing things just to be seen. I have always heard that character is who you are when no one is looking. The motive should always be to do good. The result should be that others may see your good works and works done without expecting anything in return and will ask why you do the things you do and see His light and power working through you.

Our service must be done with humility. Letting our light shine does not involve being a braggart. Mark 10:43-45 says, "But it shall not be so among you. But whoever would be great among you must be your servant, and whoever would be first among you must be slave of all. For even the Son of Man came not to be served but to serve, and to give his life as a ransom for many." I love the message in Philippians 2:1-7:

> So if there is any encouragement in Christ, any comfort from love, any participation in the Spirit, any affection and sympathy, complete my joy by being of the same mind, having the same love,

> being in full accord and of one mind. Do nothing from selfish ambition or conceit, but in humility count others more significant than yourselves. Let each of you look not only to his own interests, but also to the interests of others. Have this mind among yourselves, which is yours in Christ Jesus, who, though he was in the form of God, did not count equality with God a thing to be grasped, but emptied himself, by taking the form of a servant, being born in the likeness of men.

In a world where so many people only look out for themselves and their own interests, we need to be different. Not only is humble service the right thing to do, but it is also a way to let our light shine and draw others nearer to Christ.

Our service must be done in love. "By this we know love, that he laid down his life for us, and we ought to lay down our lives for the brothers. But if anyone has the world's goods and sees his brother in need, yet closes his heart against him, how does God's love abide in him? Little children, let us not love in word or talk but in deed and in truth" (1 John 3:16-18). I find the phrase "the world's goods" (v.17) curious here. The word choice paints a picture of an individual who covets things of the world and does not recognize that all things belong to God. I picture a person who says, "This is mine. I earned this. Get your own!" Do not be that person. We ought to perceive others' needs and display our love in our service of giving.

We have many options in life and distractions that draw us away from profitable work. Choose to fill your time with activities that build up others: "For you were called to freedom, brothers. Only do not use your freedom as an opportunity for the flesh, but through love serve one another. For the whole law is fulfilled in one word: 'You shall love your neighbor as yourself'" (Gal 5:13-14). Take caution here, knowing that some people, both men and women, do not treat themselves well. They have convinced themselves that they do not deserve love. Ruminating in this attitude will likely interfere with how they treat others. It can be a vicious cycle. Let us love one another in a way that plants seeds of change and growth, allows the love of Christ to change others, and causes a new contagious attitude—one of love, kindness, and generosity. Reflect on 1 Peter 4:7-11:

> The end of all things is at hand; therefore be self-controlled and sober-minded for the sake of your prayers. Above all, keep loving one another earnestly, since love covers a multitude of sins. Show hospitality to one another without grumbling. As each has received a gift, use it to serve one another, as good stewards of God's varied grace: whoever speaks, as one who speaks oracles of God; whoever serves, as one who serves by the strength that God supplies—in order that in

> everything God may be glorified through Jesus Christ. To him belong glory and dominion forever and ever. Amen.

Our very being and service to others bring glory to God through Jesus Christ. That is no small thing. Let us stop and think about our thoughts, our actions, our decisions, and our relationships and ask ourselves if our lives and actions bring glory to God.

We serve by building one another up, or edifying, and bearing the burdens of the weak: "And let us consider how to stir up one another to love and good works, not neglecting to meet together, as is the habit of some, but encouraging one another, and all the more as you see the Day drawing near" (Heb 10:24-25). Be a catalyst or an instigator in a good way that encourages others to be active in love and good works. When we reach out to help the weak and struggling Christian, we also need to be cautious, as Paul instructs the Galatians:

> Brothers, if anyone is caught in any transgression, you who are spiritual should restore him in a spirit of gentleness. Keep watch on yourself, lest you too be tempted. Bear one another's burdens, and so fulfill the law of Christ. For if anyone thinks he is something, when he is nothing, he deceives himself. But let each one test his own work, and then his reason to boast will be in himself alone and not in his neighbor. For each will have to bear his own load. (Gal 6:1-5)

Later in this chapter, Paul also says, "And let us not grow weary of doing good, for in due season we will reap, if we do not give up. So then, as we have opportunity, let us do good to everyone, and especially to those who are of the household of faith" (Gal 6:9-10). Many have watched Christians grow weary in doing good and may question their motivation for doing good in the first place. This may also make us wonder if they were being fed with love and support from others. What motivates you to do good works? Is it societal pressure or the power of the gospel? What keeps you energized to serve others? Is it a feeling of duty and responsibility? Those can be honorable traits, but what about watching other Christians thrive and reflecting on the glory that God receives when His people are doing what is right? Do all things for the glory of God, and let that be your motivation.

APPLICATION OF SCRIPTURE AND EXAMPLE

How can we imitate those examples and apply those scriptures to our life of service, especially regarding our service to others in the church, specifically the congregation of believers with whom we assemble? First, we must establish relationships with our brothers and sisters. Relationships involve intimacy, sharing, listening, and trusting. We can be resistant to accept help from those we do not know—so get to know people. Spend time with people. Do not rush out of the church building after worship is over. Eat together, talk about the lesson, bond over similarities, etc. Once you know each other, you can provide for the physical, material, social, emotional, and spiritual needs of those who are part of the body.

Physical and material needs may include providing for financial needs, nourishment (food), transportation (shopping, errands, doctor appointments), cleaning or other jobs within their home, or helping care for a busy mom's children (this one could fall under other categories as well). Look around and look out for the well-being of others. Are they fed, clothed, happy, and connected to others?

Social needs may involve visiting with the lonely (and not only our older adults), having conversations (think of moms who might be dying to have adult-level conversations), visiting people in the hospital, nursing home, etc., caring for children/babysitting (there are so many aspects to helping with kids), and visiting does not always involve deep conversation. Sometimes, it is meaningful to just be present.

As we read in Romans 12, emotional needs may require us to weep with those who weep and rejoice with those who rejoice. If you have not experienced it yet, you will. Your brothers and sisters will experience heartache, tragedy, loss, grief, and disappointment. They may need to talk, you to listen, or be accompanied through times of loneliness and struggles with their emotions. They may need you just to be patient with them, but they may also welcome an encouraging word, reading the Word together, singing together, or praying together. Not all emotional needs are negative, either. You will be called upon to share in another's joy. Sometimes, it is hard to share in another's joy. Sometimes, jealousy or hurt fills our hearts, but we must put our selfishness aside and rejoice with others.

Spiritual needs overlap with the above, but in being together, (the assembly, out of the assembly; large groups, small groups, one-on-one) we can encourage and edify one another, read the Bible together, deeply study the Bible together, pray together, confess, and confide in one another. The Lord provides medicine for the sin-sick soul. James encourages us with these admonitions:

> Is anyone among you suffering? Let him pray. Is anyone cheerful? Let him sing praise. Is anyone among you sick? Let him call for the elders of the church, and let them pray over him, anointing him with oil in the name of the Lord. And the prayer of faith will save the one who is sick, and the Lord will raise him up. And if he has committed sins, he will be forgiven. Therefore, confess your

> sins to one another and pray for one another, that you may be healed. The prayer of a righteous person has great power as it is working. (Jam 5:13-16)

Attending to a person's physical, social, or emotional needs often provides a remedy for their spiritual condition, or vice versa. Therefore, do not neglect these other needs, even if you are praying fervently for a brother or sister.

We can also serve in the building. I have purposefully tried to steer your minds away from the service activities we might think of first, like teaching children's Bible classes or helping clean the church building. These are good things to do, but you are ultimately not the one responsible for raising someone else's children to be godly. Older women are to teach the younger: "Older women likewise are to be reverent in behavior, not slanderers or slaves to much wine. They are to teach what is good, and so train the young women to love their husbands and children, to be self-controlled, pure, working at home, kind, and submissive to their own husbands, that the word of God may not be reviled" (Tit 2:3-5). The emphasis of Scripture is not for young ladies to teach the Bible to someone else's kids. That is a charge given to parents in Ephesians 6:4. If you feel able to do so and the church trusts you to do that, great. Again, parents ought to attend to the spiritual upbringing of their children, and congregations should know intimately those volunteering to teach children's Bible classes.

Regarding other service opportunities in the building, that will differ so much from congregation to congregation based on the size of the building and the number of members. I am thinking of cleaning, maintaining classrooms and bulletin boards if there are any, and being vigilant about structural things that need to be addressed, especially regarding any members with functional disabilities—are there rugs or transitions that are trip hazards? Are the restroom doors hard to open? Just looking out for others struggling to use the facilities can be a huge act of service.

WHAT KEEPS US FROM THIS WORK?

Sometimes, we lack good examples to imitate. Who around us is modeling behaviors and attitudes of service? When we look around for mentors and find none, look to God's word and be the example. Sometimes, we fall prey to selfishness. We are unwilling to give up time, money, or energy to serve others. Remember the widow's two mites and keep an account of where your money is going. How much have you spent on fleeting entertainment, eating out, or eating in with Uber Eats, buying just one more pair of shoes, gassing up the car for a road trip, or redecorating the house? The means are there, and we can apply the same self-examination to our accounting of our time, energy, and motivation.

Maybe we lack confidence in our abilities. We all have different abilities, some have had better (or worse) role models, some have not had the same opportunities to practice serving, or maybe we neglected to learn from those modeling these good qualities because we did not think they applied to us. Maybe you feel you are not good at talking to others. That is ok. Maybe that is not your role in the body. But maybe you can send encouraging notes to those who need to be remembered and uplifted.

Poor relationships with our brothers and sisters can interfere with our ability to serve them. Do you know those you assemble and worship with? Do you spend time together apart from meeting times? Do you have deep conversations about the gospel, each other's struggles, and what brings joy to your life? We need to form meaningful relationships with our brothers and sisters in Christ. Worshipping with a congregation is not just about sitting in a pew and being present. You are a part of the body of Christ (Rom 12; 1 Cor 12). Within a congregation, you cannot sit and do nothing, like a paralyzed limb, a deaf ear, or a blind eye. You will be required to help other parts of the body, carry out tasks, bear burdens, and complete the whole.

In conclusion, I would like to return to Romans 12 and 1 Corinthians 12. First, "present your bodies as a living sacrifice" (Rom 12:1). The sacrifices and burnt offerings we read of in the Bible are given and burned up, but we can continue to bring benefit to others when we sacrifice our lives to serve others and give glory to God. Remember, "in one body we have many members, and the members do not all have the same function" (Rom 12:4). We all have different ways we can serve and contribute to the body. One function is not greater or lesser than another, but all are necessary and complementary. "But as it is, God arranged the members in the body, each one of them, as he chose. If all were a single member, where would the body be? As it is, there are many parts, yet one body" (1 Cor 12:18-20). We cannot all serve in the same ways because God created us to carry out different tasks. So, find a way to serve that fills a current need, whether caring for physical, social, emotional, or spiritual needs. Have confidence to serve in whatever capacity, knowing your service brings glory to God.

THOUGHT QUESTIONS FOR "DEVELOPING A LIFE OF SERVICE"

1. Think about Romans 12 and 1 Corinthians 12. In your own body (congregation), can you identify ways you could better help a weaker member to get stronger, or to provide a service that is lacking?

2. The scriptures urge us: "Do not neglect to do good and to share what you have, for such sacrifices are pleasing to God" (Heb 13:16). Also, "Do not withhold good from those to whom it is due, when it is in your power to do it" (Pro 3:27). What things in your life often hold you back from doing good or serving others?

3. What are some ways that women can take part in spreading the gospel, as seen in scripture?

4. What biblical example most inspires you to serve? How can you inspire others to serve?

ALL THE WAY MY SAVIOR LEADS ME

by Fanny Crosby

All the way my Savior leads me–
What have I to ask beside?
Can I doubt His tender mercy,
Who through life has been my guide?
Heav'nly peace, divinest comfort,
Here by faith in Him to dwell!
For I know, whate'er befall me,
Jesus doeth all things well;
For I know, whate'er befall me,
Jesus doeth all things well.

All the way my Savior leads me–
Cheers each winding path I tread,
Gives me grace for ev'ry trial,
Feeds me with the living bread.
Though my weary steps may falter
And my soul athirst may be,
Gushing from the rock before me,
Lo! a spring of joy I see;
Gushing from the rock before me,
Lo! A spring of joy I see.

All the way my Savior leads me–
Oh, the fullness of His love!
Perfect rest to me is promised
In my Father's house above.
When my spirit, clothed immortal,
Wings its flight to realms of day,
This my song through endless ages:
Jesus led me all the way;
This my song through endless ages:
Jesus led me all the way.

WE ARE FC

Florida College was chartered in 1944 as a private, independent school of higher learning originally called Florida Christian College. It enrolled its first 100 students in the fall of 1946 and in 1954 received accreditation from the Southern Association of Colleges and Schools (SACS) to offer the associate of arts degree. In 1963, the name changed to Florida College and in 1996 was approved by SACS to offer its first bachelor's degree in Biblical Studies. As of 2024, along with the long-standing AA degree, Florida College serves nearly 600 students studying bachelor's degrees in 23 majors with 9 added specializations.

Florida College has one campus located along the banks of the Hillsborough River in Temple Terrace, an incorporated city ten miles from downtown Tampa. This private, liberal arts college provides a comprehensive experience designed to develop students spiritually, mentally, physically, and socially; to integrate into their lives the Bible as the revealed will of God; and to prepare them for lives of service to their Creator and humanity. The Board of Directors, administrators, faculty, and staff are members of churches of Christ.

The school maintains an independent status without accepting financial support from churches, entirely through tuition paid by students and through donations by individuals, corporations, and non-church entities. A dedicated network of alumni and friends across the nation generously donate time and resources to support the school's mission through Hutchinson Bell chapters and 23 summer camps and a growing number of winter camps. In addition to its collegiate curriculum, Florida College is accompanied by a K-12 academy and dual enrollment opportunities.

The student body of Florida College is diverse, having a balanced gender ratio with 23% minority representation. The 86% of students living in residence halls creates a vibrant on-campus community. Beyond its academic rigor, the school hosts NAIA basketball, cross country, golf, soccer, track and field, and volleyball teams and a cheerleading squad. Students can join campus societies for social enrichment and community service and participate in numerous student-led clubs and activities. To learn more about the school, visit floridacollege.edu.

We are FC: We follow Christ.

Made in the USA
Coppell, TX
14 February 2026